2003 THE TOUR DE FRANCE

100TH ANNIVERSARY TOUR

John Wilcockson

VELO press

BOULDER, COLORADO

For Rivvy Neshama

Printed in the United States of America.

10 9 8 7 6 5 4 3 2 1

Distributed in the United States and Canada by Publishers Group West.

International Standard Book Number: 1-931382-26-3

Library of Congress Cataloging-in-Publication Data available

VeloPress®
1830 North 55th Street
Boulder, Colorado 80301–2700 USA
tel 303/440-0601 • fax 303/444-6788 • e-mail velopress@7dogs.com

To purchase additional copies of this book or other VeloPress® books, call 800/234-8356 or visit us on the Web at velopress.com.

Cover photos: Lance Armstrong, Luz-Ardiden, © Graham Watson. Armstrong, Jan Ullrich, and Alex Vinokourov, winner's podium, © Cor Vos.

Cover and interior design by Erin Johnson.
Composition by Erin Johnson, with Paula Megenhardt.

TABLE OF CONTENTS

What a Race!

What's going to happen next? That was the thought every day, every moment of a palpitatingly dramatic centennial Tour de France that Lance Armstrong eventually won because he had more resilience, more motivation, more patience and, in the end, more luck than all of his opponents. As a result, the mighty Texan now stands alongside Jacques Anquetil and Eddy Merckx, Bernard Hinault and Miguel Induráin, as a legendary figure in cycling, a five-time winner of the world's most demanding, most storied bicycle race.

It was a Tour that sucked the emotions dry. There were terrifying crashes and electrifying attacks, mind-jarring sprints and heart-stopping chases, stunning failures and dramatic turnarounds, along with awesome acts of heroism and goodwill. The suffocating heat down south almost downed the favorite, and an Atlantic storm did down his main challenger.

Armstrong's eventual one-minute, one-second margin of victory over a resurrected Jan Ullrich made this the closest Tour since Greg LeMond overcame Laurent Fignon in 1989, and the sixth closest of all time. And had challengers like Joseba Beloki, Tyler Hamilton, and Levi Leipheimer not been eliminated or handicapped by high-speed accidents then we would probably still be asking: What's going to happen next?

The thrills and drama of a Tour celebrating its one-hundredth anniversary took center stage in a contest that fully honored and remembered the pioneers who contested the first Tour in 1903—as well as all of the racers who competed in the races in between. There were constant reminders of the Tour's history when ceremonial appearances were made by past champions like 70-year-old Charly Gaul (the 1958 winner), 75-year-old Federico Bahamontes (1959 winner), and 84-year-old Ferdi Kubler (1950 winner).

The Tour's 100-year-history is the subject of the opening section of this book, starting with the November 1902 meeting in Paris that gave birth to the race. There follows a comprehensive timeline of how the Tour changed through the twentieth century, along with some tactical and technical stories that forged the Tour's identity. This section closes with a detailed look at the tough times experienced by Anquetil, Merckx, Hinault, and Induráin in taking their fifth Tour victory—and attempting to win a sixth.

The second section of the book traces the growing popularity of the Tour de France in North America, and details the performances of all the North Americans who have ridden in the Tour. Separate chapters are devoted to the only American Tour winners, LeMond and Armstrong, highlighting their breakthrough first victories in 1986 and 1999, respectively.

The second half of the book is devoted to the 2003 Tour itself, divided into three weekly sections that trace Armstrong's quest to win a fifth Tour, with detailed accounts of every stage, along with diary entries from American hero Tyler Hamilton and Australian rookie Michael Rogers.

With Gratitude...

Without the three thousand athletes who have contested the Tour de France since 1903, the journalists who have written about them, and the race personnel that has organized the Tour, this book could not have been produced. I would like to give particular thanks to the late J.B. Wadley, Pierre Chany, Geoffrey Nicholson, and Jacques Goddet, who all wrote about the Tour with such great feeling and skill. They remain an inspiration. Many others have contributed to my own love and knowledge of the Tour over the past thirty-five years, including traveling companions Samuel Abt, Susan Bickelhaupt, Rupert Guinness, Andy Hood, Bryan Jew, Andrew Juskaitis, Felix Magowan, Robin Magowan, Kip Mikler, Charles Pelkey, Chico Perez, James Startt, Noël Truyers, Louis Viggio, Alberto Villareal, David Walsh, Graham Watson, Steve Wood, and Lennard Zinn. I'd like to thank especially all the American, Australian, British, Canadian, Irish, Mexican, and New Zealand riders who have shared their experiences during the Tour and provided so many memorable moments. For invaluable help with my writing over the years, I want to thank Rivvy Neshama and Evelyn Spire. And, finally, a thank-you to my editors at VeloPress, Renee Jardine, Amy Rinehart, and Theresa van Zante, for their encouragement, patience, and support.

PART I

The Centennial Challenge

LANCE ARMSTRONG WAS AIMING TO BECOME THE
TOUR'S FIFTH FIVE-TIME WINNER IN 100 YEARS.

———————————◉———————————

nniversaries are big in France. Take the year 1989, which was the bicentennial of the French Revolution. (Remember the storming of the Bastille in 1789?) The bicentennial's big celebration came on the Fourteenth of July, Bastille Day, and the Tour de France organizers just happened to schedule that day's stage to finish in Marseille, the city after which the French national anthem, the "Marseillaise," is named. On July 14, 1989, the race saw plenty of attacks by French riders, and a blond rider from Normandy, Vincent Barteau, won the stage in a late solo attack. His victory and the very special day were celebrated on a hot, steamy night by huge crowds of people, who watched a mammoth fireworks display exploding in brilliant cascades over Marseille's ancient harbor as synchronized orchestral and French techno music resounded through the city's decorated streets. There would be similar celebrations in 2003 at many of the nineteen stage towns, even though there was no bicentennial of the French republic to remember. The reason, of course, was the centennial of the Tour de France. The year 1903 must have been a particularly creative one as it also saw the founding of the Ford Motor Company, Harley-Davidson motorcycles, and the New York Yankees, as well as the first powered flight by the Wright brothers.

There would be many reminders of the Tour's 100th anniversary throughout the July 5–27 event, which was actually the ninetieth edition because of the combined eleven years lost during the twentieth century's two world wars. Notable in the commemoration of the original Tour was the actual race route, which was structured around the six cities that greeted the Tour pioneers: Lyon, Marseille, Toulouse, Bordeaux, Nantes, and Paris. Symbolically, the prologue time trial would start in Paris, at the foot of the Eiffel Tower, while the opening road stage would begin from outside the Auberge au Réveil Matin (the "Alarm Clock Inn"), in Montgeron, where the 1903 Tour launched its historic journey.

To celebrate some of the race's leading personalities, the centennial Tour would visit the memorials erected for Tour founder Henri Desgrange (on the Col du Galibier in the Alps) and longtime race director Jacques Goddet (on the Col du Tourmalet in the Pyrénées), while a wreath would be placed on the grave of co-founder Géo Lefèvre in Vitry-le-François on the day that the team time trial finished at nearby St. Dizier. The centennial Tour would also pass the memorials placed for notable race winners Fausto Coppi and Louison Bobet (on the Col d'Izoard in the Alps) and fallen hero Fabio Casartelli (where he died on the Col du Portet d'Aspet in the Pyrénées in 1995).

Significantly, the 2003 Tour was also the one at which an American who was a teammate of Casartelli, Lance Armstrong, would attempt to become the event's fifth five-time winner—to follow Spaniard Miguel Induráin (1991–95), Frenchman

Two years after becoming the Tour's first five-time winner, Jacques Anquetil abandoned the race in 1966 after guiding his Ford teammate Lucien Aimar to victory.

Bernard Hinault (1978–79, 1981–82, 1985), Belgian Eddy Merckx (1969–72, 1974) and the late Frenchman Jacques Anquetil (1957, 1961–64).

During the reigns of the earlier quintuple winners, there were times when people said that the dominance displayed by those champions made the race a bore. What the critics tended to forget was the confidence, resilience, and determination those men had to display to match their natural talent. And each of their fifth victories was usually their toughest.

By 1964, Anquetil had lost some of the greyhound qualities that previously enabled him to gain handfuls of minutes in the time trials while calmly matching the best the climbers could throw at him. Anquetil went into the 1964 Tour fatigued by an exhausting win at the Giro d'Italia and was in trouble on many of the climbs. He was dropped for several minutes on the Port d'Envalira in the Pyrénées, but fought back with the help of a teammate and a risky downhill chase through thick fog. Then, on the Tour's last peak, the Puy de Dôme, he raced elbow to elbow with his French rival Raymond Poulidor until Anquetil cracked less than a kilometer from the top. Poulidor gained 40 seconds that day, to come within 14 seconds of the leader going into the last day's time trial. But the incentive of taking his fifth overall win was enough for the defending champion to overcome Poulidor and earn a final winning margin of 55 seconds.

Ten years later, Poulidor—by now thirty-eight years old—came close to toppling Merckx, the Belgian superstar, who showed considerable frailty in taking his fifth victory. Merckx was fortunate that his two strongest opponents, Joop Zoetemelk and Luis Ocaña, were absent because of injuries, and in the race itself he was dropped on several climbs— notably suffering a humiliating defeat to Poulidor at the St. Lary summit finish. The Belgian even lost the final time trial, but his strength in the flatter stages enabled Merckx to persevere and beat runner-up Poulidor by

Poulidor, 38, challenged Merckx (right) on the Tour climbs in 1974.

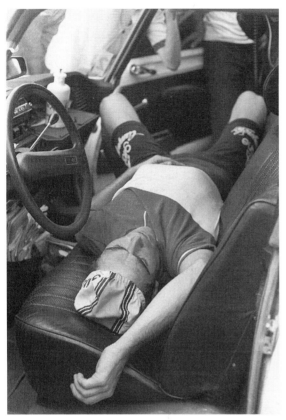

Hinault often rode to his limit, as he did on this stage at his debut Tour win in 1978.

8:04, which was actually the narrowest winning margin of his five successes.

Hinault's fifth victory, in 1985, was also labored. If eventual runner-up Greg LeMond hadn't been the Frenchman's teammate, the American would probably have won that Tour. Why? On the Col du Tourmalet, LeMond was the strongest and might well have taken the yellow jersey had his team not ordered him to slow down. LeMond then defeated Hinault in the final time trial and was only 1:42 behind his team leader by the time the race ended in Paris.

As for Induráin, in 1995, he somewhat preempted his opposition with a devastating attack on the hilly stage 7 to Liège and then took the next day's time trial to move into an overall lead that he never relinquished. But the Spaniard fought hard to keep the yellow jersey, particularly when he and his team were forced to chase a breakaway group led by Laurent Jalabert that gained almost 10 minutes on the stage to Mende.

So would Armstrong be similarly challenged by his attempt to win his fifth Tour? Conventional wisdom said no, but there were many more potential opponents in 2003 than in any of his four previous successes. The danger list was again headed by the 1997 winner, Jan Ullrich of Germany, who had twice finished second to Armstrong, but appeared to have renewed energy with Bianchi, a squad that had risen like a phoenix from the ashes of the Coast team. Riders who had greater ambition—or greater strength than ever before—included America's Tyler Hamilton of CSC; Kazakhstan's Alex Virokourov of Telekom; the Spaniards Aitor Gonzales of Fassa Bortolo, Joseba Beloki of ONCE-Eroski, and Iban Mayo of Euskaltel-Euskadi; and the Italians Gilberto Simoni of Saeco, Stefano Garzelli of Vini Caldirola, and Ivan Basso of Fassa Bortolo.

Induráin makes the attack on the Mont Theux climb during the stage to Liège. This proved to be the move that earned him his fifth Tour win, in 1995.

Armstrong himself believed that all those men would give him his toughest challenge yet, and given the experiences of Anquetil, Merckx, Hinault, and Induráin, winning a fifth Tour would not come easily. Should Armstrong take this Tour, it would mean that of the twenty-three Tours contested by Americans since Californian Jonathan Boyer debuted in 1981, eight would have resulted in overall victories. That's a winning average of .347—which compares with the .382 of the most successful nation in the Tour's history, the French.

Even though a Frenchman wasn't likely to win this centennial Tour—unless you believed in miracles—we knew that after the finish on the Champs-Élysées a few hundred thousand Parisians would be in celebratory mood. Anniversaries are big in France.

The Birth of the Tour

IN THE PARIS WINTER OF 1902, AN OUTRAGEOUS PLAN
IS ABOUT TO CHANGE THE COURSE OF CYCLING HISTORY.

t is a chilly Thursday morning in Paris; the date is November 20, 1902. Henri Desgrange, editor-in-chief of the French daily sports newspaper *L'Auto-Vélo*, is chatting with two colleagues in a high-ceilinged office. Through the windows of the five-story Victorian building come the distant sounds of the Boulevard Montmartre muffled by falling snow: the klaxons of newfangled automobiles and the ringing of bicycle bells mixed with the clacking of horseshoes and the rumble of cartwheels on the cobblestones.

L'Auto-Vélo has just celebrated its second year of publishing, but the paper is having a hard time financially, particularly as Desgrange's big rival, Pierre Giffard of *Le Vélo*, has just won a suit that will force the publication's title to change to simply "*L'Auto*." This could impact the paper's circulation, which is already at a precarious level—25,000 a day compared with *Le Vélo*'s 80,000.

This morning Desgrange, dressed in his usual dark dress suit and bow tie, is discussing the circulation problems with the newspaper's automobile editor, Georges Prade, and cycling editor, Géo Lefèvre. Looking at Lefèvre—who joined *L'Auto-Vélo* after being fired by Giffard a year ago—Desgrange says, "It's absolutely necessary that we invent something to shut Giffard up. . . . Do you have any ideas?"

It's something that the young cycling editor has clearly been thinking about because Lefèvre answers, "Why not a cycling tour of France?"

Desgrange is stunned by what seems a preposterous idea. The only road events organized to date have been one- to two-day point-to-point races like Paris-Roubaix (280 kilometers), Bordeaux-Paris (575 kilometers), and the longest, Paris to Brest and back (1,196 kilometers)—all organized by Desgrange and his team.

Lefèvre continues, "Yes, a race over several days, longer and harder than all those that already exist. Something like the six-day races on the track, but on the road. The big cities in the provinces are clamoring for the bike racers, they'll buy into the idea."

"And what name will this race have?" asks a still-skeptical Desgrange.

Lefèvre shoots back, "The Tour de France, of course!"

Intrigued by the suggestion, Desgrange, thirty-seven years old, thinks for a moment then invites the twenty-five-year-old Lefèvre to lunch, even though in the protocol of the day such social interaction was frowned upon. They put on their heavy winter coats and derby hats to walk the few blocks up the narrow Rue du Faubourg-Montmartre to the Zimmer café, just around the corner on the Boulevard Montmartre.

Desgrange, who a decade before had set track cycling's first world hour record by riding 35.325 kilometers in 60 minutes on the Buffalo velodrome in Paris, is a health freak. He orders his usual *plat du jour* and fruit salad, along with a glass of water. The younger man asks for something more substantial to eat and a carafe of wine. Their discussion about the new bike race continues.

"Your idea is not as crazy as I first thought," says Desgrange. "Let's talk some more about it."

Lefèvre is persuasive. He tells his boss that, based on the speeds of their existing road races, each stage of the new event will probably take between 12 and 18 hours to complete. The stragglers could take twice that time, so two or three rest days will be scheduled between the stages. Desgrange likes what he hears from his employee and warms to the subject. He can see that there will be stories for three or four weeks to boost the daily circulation of his newspaper. After paying the bill, he tells Lefèvre, "All we need now is for Goddet to decide that this is possible."

Back in the offices of *L'Auto-Vélo*, Desgrange visits the newspaper's financial controller, Victor Goddet. The genial Goddet, a big man with a handlebar mustache, listens attentively to his partner's ideas and, without hesitation—and much to Desgrange's surprise—Goddet does something totally out of character: He offers Desgrange the keys to the strongbox and says quite simply, "Take what you need."

The Tour de France is born.

Two months later, on January 19, 1903, *L'Auto* (with "*Vélo*" dropped from its name) made an announcement on its front page: "The biggest cycling event in the world, the Tour de France, will take place on a course from Paris-Lyon-Marseille-

Toulouse-Nantes-Paris—20,000 francs in prizes—start June 1—finish July 5 at the Parc-des-Princes."

The French press (and even the *New York Herald*) was impressed. *Le Figaro* wrote, "A colossal event has been announced by *L'Auto*." Only Giffard at *Le Vélo* ignored the big news. Miffed by this, Desgrange sarcastically wrote in the next day's *L'Auto*, "The newspaper that is now the only one called *Le Vélo* hasn't deigned to devote one line, you heard me right, not one line, to the most sensational bike race to be organized since the invention of cycle sport. *There* are some well-informed readers."

Giffard had no choice now but to mention the new race in the next day's paper, but he did it in just two lines and with no reference to *L'Auto*. Seven months later, after the inaugural Tour de France was a huge success, the circulation of *L'Auto* soared to 60,000 . . . and *Le Vélo* began a steady decline that put it out of business by 1905.

The Tour itself experienced major logistical problems that first year, but the indefatigable Lefèvre saved the event by working around the clock as the race director, referee, finish-line judge, and timekeeper—in addition to writing long race reports for the newspaper!

Describing his duties during the Tour's first two years—which featured ultra-marathon stages of up to 471 kilometers, usually starting in the wee hours or going through the entire night, with some riders being on the road for 40 hours—Lefèvre said, "I took the train before the racers started to go and surprised them on the road and in the night with rolling controls." Even so, particularly in 1904, many riders cheated by hitching rides in cars (or trains!), having illicit feeds, or switching race numbers with other riders. There were even cases of mobs delaying their hero's rivals by scattering carpet tacks on the roads or blocking the road. Fifteen riders were disqualified for cheating during the 1904 Tour, a fact that appalled Desgrange, as did the chaos caused by the huge crowds at each of the six stage finishes.

One of the worst incidents took place early in the Tour's second stage, Lyon-Marseille, a couple of hours after the peloton left the streets of St. Etienne at about 3 a.m. (That 374-kilometer stage began at midnight and the winner finished after 3 p.m.) As the leaders approached the 3809-foot summit of the 13-kilometer Col de la République climb, in the half-light of dawn, local rider Alfred Faure made a sharp acceleration. Only one man, Lucien Pothier, went with him. Then as soon as they passed, one hundred or so spectators—Faure supporters—proceeded to block the road. They swung cudgels, threw stones, and shouted, "Knock down Garin! Long live Faure! Kill the others!"

A rock hit Maurice Garin's cheek, and he took severe blows on his knee and arm. His brother César was struck on the neck and back. And the Italian Giovanni Gerbi fell unconscious under a rain of blows. As the riders fought their way clear, a race official in one of the blocked cars fired a revolver several times into the air, scaring the Faure fans, who scattered into the adjacent pine forest.

Shots were fired to disperse another mob in a different town three days later. The disgruntled fans this time were from Alès, the hometown of Ferdinand Payan, who was thrown out of the Tour at Marseille for drafting behind a team of riders not in the race. The Payan supporters spread carpet tacks on the road in a couple of places before gathering at the Nîmes race control. There, in a city square packed with thousands of late-night revelers, about 150 of the Payan fans attacked the race, yelling "Death, kill them" as they threw stones, bottles, and punches at the peloton and smashed bikes. Riders took refuge in cafés before a troop of soldiers charged the mob to clear a passage.

The day after the 1904 Tour ended, a distraught Desgrange wrote: "The Tour de France is over and its second edition could have, I truly believe, been the last. It will be dead from its own success."

Two months later, however, Desgrange changed his mind. But then in late November, four months after the finish, he and the rest of the race organizers were appalled when the French cycling union sanctioned twenty-nine of the Tour competitors, disqualifying the winner, Maurice Garin, and the next three finishers. Garin was handed down a two-year suspension from cycling while runner-up Lucien Pothier was banned for life.

Desgrange was indignant that the sport's governing body had treated his race so badly; but the scandal did cause some improvements to the Tour. Lefèvre suggested that the stages be shortened to avoid the through-the-night rides, which was when most of the cheating took place. So in 1905, the Tour was split into eleven stages, and further interest was added in the form of mountain climbs—notably the Ballon d'Alsace in the Vosges mountains and the Laffrey and Bayard passes in the Alps.

After those "mini" steps toward the Tour de France that we know today, the biggest leap was taken in 1910, when the race ventured into the high mountains for the first time. After seven editions of the race, Desgrange felt that the event was stagnating and asked his staff to come up with some new ideas. He didn't expect, however, that his course expert, Alphonse Steinès, would propose the inclusion of the largely unexplored goat tracks that crossed the highest passes in the Pyrénées.

On hearing the suggestion at a January 1910 meeting, Desgrange replied, "Steinès, you're going crazy!"

"But you believe that we should enlarge the Tour?" asked the course wizard.

"Yes, but not in this crazy fashion," stated Desgrange.

The boss pointed out that there weren't even any real roads over the passes, notably the Tourmalet and Aubisque.

"So, you want me to go and take a look?" asked Steinès.

"That's right," Desgrange said. "Leave, and we'll talk later."

On arriving in the south of France, Steinès heard about a car that had recently crashed into a ravine descending the Aubisque, causing damage to the road. So he visited the local highway department and got them to agree to repairs in exchange for a payment of 5,000 francs—an amount that Desgrange, by phone, then had reduced to 2,000 francs.

Steinès next went to the Tourmalet and asked an innkeeper at Ste. Marie-de-Campan if it was possible to go over the pass at that time of year. "It's been snowing up there," he was told. "In theory, you can barely cross it in July."

That didn't deter the Tour official, who jumped into his chauffeured car and told the driver to head up the Tourmalet. About 4 kilometers from the top, snowdrifts blocked the road. Steinès said he would continue on foot, and he told his driver to backtrack via the valley roads to meet him on the other side of the pass. Even though it was 6 p.m. and night was falling, the Paris businessman ascended the narrow path, where the snow was 13 feet high in places. Struggling through the deep drifts, Steinès followed the tall marker posts heading for the summit.

Meanwhile, the driver had alerted the authorities and search parties were dispatched from Barrèges, located on the west side of the mountain pass. Around 3 a.m., Steinès, having followed a mountain stream down from the summit, arrived on the edge of the village. "Who goes there?" asked a voice in the dark. Steinès hesitated. The voice repeated, "Say who's there, or I'll shoot." It wasn't uncommon for bears to be on the prowl in that part of the Pyrénées.

Luckily, the voice belonged to the local correspondent of *L'Auto*, who then took the disheveled Steinès for a meal, a hot bath, and a warm bed. On awakening, Steinès met with the relieved members of the search parties, and then sent off a telegram to Desgrange. It said: "Crossed Tourmalet. Stop. Very good road. Stop. Perfectly practicable. Stop. Signed Steinès."

1910 Tour winner Octave Lapíze had to walk up the Col du Galibier the first time it was included in the Tour route, in 1911.

Six months later, on July 21, the Tour's 326-kilometer stage 10 from Luchon to Bayonne took the winner, Octave Lapize, 15 hours to complete. After crossing the Peyresourde, Aspin, and, yes, the Tourmalet, Lapize pushed his 35-pound bike most of the way up the Aubisque, and when he saw race director Victor Breyer—who was standing in for Desgrange who'd had to return to Paris for a couple of days—the French cyclist shouted at him: "You're murderers! Yes, murderers!"

Only forty-six riders survived the Tour's first confrontation with the high mountains, but Steinès's crazy scheme proved a big hit with the public, and the Tour was on its way toward living up to Desgrange's claim that it would be the biggest cycling event in the world. As for his newspaper, *L'Auto* changed its name in 1946 to *L'Équipe*, which today is France's most successful publication and the biggest daily sports newspaper in the world.

Little Géo Lefèvre's idea to create a cycling tour of France wasn't so bad after all.

A Century of Tours

WHAT BEGAN AS A PAWN IN A NEWSPAPER
CIRCULATION WAR BECOMES THE GREATEST
ANNUAL SPORTS EVENT THE WORLD HAS SEEN.

———————————⊙———————————

Tour de France founder Henri Desgrange, the owner and editor-in-chief of the
Paris sports daily *L'Auto* (which changed its name to *L'Équipe* after World War II),
was so upset by the cheating that went on during the event's second edition that
he threatened to abandon the whole project. Thankfully, he changed his mind, and
the race gradually grew in popularity, producing some of the most dramatic stories
in sports history. Today, the slick organization, live television images, and international renown are taken for granted. It wasn't always so . . .

1903—Sixty cyclists start the first stage of the inaugural Tour de France, sponsored by
the sports newspaper *L'Auto*, from Montgeron, just outside the Paris city limits, at pre-
cisely 3:16 p.m. on July 1. Each rider pays 10 old francs to enter the race and competes
for 20,000 francs in prizes (about $250,000 in today's currency), with 3,000 francs
($37,500) for the overall winner. Frenchman Maurice Garin takes the 467-kilometer
opening stage to Lyon in 17:45:44. Note that this is an estimate, since Garin crosses the
line before race director Géo Lefèvre had arrived. Garin wins three of the six stages to
become the first overall winner. The circulation of *L'Auto* doubles as a result of the event.

1904—The first controversy of the Tour. Despite the additions of assistant race director Jacques Miral and controller Gaston Rivière, the second Tour is marred by many
problems. Maurice Garin, Lucien Pothier, César Garin, and Hyppolite Aucouturier—
the first four on General Classification—are later disqualified by the French cycling
union. Henri Cornet, the twenty-year-old who finishes three hours behind Garin,
inherits the victory. He remains the youngest winner in the history of the Tour.

The first winner of the Tour de France, Maurice Garin, also finished first in 1904 before being disqualified a few months later.

1905—To avoid racing at nighttime, race organizer Henri Desgrange decides to reduce the length of each stage, but increase their number from six to eleven. The overall classification is not established by time but by points for placings on each stage, a formula that lasts until 1912. The first climb of a true mountain pass is made on the stage from Nancy to Besançon on July 11. Remarkably, René Pottier ascends the Ballon d'Alsace in the Vosges mountains at almost 20 kilometers per hour.

1906—This year marks the creation of the small red kite that indicates the last kilometer of each day's stage.

1907—For the first time, the Tour goes beyond the French border. It passes through Geneva, Switzerland, during the Lyon-Grenoble stage. Mountain climbs in the Chartreuse massif are added.

1909—The first non-French winner of the Tour is Luxembourg's François Faber.

1910—The first crossing of the Pyrénées takes place on July 21, with the riders climbing the Peyresourde, Aspin, Tourmalet, and Aubisque mountain passes on the stage from Luchon to Bayonne. Gustave Garrigou, the only one to climb the Tourmalet without putting a foot down, receives a cash bonus of 100 francs.

1911—The Tour enters the high Alps for the first time on July 10, with the climbs of the Col du Télégraphe and Col du Galibier on the stage from Chamonix to Grenoble.

1912—Odile Defraye is the first Belgian to win the Tour.

1913—The Tour takes a counterclockwise direction around France for the first time: The Pyrénées are climbed before the Alps. An eighteen-year-old Tunisian, Ali Neffati, becomes the youngest rider to participate in the race.

1914—Race numbers affixed to the riders' bike frames are introduced. Don Kirkham and Snowy Munro are the first Australians to compete in the Tour.

1919—The Tour returns after four years of World War I, but without three of its winners who were killed during the combat: Lucien Petit-Breton (1907, 1908),

Top left: Philippe Thys was the first three-time winner in 1920. **Top right:** Ottavio Bottecchia (left) was the first Italian to win the Tour (in 1924 and 1925). **Lower:** Vicente Trueba (left) was the first winner, in 1930, of the King of the Mountains competition.

François Faber (1909), and Octave Lapize (1910). The yellow jersey (*maillot jaune*) is introduced. Eugène Christophe is the first one to don it, at Grenoble on July 19.

1920—Philippe Thys of Belgium becomes the Tour's first three-time winner, while his countrymen take the following six places.

1923—Time bonuses for winners of the stages are created. Outside mechanical assistance is allowed for the first time, and the total purse reaches 100,000 old francs at a time when a one-pound loaf of bread costs about half an old franc. *L'Auto* achieves a press run of one million the morning after Henri Pelissier's overall victory.

1924—Ottavio Bottecchia is the first Italian to win the Tour.

1926—For the first time, the Tour doesn't start in the Paris region, but from the provincial town of Évian. The race distance is a record 5,745 kilometers, and few take notice of the first Japanese rider, Kisso Kawamuro, who abandons on the opening stage.

1927—All the flat stages are contested by each team starting separately, like team time trials.

1930—Henri Desgrange creates new rules that declare national and regional teams, and in doing so ends the run of trade teams. All the bicycles are supplied by the organization and painted a uniform color: yellow. Sponsorship is achieved through a pre-race caravan of promotional vehicles. The first live radio reports, hosted by Jean Antoine and Alex Virot, debut this year.

1933—The first King of the Mountains competition takes place and is won by Vicente Trueba of Spain.

1934— Race leader Antonin Magne of France wins the first individual time trial, 90 kilometers between La Roche-sur-Yon and Nantes.

1935—The victim of a heavy fall descending the Galibier, Spanish rider Francesco Cepeda dies. This is the first death of the Tour.

1936—Taken sick, race founder Henri Desgrange leaves the Tour after the second stage. The young editor of *L'Auto*, Jacques Goddet, succeeds him.

1937—The use of derailleurs is permitted for the first time at the Tour.

1947—After a seven-year interruption for World War II, the Tour returns. For the first time, Félix Lévitan appears in the organization of the race as Goddet's assistant. Frenchman Albert Bourlon completes the Tour's longest-ever successful solo break, 253 kilometers between Carcassonne and Luchon, winning the stage by 16:30.

1950—Both Italian teams (including race leader Fiorenzo Magni) abandon the Tour at St. Gaudens after race favorite Gino Bartali felt threatened by the aggressive actions of French spectators on the Col d'Aspin. Ferdi Kubler is the first Swiss to win the Tour.

1952—For the first time on the road stages, television is present at the Tour. Henri Persin holds the camera to shoot daily newsreels, while Georges de Caunes commentates. The Tour has its first mountaintop finishes at L'Alpe d'Huez, Sestriere, and the Puy de Dôme.

1953—The green jersey, awarded to the sprint points leader, is introduced.

1954—The Tour begins at Amsterdam in the Netherlands. This is the first time the Tour begins outside France.

1955—The photo-finish camera is introduced to help judge close sprints.

1959—Federico Bahamontes is the first Spaniard to win the Tour.

1960—The first transfer by train between stages occurs.

1962—For the first time since 1929, the Tour ends the national team rule and, once again, institutes the inclusion of trade teams. The race crosses the highest peak in its history, the Col du Restefond, at an elevation of 2,802 meters (9,192 feet). Tom Simpson becomes the first British rider to wear the yellow jersey.

Top: Father of the Tour Henri Desgrange sits with his eventual successor Jacques Goddet at a time trial start in 1939. **Left:** Goddet (in car) directed the Tour for half a century, half of the time with Félix Lévitan (standing with Jacques Anquetil in 1964). **Right:** Tom Simpson was the first British rider to wear the yellow jersey, in 1962.

Here riding a time trial at the 1962 Tour,
Anquetil was the first five-time winner.

1963—To celebrate the Tour's fiftieth edition, the race starts in Paris for the first time since 1950. Shay Elliott becomes the first Irishman to wear the yellow jersey.

1964—Jacques Anquetil of France becomes the first five-time winner of the Tour.

1965—The use of a starting ramp for individual time trials is allowed for the first time.

1966—Unofficial drug controls arrive at the Tour, carried out in Bordeaux by the French police. Raymond Poulidor is the first rider tested, and the next day, the peloton stages a demonstration as a sign of protest.

1967—The first prologue time trial is held at the Tour at the start in Angers. There is a return to the national team formula for the first of two Tours. Tom Simpson of Britain dies near the summit of Mont Ventoux after collapsing from heat exhaustion brought on by ingesting drugs and alcohol.

1968—Systematic antidrug controls are instituted by the Union Cycliste Internationale (UCI). Jan Janssen is the first Dutch winner of the Tour.

1969—A return to the trade team formula is instigated. This is Eddy Merckx's first Tour and his first Tour victory. During his prestigious career, he will wear the yellow jersey for ninety-six days and win thirty-four stages, both of them records that still stand.

1970—This is Dutchman Joop Zoetemelk's first Tour. He will participate in sixteen Tours, completing all of them, with twelve finishes in the top ten, a performance yet to be equaled.

1971—First transfers by air between certain stages occurs.

1974—The first visit of the Tour to England. Dutchman Henk Poppe wins the stage at Plymouth.

1975—This year notes the creation of the white jersey to reward the best young rider, and the polka-dot jersey is introduced to mark the best climber. Also, for the first time, the Tour finishes on the Champs-Élysées in Paris.

1978—After the stage finish at L'Alpe d'Huez, Belgian Michel Pollentier, the yellow jersey holder, is disqualified for attempting to cheat the drug control.

1981—Jonathan Boyer is the first American to start the Tour, and Phil Anderson becomes the first Australian to wear the yellow jersey.

1983—This year marks the debut of open racing with the participation of amateur racers from the Colombian national team, a move that attracts thirty-two reporters from their homeland.

1984—Luis Herrera, a Colombian, wins the Alpe d'Huez stage, the first South American stage winner in history.

1985—Greg LeMond is the first North American to win a stage of the Tour, taking the individual time trial at Lac de Vassivière.

1986—First participation of an American-based team, 7-Eleven, whose Alex Stieda becomes the first Canadian to wear the yellow jersey. Greg LeMond becomes the first American to win the overall title; his compatriot and La Vie Claire team-mate, Andy Hampsten, takes the white jersey.

Until he left the direction of the Tour in 1988, in his late eighties, Goddet penned a daily column for *L'Équipe*.

Steve Bauer was the first Canadian to win a Tour stage, in 1988, and wore the yellow jersey for five days that year, and for another nine days in 1990.

1987—The Tour starts in West Berlin, Germany, where Lech Piasecki becomes the first Polish rider to wear the yellow jersey. Félix Lévitan leaves the organization after misappropriation of funds. Stephen Roche is the first Irishman to win the Tour.

1988—The *Village Départ*, the tented sponsor compound at the stage starts, is created. Steve Bauer is the first Canadian to win a stage, taking the opening stage at Machecoul.

1989—The departure of the elderly Jacques Goddet leaves the door open for a new Tour organization led by Jean-Marie Leblanc, a former Tour racer and sports journalist, who takes over as director of competitions. Team invitations are based on UCI rankings for the first time, with a half-dozen wild cards issued to complete the list of starting teams. Greg LeMond and the 7-Eleven team introduce aero bars to the Tour. Raúl Alcalá is the first Mexican to win a stage, at Francorchamps, Belgium. LeMond wins the race by its smallest margin (8 seconds) after riding the fastest-ever Tour time trial at 54.545 kilometers per hour.

1990—A first stage victory for a Russian rider, Dmitri Konyshev, is recorded.

Using aero bars for the first time that year, Greg LeMond came from 50 seconds back on the final day to win the closing time trial and take the Tour by 8 seconds.

Lance Armstrong took his second consecutive Tour victory, in 2000.

1991—On being taken ill (drugs are suspected), all the riders from the world's No. 1 team, PDM, pull out of the race after eleven stages.

1992—To celebrate the European Union, the Tour passes through seven countries: Spain, France, Belgium, the Netherlands, Germany, Luxembourg, and Italy.

1993—At age twenty-one, Lance Armstrong competes at the Tour for the first time, winning stage 8 at Verdun before pulling out of the race in the Alps.

1994—Chris Boardman of Britain sets a record speed for a prologue time trial, completing the 7.2-kilometer course in Lille at 55.152 kilometers per hour.

1995—The Italian Fabio Casartelli, a Motorola teammate of Lance Armstrong, is killed when he crashes into a concrete post on the descent of the Col du Portet d'Aspet in the Pyrénées. The Italian team Gewiss-Ballan races the 67-kilometer Mayenne-Alençon team time trial at 54.930 kilometers per hour, a Tour record.

1996—Snow and high winds cause the major alpine stage to be cut from 190 kilometers to 46 kilometers, with the climbs of the Iseran, Télégraphe, and Galibier abandoned. Bjarne Riis of Denmark is the first Scandinavian to win the Tour.

1997—Jan Ullrich is the first German to win the Tour, sixty-five years after his countryman Kurt Stöpel was runner-up to André Leducq in 1932.

1998—The Festina doping scandal rocks the Tour as the race starts in Ireland for the first time, while the subsequent drug raids by French police on team hotels almost force the Tour to be abandoned on two occasions.

1999—Cancer survivor Lance Armstrong wins the 3,870-kilometer Tour at a record average speed of 40.276 kilometers per hour. Mario Cipollini sets a record speed for a road stage, completing the 194.5-kilometer stage from Laval to Blois at 50.355 kilometers per hour.

2001—A breakaway group finishes almost 36 minutes ahead of the peloton on the 222-kilometer stage 8 from Colmar to Pontarlier, the widest margin in postwar history.

2002—Lance Armstrong becomes the fifth rider to win a fourth Tour; the others all went on to win a fifth.

2003—The ninetieth edition of the Tour has 198 starters from twenty-two professional teams competing for about $3 million in prizes, with $400,000 to the winner.

Tales of the Unexpected

TOUR DE FRANCE HISTORY IS
FULL OF STRANGE GOINGS-ON.

For as long as the Tour de France has existed, riders and teams have bent the rules, made secret deals, or used questionable tactics to affect the outcome of the race. There have been some memorable, sometimes bizarre, incidents.

1911 TOUR DE FRANCE: A DOCTORED DRINK

There is a well-known story about Eddy Merckx who, after being disqualified for a positive drug test while leading the Giro d'Italia in 1969, claimed that someone had doctored one of his drinks. This was nothing new.

Almost sixty years before that incident, the French rider Paul Duboc was challenging eventual winner Gustave Garrigou for the leadership of the 1911 Tour de France. Duboc, who rode for a French team, La Française, had beaten Garrigou, leader of the rival Alcyon team, by 2 minutes on the mountain stage from Perpignan to Luchon in the Pyrénées. The next day, Duboc was 10 minutes ahead of Garrigou after the first two climbs and seemed to be headed for overall victory. Then partway up the next climb, the Col d'Aubisque, Duboc collapsed by the roadside and, doubled up with stomach pains, vomited a black liquid.

A few minutes earlier he had taken a bottle at a feed zone and downed the contents. Duboc was incapacitated for more than an hour before he could continue. It was revealed a few years later that a *soigneur* from Garrigou's Alcyon team was secretly banned for life from working in cycling, apparently for dubious practices that are believed to have included putting poison into Duboc's bottle.

Remarkably, Duboc recovered enough to win the next day's stage in Bordeaux, then another at Le Havre, and still finished second overall in Paris.

And Merckx and the doctored drink at the 1969 Giro? Well, the Cannibal was given the benefit of the doubt and his suspension was lifted in time for him to make his debut at the Tour de France—which he won by 17:54 over the runner-up.

1931 TOUR DE FRANCE: A FORTUITOUS LETTER

When you look at the factors that have helped riders win the Tour de France, you can cite things like strong time trialing, superb climbing, a dedicated team, or a smart directeur sportif. Antonin Magne of France had some of those things going for him at the 1931 Tour, but in the end it was a letter from a fan that helped him keep the yellow jersey. A letter? Well, read on . . .

The night before the Tour's penultimate stage, Magne was having trouble sleeping in his Charleville hotel room. His tossing and turning awoke roommate André Leducq, the winner of the previous Tour.

"I'm tired, but I can't sleep," Magne said. "I've too many things on my mind."

"Why don't you do some reading," replied Leducq. "You have a pile of fan mail on the table there."

One of the envelopes was slightly bigger than the others, yellow with a Belgian postage stamp. Magne picked it up. Written on a sheet of squared paper was a short, anonymous note: "Monsieur Antonin Magne, I want to tell you that Rebry wrote to his mother that he's going to make a big attack with Demuysère on the Charleville-Malo stage. Greetings."

"It's a joke," said Leducq.

"No," the Tour leader answered. "Look at the postmark, it's from Rebry's village."

Gaston Rebry and Jef Demuysère, the leaders of the Belgian national team, were both experts at riding the cobblestones of northern France, where the Charleville-Malo-les-Bains stage was headed. Rebry, known as "the Bulldog," won that spring's Paris-Roubaix, and was fighting hard at the Tour for Demuysère, who was lying third on General Classification, 12:56 down on Magne. The contents of the letter only gave Magne one more thing to worry about during his restless night.

It was a gray morning with rain forecast for most of the day. In the early part of the 271-kilometer stage, the forty-one survivors of the three weeks of racing stayed huddled together against the heavy rain. Magne stayed resolutely on Demuysère's wheel, while also keeping an eye on the Italian Antonio Pesenti, who was second on General Classification, 4:58 back.

Maybe the two Belgians weren't going to attack. . . . Then in the village of Bas-Lieu, 94 kilometers into the stage, Rebry suddenly accelerated on a rough cobblestone turn, taking Demuysère with him. Magne went wide and was 10 meters back when his friend Leducq shouted to him, "Hop! Hop!"

A superhuman effort by the yellow jersey closed the gap, but he managed to stay with the two charging Belgians. As they opened up a big gap over the rest of the field, Magne had to repeatedly chase after the Belgians as they kept on attacking him over the remaining 177 kilometers. The Frenchman was gapped again and again by the two Belgians, who adroitly switched from cobbled roadway to dirt path and back. The biggest gap Magne had to close was 150 meters when he had a small mechanical problem in the city of Valenciennes. By the finish, the three men arrived in Malo-les-Bains almost 18 minutes ahead of the chase pack led by Pesenti.

That time gap would have cost Magne the Tour if he had missed the break, but thanks to the fan letter from Belgium, he was forewarned and the yellow jersey was saved.

1947 TOUR DE FRANCE: SERVICES FOR HIRE

The mercurial Jean Robic is the only rider to have pulled off an overall victory at the Tour de France in a final-day road race (as opposed to the last-day time-trial turnarounds achieved by Jan Janssen in 1968 and Greg LeMond in 1989). Robic achieved his sensational success in 1947.

Before the final stage, a rolling 257 kilometers from Caen in Normandy to Paris, this was the overall classification:

> Pierre Brambilla (Italy), 140:44:38
> Aldo Ronconi (Italy), at 0:53
> Jean Robic (West France), at 2:58
> René Vietto (France), at 5:16
> Edouard Fachleitner (France), at 6:56

With two men on the Italian national team first and second, it seemed that all the Italians had to do was sit on Robic all day, while making sure that neither Vietto nor Fachleitner of the French national team escaped in a breakaway. Sounds simple, but Brambilla was an Italian who lived in France and his five remaining teammates didn't consider him one of them. Also, there were only fifty-three riders left in the race, and most of them were fatigued, particularly from a marathon 139-kilometer individual time trial two days earlier.

Even so, this final stage seemed routine when seven riders more than an hour down on General Classification escaped early on. But then, halfway through the stage, on leaving the crowd-packed streets of Rouen, Robic spotted that Brambilla was riding in the center of the small peloton. The slightly built Robic, a climber who had earlier won two mountain stages, now saw his chance. He attacked on a smoothly cobbled hill that went up for 2 kilometers to the chapel of Bonsecours.

Robic took 50 meters before Brambilla extricated himself from the pack and chased down the Frenchman. They slowed, and Robic went again, forcing the race leader to make another all-out effort. They slowed again; three others joined them, including Fachleitner, who rolled off the front. Brambilla got out of the saddle a third time, with Robic on his wheel, but before catching Fachleitner, Brambilla cracked.

Robic saw his chance, and even though he too was in the red zone, he dug deep to bridge across to Fachleitner. A 50-meter gap at the top of the hill soon stretched to a minute. With an overall deficit of almost 7 minutes, Fachleitner knew his odds of winning the Tour were minimal, while there was little chance of them catching the break that by now was 10 minutes up the road.

So why did Fachleitner then decide to pull and work with Robic? Well, as Robic later revealed, Fachleitner said, "You give me 50,000 francs and I'll work for you." Robic agreed to the deal, and again, a little later, when his rival upped the price to 100,000 francs (20 percent of the Tour winner's overall prize, which in today's terms would be about $40,000!).

By Paris, Robic and Fachleitner were 13 minutes ahead of the Brambilla-Ronconi-Vietto group. The Tour was Robic's, with Fachleitner runner-up—although there was a late twist.

The French national team sent back its rider in the break, Lucien Teisseire, to help Fachleitner. Robic claimed that Teisseire then bumped his rear wheel, causing both of them to crash, while Fachleitner rode clear. But Robic wasn't going to stand for that. Despite a damaged derailleur, he dashed back to his rival . . . and later paid him the 100,000 francs.

1987 TOUR DE FRANCE: BREAKING PROTOCOL

One of the oldest tricks in the pro cyclist's book is an attack through the feed zone. Technically, it is not against the rules. But it is a breach of race protocol, in the same league as attacking when riders have stopped for a pee. There was such an incident at the 1957 Giro d'Italia that cost Luxembourger Charly Gaul the overall victory. While he was relieving himself, Gaul's rivals Louison Bobet and Gastone Nencini and their teams made a joint attack, leaving the race leader almost 10 minutes behind. Although on that occasion, it was later revealed that when Gaul was at the roadside he provoked the attack by making an obscene gesture at Bobet.

The circumstances were much grayer at the 1987 Tour de France when a pre-meditated feed-zone attack by the Système U team caused Frenchman Jean-François Bernard to lose the yellow jersey.

Bernard, the French leader of the Toshiba team, took the race leadership by winning the time trial up Mont Ventoux. That win gave him the overall lead by 2:35 over Stephen Roche, the Irish leader of the Italian squad Carrera, and 2:47 on the former yellow jersey, Charly Mottet of French team Système U. On the next day's 185-kilometer stage 19, the top three all put teammates in an early break that gained 6 minutes before the first of the many climbs.

Roche made a couple of exploratory attacks up the narrow, sinuous Col de Tourniol that Bernard easily countered, but the race leader flatted just before the summit. After getting a wheel from a teammate, he managed to catch the end of the single file of 150 riders just as they reached the village of Léoncel, where they crossed a narrow bridge before reaching the crowded feed zone.

It looked as though Bernard would soon be back at the front. Unluckily for him, the Système U director, Cyrille Guimard, had other plans: He had given his men extra food before the start so they could attack through the feed zone and not slow down to grab their musette bags.

The attack was launched by Système U's Martial Gayant, and he was soon joined by teammates Mottet and Laurent Fignon, along with Roche and half-dozen others. Bernard was blocked at the back and was left chasing for the rest of the day. Roche took the yellow jersey with a 41-second lead on Mottet, while Bernard fell to fourth, 1:39 back.

Roche, who went on to win the Tour, later said he knew nothing of the premeditated feed-zone move and just followed his instincts in sensing that an attack was in the making. "I wouldn't have attacked because Bernard had punctured just before," he said. Not everyone has the same high standards.

1998 TOUR DE FRANCE: IT HELPS TO HAVE FRIENDS

Except in the individual time trials, the Tour de France is rarely a one-on-one battle between the strongest riders. For sure, a leader needs a strong team to control the pace on the long, flat stages so that breakaways are kept in check, but when his teammates have been dropped in the mountains other forces come into play. Such was the case on the dramatic alpine stage from Grenoble to Les Deux-Alpes in 1998.

The day began with defending champion Jan Ullrich of Germany leading the Tour by 1:11 over second-place Bobby Julich of the United States, with the dangerous climber Marco Pantani of Italy at 3:01. Pantani knew that if he were to have a chance of winning the Tour he would have to attack on the long climb of the Col du Galibier, even though it was followed by a 34-kilometer-long descent before the final short climb to the finish.

The weather worsened the higher the Galibier climbed, and a trio of climbers gained 3 minutes before reaching the toughest sections, which were about 6 kilometers from the 2,645-meter (8,677-foot) summit. Thick clouds cloaked the ice-lined peaks, suddenly unleashing sheets of bone-numbing rain as the temperatures dropped into the 40s (°Fahrenheit).

Race leader Ullrich hated cold, wet conditions, so this was the moment chosen by Pantani to unleash a furious attack. By the summit he had overtaken all those ahead of him and left the small Ullrich-Julich group 2:40 behind.

Matters seemed to improve for Ullrich on the first part of the long descent, and he turned onto a wider, less steep section only 2:11 behind Pantani. Riders were catching back to Ullrich, and his group was soon thirteen strong. Unfortunately, none of the other dozen men were teammates, and only Julich offered to help the German in the pursuit of Pantani.

Ahead, four other climbers had joined the Italian: Kelme teammates Fernando Escartin and Marcos Serrano of Spain, Casino team rider Rodolfo Massi of Italy, and Frenchman Christophe Rinero. As Rinero was one of Julich's team colleagues, he wasn't going to help Pantani. But Massi, a good friend, was soon making strong pulls for his fellow Italian, while the Kelme pair worked hard, knowing they had a chance of winning the stage at Les Deux-Alpes.

Even though there were only five riders in front and thirteen behind, the Pantani group started to gain time: 2:18 at the village of La Grave, where the road leveled out; 2:33 in the next 5 kilometers; and 3:14 before reaching the final 8.5-kilometer climb. On the uphill, Pantani raced clear to beat the runner-up Massi by 1:54, while Ullrich fell to pieces on the cold, wet ascent to the finish, crossing the line 8:57 back.

Pantani kept the yellow jersey all the way to Paris. But he wouldn't have had that opportunity without those friends on rival teams.

Techniques and Technology

BICYCLES AND EQUIPMENT HAVE CHANGED RADICALLY IN THE 100 YEARS SINCE THE FIRST TOUR DE FRANCE.

W hen you watch the closely packed peloton heading for the Tour de France finish line on the Champs-Élysées—the elbows of the colorful, Lycra-clad sprinters only inches apart as they weave through the pack at 45 miles per hour, their derailleurs shifting effortlessly into top gear, their skinny tires singing on the pavement—you are awestruck by the sight. You rarely give a thought to either the engineering technology that has created the racers' ultralight aluminum-alloy and carbon-fiber frames and components, or to the manufacturing skills that made their aerodynamic uniforms and helmets. These products are a quantum leap from the crude, heavy, single-gear bikes that the Tour pioneers trundled over dirt roads in the first years of the twentieth century. The story of how the equipment evolved is as fascinating as the race itself.

Let's go back to the Tour of 1907, to the 311-kilometer (194-mile) stage from Lyon to Grenoble. For the first time, the riders had to race through the mountainous Chartreuse massif, climbing the difficult Col de Portes before a 16-kilometer (10-mile) plunge to the finish. A Frenchman, Emile Georget, and a Luxembourger, François Faber, rode away from the field, topping the mountain pass several minutes ahead of the third rider. Today the pair would likely finish together to contest the stage win, but this was 1907 and Georget was the only one riding a bike with a freewheel, which wasn't an item in common use. The other racer, Faber, was riding a bike with a fixed wheel, which meant that he had to pedal all the way down the long descent. He couldn't keep up with the Frenchman and finished in Grenoble 7 minutes behind him.

Soon everyone fitted freewheels, but it was another thirty years before derailleurs were permitted at the Tour. Founder and race director Henri Desgrange

Even the motorcyclists following the Tour couldn't cope with the often muddy conditions during the early years of the race.

was not enthusiastic about the technical developments, and even though practicable derailleurs were in use by cyclo-tourists in the mid-1920s, he did not sanction their use until the 1937 Tour. Prior to then, the racers had to shift gears by stopping, loosening the rear wheel, and moving the chain by hand to another sprocket.

The typical pre-1937 Tour bike was fitted with one chainring and four sprockets, two on each side of the rear hub. In the mountains, a 46-tooth chainring would be used with a 22-tooth sprocket for a bottom gear of 52 inches (compared with a typical low gear today of 39x23, or 46 inches). A typical high gear seventy years ago was 46x16 (or 77 inches), vastly smaller than today's typical high gear of 53x11 (or 130 inches).

Besides the restrictions on the size and number of gears, the racers of the 1930s had to choose when and where to stop to effect their gearshifts. Those with local knowledge could sometimes remain on a higher gear for a climb, knowing that it wasn't too long, while others would have to stop twice: once to turn the wheel for the uphill and again for the descent.

Another problem racers experienced at the time was bruised or broken toenails. The simple cleat had yet to be invented, and racers had to strap their feet tightly into their pedals and toe clips to prevent their shoes from slipping. That fact is all the more

An early form of the derailleur gear, here used by René Vietto, was first sanctioned at the 1937 Tour.

surprising when you realize that a prototype toe clip was already in use at the first Tour, while well-designed toe clips and straps were in use by 1910. Today, of course, the toe clip is obsolete, and everyone uses click-in pedals that were pioneered in 1984 by the Look Company. Broken and blackened toenails are a thing of the past.

One of the lasting images of the early Tours is of the woolen-jerseyed *coureur* with a sheaf of tubular tires looped over his shoulders. Until 1908, riders used wired-on clinchers; when they flatted, they had to remove the wheel and tire and replace the inner tube. The one-piece tubular first made its appearance in 1908, although the racers still had to change the tires themselves, even if the procedure was simpler. It was not until 1923 that racers were allowed to receive replacement equipment from a support vehicle—and the draconian Desgrange only agreed to this after two men had been robbed of Tour victories because of mechanical breakdowns.

The most famous incident happened in 1913 when Eugène Christophe snapped his frame while leading the race on the Col du Tourmalet in the Pyrénées. He wasn't allowed a replacement bike (as he would be today), so he had to run for 16 kilometers (10 miles) down the rough mountain road with his heavy, broken machine slung over his shoulder to the village of Ste. Marie de Campan. There, he was directed to a forge normally used for making and fitting horseshoes. For three hours, Christophe worked on brazing together the broken tubes, watched by officials to ensure that nobody helped him. Such were the rules. (After the rider allowed a boy to pump the bellows for him, the officials slapped an extra time penalty on Christophe!)

Frenchman Christophe may have lost the race, but his disappointment was somewhat mitigated by his Peugeot teammate Marcel Buysse of Belgium taking over the leadership. Incredibly, three stages later, lightning struck the Peugeot team a second time. On the Esterel climb, Buysse's handlebars snapped. He too had to run 16 kilometers to the nearest town, Cannes, and even with Christophe's help he lost three hours. Despite going on to win six stages of that 1913 Tour, Buysse ended up in third place overall—just over 3 hours behind fellow Belgian Philippe Thys.

Buysse never came close to winning the Tour again (although his brother Lucien succeeded in 1926). But Christophe looked like a certain winner in 1919, the first Tour after World War I. Incredibly, he crashed while wearing the yellow jersey on the second-to-last stage—and his frame broke! Christophe was forced to repair the damage once more: two hours, and the Tour, were lost.

These incidents were among the ingredients of the battle for supremacy between the major bicycle manufacturers of the time: Alcyon, Automoto, and Peugeot. The monetary aspect of this commercial war intensely annoyed Desgrange, and in 1930 he produced a brilliant scheme to overcome the manufacturers' influence on the racing. He decided that the Tour would be contested by national teams, not trade teams sponsored by the bike companies, and that every racer would use an anonymous yellow bicycle supplied by the organization. To make up for the advertising fees his newspaper lost, Desgrange generated revenues for a publicity caravan, a parade of commercial vehicles displaying a wide variety of products that preceded the race by an hour or so.

Desgrange won this particular battle because the national team formula produced a string of popular French winners, but he was on a losing pitch with the bicycle industry, which needed the Tour de France to give its products the exposure to mass publicity. In 1939—the year he relinquished his control of the Tour—the aging Desgrange relented and allowed manufacturers to supply racers with brand-name bikes. Since World War II, the rivalry between both bicycle and equipment manufacturers has stepped up. Companies such as Campagnolo, Shimano, and Mavic test many of their products at the Tour to develop new lines. So the next time you watch the peloton speeding toward the finish line on the Champs-Élysées, remember a whole century of evolution made that beautiful sight possible.

Five-Time Champions

WINNING MULTIPLE TOURS IS A
COMPARATIVELY RECENT PHENOMENON.

———————◉———————

Given the greater number of teams, higher speeds, and increased competition at modern Tours de France, the chances of a rider taking multiple victories would appear to be more difficult. And yet seven riders have won three or more Tours in the past fifty years of the race, compared with only one such winner in its first fifty years. The first multiple champion was a Belgian, Philippe Thys, who won the Tour in 1913, 1914, and 1920. If World War I had not interrupted his streak, Thys might well have become the Tour's first five-time champion.

Similarly, World War II—when the Tour was put on hold for seven years—stopped Italy's legendary Gino Bartali and Fausto Coppi from having their shot at quintuple glory. Bartali had won the Giro d'Italia twice and the Tour once before the war; and he would go on to take a second Tour, ten years after the first, and a third Giro. Coppi won his first Giro before the war, and after the conflict he went on to dominate two of the three Tours he contested and became a five-time Giro champion.

Besides the hiatus of the two world wars, several other factors worked against riders taking multiple victories in the Tour's first half-century. More than one Tour was lost because of antiquated Tour rules that prevented the replacement of broken equipment and forced competitors to make their own repairs. Also, riders were more likely to drop out of the race because of sickness, saddle sores, or injuries from crashes because of the often atrocious condition of the roads and the less effective medical treatment. And in the era of the Tour being contested by national teams (1930–61), rather than the current trade-team system, the best riders often were not selected to ride the Tour and sometimes their countries simply did not compete. That's why, for example, Coppi started only three Tours.

Top: Would Coppi (left) and Bartali, here seen on their famous attack on the Col d'Izoard in 1949, have won five Tours without the hiatus of World War II? **Bottom:** During the era of national teams (made up of riders from different trade teams), Jacques Anquetil (here riding with teammate Roger Rivière) finished only third at the 1959 Tour.

In fact, in the national-team era, the only man who managed to put together three Tour victories (out of ten starts) was Louison Bobet of France. It wasn't until the change to trade teams, with their more professionally structured and cohesive organizations, that multiple wins became more frequent. Although Bobet's younger compatriot Jacques Anquetil did win two Tours as a member of the French national team (in 1957 and 1961), he became the event's first five-time champion with his St. Raphaël trade team, which helped him take his last three Tour victories in consecutive years. Trade teams also propelled Belgium's Eddy Merckx (between 1969 and 1974), France's Bernard Hinault (1978 to 1985), and Spain's Miguel Induráin (1991 to 1995) to their five Tour titles.

Besides the greater sophistication of modern professional cycling teams, another factor in the higher incidence of multiple wins has been the almost exclusive focus that a rider today can devote to the Tour. In contrast to the now accepted method of building up to the Tour with targeted training rather than random racing, riders like Merckx (and Hinault to a lesser extent) were winning races all year long. In 1970, for example, Merckx took fifty-two victories! Among the races he won before starting the Tour (which he also won) were the Giro d'Italia (including five stage wins), Paris-Nice, the Tour of Belgium, and four major single-day races: Paris-Roubaix, the Flèche Wallonne, Ghent Wevelgem, and the Belgian national championship. Without such

The Tour's first three five-time winners Eddy Merckx (left), Bernard Hinault (center), and Jacques Anquetil wore the yellow jersey for a publicity shot before Anquetil's death in 1987.

profligacy, and with a greater focus on the Tour, Merckx might well have won the Tour six or seven times.

However, whatever the merits of the more focused programs followed by riders in recent times, winning the Tour remains an inexact science. The vagaries of the weather, a rider's health and motivation, and the strength of his opponents still make the annual three-week trek around France one of the world's toughest sports events to win. To illustrate this, in a year when America's Lance Armstrong was attempting to join the exclusive five-win club, here is an analysis of how difficult it was for Anquetil, Merckx, Hinault, and Induráin to win a fifth Tour (and fail to take a sixth).

JACQUES ANQUETIL

If it hadn't been for a bicycle mechanic named Loulou Boulard, it's doubtful that Jacques Anquetil, in 1964, would have won a fifth Tour de France. Boulard was the mechanic for the Mercier team—the team of Anquetil's arch French rival, Raymond Poulidor. That year, the two French icons fought one of the closest battles the Tour has ever seen. After thirteen of the twenty-two stages, Anquetil was leading Poulidor by only 31 seconds. That was virtually nothing when you consider that a few days earlier, in a sprint finish to stage 9 on a cinder running track in Monaco, Poulidor missed winning a 30-second time bonus because he sprinted for the victory one lap too soon.

Analyzing the situation on the rest day in Andorra—where another Frenchman, Georges Groussard of the Pelforth team, held the race lead by a minute over Anquetil—observers felt that Anquetil still held the advantage. But the pressure of a feisty challenger had gotten to Anquetil. He was tired coming into the Tour, which began only two weeks after he won the Giro d'Italia—where he defended the leader's pink jersey for seventeen straight days. In contrast, Poulidor, two years younger, had started this, his third Tour, in perfect condition. His preparation included winning the Vuelta a España (then held in April-May) and finishing second at the nine-day Dauphiné Libéré.

Poulidor was a climber who could time trial, while Anquetil was a time trialist who could climb. And with more mountain stages than time trials in the second half of the 1964 Tour, Poulidor seemed to have the momentum turning his way.

That view was endorsed when Anquetil was dropped on the long climb out of Andorra. (He later admitted that he was wrong not to ride his bike on the rest day and instead attend a much-publicized party, munching on barbecued lamb and drinking sangria.) Looking sick, Anquetil slowly pedaled up the 20-kilometer Envalira climb, paced by his teammate Louis Rostollan. Without Rostollan's encour-

After having barbecued lamb and sangria at a rest-day picnic in Andorra (top left), Anquetil lost 4 minutes on the next day's first climb where teammate Louis Rostollan saved him from quitting (top right). Anquetil ended the race in Paris with a tiny 55-second margin over Raymond Poulidor to take his fifth Tour.

agement, Anquetil said he would have quit. As it was, he topped the mountain pass 4 minutes down on Poulidor's group, took a swig of champagne handed to him by his team director, Raphaël Geminiani, and set off at a terrifying speed through thick fog down the other side.

Anquetil quickly dropped Rostollan and passed two or three of his other teammates. "I had to catch Groussard's group or I'd have been finished," Anquetil said.

He did achieve that initial goal, and he was then helped by Groussard and his four Pelforth teammates, who were chasing the leaders to save their yellow jersey. Anquetil caught back to the fifteen-strong front group—led by Poulidor and the Spanish star Federico Bahamontes—exactly 114 kilometers into the 185-kilometer stage. With flat roads the rest of the way to the day's finish in Toulouse, things calmed down, and the stage appeared to be headed toward a sprint finish between the twenty-two leaders.

In such a small group, mostly climbers, it seemed likely that Poulidor might win one of the top-three time bonuses. But then, with 25 kilometers to go, some spokes snapped in Poulidor's rear wheel and he stopped to have the wheel replaced. This is where mechanic Boulard entered the picture. Although the routine wheel change took just a few seconds, Poulidor was off-balance when Boulard pushed him off again; he shoved so hard that Poulidor was knocked to the ground. He picked himself up, remounted—and then saw that his chain had fallen off the chainwheel.

By this time, the leaders had disappeared up the wide highway. Normally, Poulidor would have been able to chase back through the line of team and press cars following the first group. But the vehicles were all stuck behind Poulidor, mainly because the journalists wanted to see the chase, while Geminiani, Anquetil's team director, purposely blocked the other team cars from going ahead until the gap was too wide for Poulidor to close on his own. Unlucky "Poupou" was eventually caught by the next group and finished the stage 2:36 back. Because of Boulard's overly enthusiastic push, Poulidor now had a 3-minute deficit on Anquetil.

The picture changed again the next day when Poulidor, piqued by his bad luck, made a ferocious solo attack on the Portillon climb to win the stage into Luchon. The time he gained in addition to a 1-minute victory bonus took Poulidor back to within 9 seconds of Anquetil. That was still the situation two days later when they started a 42.5-kilometer time trial into the coastal town of Bayonne. Would Anquetil's time-trial skills carry the day, or would the resurgent Poulidor be stronger?

Over the first part of the course they seemed to be evenly matched, and with time bonuses of 20 seconds and 10 seconds for the two fastest riders, Poulidor had a real chance of taking the yellow jersey. (Groussard was a poor time trialist and would lose more than 3 minutes on that stage.) Poulidor was looking stronger as the kilometers ticked by. Then, up went Poulidor's hand to signal to his team car that he had flatted. Mechanic Boulard had a spare bike on his shoulder, ready to jump from the car and give to his rider. But in his eagerness he jumped out before the car had completely stopped and as its brakes went on, Boulard took a dive, with the new bike clattering on the tarmac. Poulidor picked it up, hopped on it, and was given a push start by another team helper. Unfortunately, the handlebars had twisted to the side when the bike fell, and Poulidor had to stop again. Boulard came running up to help straighten the bars, but in his panic forgot to give Poulidor a push start while he was trying to put his cleats into the toe clips. More seconds lost.

Even after all those delays, Poulidor still finished second on the stage, only 37 seconds slower than Anquetil. "I feel cursed," said Poulidor. "The slightest little problem becomes a catastrophe when it concerns me. I'm not criticizing [the mechanic]. I'm certain he's unhappier than me, because I'm sure it's panic that's causing all this."

But if Loulou Boulard had kept his cool, Poulidor—who finally lost the Tour by just 55 seconds—would have won that year. And Anquetil would not have been the first man to take five.

EDDY MERCKX

When the readers of French cycling magazine *Vélo* were asked in the spring of 2003 who they thought was the most dominant rider in Tour de France history, Eddy Merckx was named by 88 percent of them. Perhaps that was not a surprise, because in just seven appearances, Merckx won five Tours and finished second and sixth in the other two; he also set a number of all-time records, including the most career stage wins (thirty-four) and the greatest number of days in the leader's yellow jersey (ninety-six).

The Belgian superstar was taller and heavier than most Tour winners—6 feet and 165 pounds—and toward the end of his career his size made it more difficult for him to match the more lightly built climbers. In his first Tour victory, in 1969, he dominated in the mountains. When he took off over the summit of the Col du Tourmalet on stage 17, he continued alone for the next 130 kilometers of descending and climbing to finish the day some 8 minutes ahead of the runner-up. Riders leading the Tour de France weren't supposed to make risky breakaways like that.

Merckx wasn't capable of such an exploit five years later, at age twenty-nine, when he won his fifth Tour. In fact, he conceded time on virtually every mountain climb. On the two stages that had summit finishes, he was badly beaten by a man aged thirty-eight—the remarkable Raymond Poulidor—who, ten years earlier, had almost deprived Jacques Anquetil of his fifth win. Even in his twelfth Tour, the 5-foot-8, 152-pound Poulidor remained a talented climber, and on the two summit finishes in the Pyrénées he beat Merckx by 1:49 and 0:42 respectively. Luckily for

Eddy Merckx dominated his debut Tour, in which he made a solo attack over the Aubisque Pass to win stage 17 by almost 8 minutes.

Merckx, all the other mountain stages finished in the valleys, and he remained perhaps the fastest, most impressive descender in Tour history.

Merckx's downhill speed was useful the first day he was challenged by Poulidor, over the ultrasteep, but fairly short, Col du Chat on stage 10 into Aix-les-Bains. Merckx couldn't respond to the sharp uphill attack made by Poulidor, and he was more than a minute behind at the summit. Merckx descended the steep, narrow mountain road at a crazy pace to catch the French veteran.

After the Tour, Merckx revealed that part of the reason for his poor climbing form was a saddle sore that was operated on just before the race started. "The wound wasn't totally healed," Merckx said. "I finished the prologue with my shorts all bloody, and I suffered for the whole three weeks, without saying anything. It was worst on the climbs, where to lessen the pain I tried to climb standing on the pedals, and so I used up a lot more energy. It was because of this that I wasn't feeling at ease on the Col du Chat.

"I tried to find the least uncomfortable position, the opposite to Poulidor, who was superb that day. He really scared me, and it was because of that I chased after him like a madman on the descent. I've never gone downhill so fast."

Merckx then made a telling remark on why he didn't want Poulidor to win that day. "I couldn't let him believe that I was vulnerable. In the Tour, you sometimes have to bluff to stay on top of an opponent."

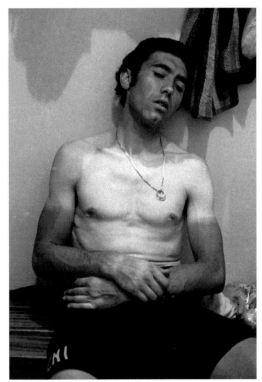

A kidney punch laid Merckx low in his bid for a sixth Tour win.

Bluffing was again part of his strategy the following year, when in his bid to win a sixth Tour Merckx had to deal with a much younger French opponent, Bernard Thévenet. Once again, Merckx struggled somewhat on the mountaintop finishes. He conceded 49 seconds to Thévenet at Pla d'Adet, then 34 seconds on the Puy de Dôme—where Merckx was punched in the kidneys by a spectator (who was later arrested, tried, and found guilty of assault). That stage was followed by a rest day and a transfer by plane to the French Riviera, giving Merckx a little time to recover, but in the alpine stages ahead he would have to fight through pain just as he had the previous year.

Going into the long climbing stage from Nice to Pra-Loup, Merckx was the race leader by 58 seconds over Thévenet, who vowed to attack the Belgian in a bid to wrest the yellow jersey from the defending champion. Thévenet was as good as his word, making six separate attacks on the day's longest climb, the Col des Champs. Merckx clawed his way back to the young Frenchman every time, and when the Belgian placed his own attack just before the summit of the penultimate climb, the Col d'Allos, it seemed that Thévenet had lost his chance to win.

Just as he did on the Col du Chat downhill in 1974, Merckx was unstoppable on the Allos descent. He reached the valley 1:10 ahead of Thévenet, with just a climb of 6.5 kilometers to the finish at Pra-Loup. It appeared that Merckx was on his way to a sixth Tour victory. But partway up that final climb, Merckx suddenly ran out of gas: Was it his aging legs, was it the effects from that kidney punch, or was it, as he later claimed, the back pain he sometimes felt on climbs following a frightening high-speed crash that cracked one of his vertebra in September 1969? Whatever it was, the five-time Tour champion slowed dramatically, riding on automatic. Thévenet caught him and in the last 3 kilometers left Merckx almost 2 minutes in his wake.

"I tried everything I could," said Merckx, "and I lost. I don't think I'll win this Tour. It's finished."

BERNARD HINAULT

The story of Bernard Hinault's fifth Tour de France win in 1985 (and his attempt to win a sixth in 1986) is inextricably connected to Greg LeMond. In those two Tours, the Frenchman and the American were co-leaders of La Vie Claire, then the strongest cycling team in the world. La Vie Claire was a French-sponsored team, but it had a multinational roster and its directeur sportif and coach was a Swiss, Paul Köchli.

Going into the 1985 race, Hinault, thirty years old, was his country's biggest sports star: the four-time Tour de France champion, two-time Giro d'Italia winner, world champion, and the winner of major classics like Paris-Roubaix, Liège-Bastogne-Liège, and the Tour of Lombardy. LeMond, twenty-four years old, was the precocious newcomer who, like Hinault, had won the world title, and on his Tour debut the previous year he had finished third overall after helping his then team-mate Laurent Fignon win the race. LeMond had then signed with La Vie Claire at what was a world cycling salary record of a million dollars over three years. As preparation for the 1985 Tour, LeMond finished third at the Giro, won by Hinault. With the two teammates almost equal in strength, the cycling world was wondering whether they would race as friends or rivals at the Tour.

Hinault was not only a talented athlete but also a master tactician who could control a race by his sometimes belligerent style. He acted as the boss of the peloton and he wouldn't put up with riders "disobeying" his orders. A famous example came in stage 12 of the 1985 Tour, when the young Frenchman Joël Pelier made an attack on the day's first climb, the Col de la Colombière, after Hinault had made it clear that early breaks wouldn't be tolerated on the very long stage of 269 kilometers. Hinault raced up to Pelier, shouted some abuse at him, and sent him back to the peloton.

In his bid to win a fifth Tour, in 1985, Bernard Hinault made a crafty break with Colombian Luis Herrera in the Alps (top left), but things started to fall apart when he crashed and broke his nose at St. Étienne (top right). He was left behind on the Tourmalet stage in the Pyrénées, but his teammate Greg LeMond was told to wait for him.

By that point in the 1985 Tour, Hinault was already wearing the yellow jersey. He had won the prologue and the 75-kilometer time trial at Strasbourg, and on the first mountain stage he had made an audacious attack with the Colombian, Luis Herrera, while the surprised LeMond had to sit back and watch like a dutiful teammate.

The American was frustrated that he couldn't fully use his true abilities, and although he was lying in second place coming out of the Alps, he was already 5:23 behind Hinault. He did pull back some time on the stage into St. Étienne, when he covered a break by some potentially dangerous climbers, including the Spaniard Pedro Delgado, as Hinault remained with a sixteen-strong chase group with La Vie Claire teammates Steve Bauer and Dominique Arnaud. Rounding the final turn, as the chasers sprinted for 10th place on the stage, four riders crashed into the barriers, including Hinault and Australian Phil Anderson, who was on the rival Panasonic team and a good friend of LeMond's.

Hinault fell heavily on his face and limped across the line looking more like a boxer than a cyclist, with blood streaming from a cut eyebrow. His X rays later showed that he'd broken his nose. The race leader—who didn't lose any overall time because the accident happened in the final kilometer—accused Anderson of causing the crash, which the Australian vigorously denied.

Hinault's injuries caused him considerable pain in the ensuing days, and there was speculation that he would have trouble on the climbs coming up in the Pyrénées. The speculation proved correct. On the stage that went over the mighty Col du Tourmalet and finished at the top of the next climb, Luz-Ardiden—the same ending as stage 15 of the 2003 Tour—Hinault couldn't follow the leaders' pace up the Tourmalet, while LeMond was in the front, riding with third-place rider Stephen Roche of Ireland. It looked as though the American, now only 3:38 behind teammate Hinault overall, would ride into the yellow jersey. Just then, the second La Vie Claire team car, driven by assistant director Maurice Le Guilloux, a Frenchman, moved up alongside LeMond. Le Guilloux told LeMond to stop his effort and reminded him that the goal was to keep Hinault in yellow. LeMond reluctantly backed off. He finished the stage in a small group with Anderson, Roche, and another Irishman, Sean Kelly.

Normally LeMond would have finished a steep climb like that final one to Luz-Ardiden several minutes ahead of Kelly, who was a sprinter rather than a climber. In fact, the American would have probably finished with the stage winner Delgado. As for Hinault, after being with LeMond's group at the foot of the last climb, he fell back to finish the stage in 18th place, 1:13 behind LeMond and 4:05 behind Delgado. The stage winner's advantage would have been more than enough to put LeMond into

On the 1985 Paris podium, the look on LeMond's face revealed his despair in conceding victory to teammate Hinault, who chats with then Paris Mayor Jacques Chirac.

the race lead, and he knew it. He was bitterly upset, but the American again held off in the next morning's half-stage up the Col d'Aubisque (won by Roche).

LeMond took some consolation three days later in becoming the first American to win a stage of the Tour de France, defeating Hinault by just 5 seconds in the 45.7-kilometer time trial at Lac de Vassivière. The Tour ended the next day in Paris with Hinault taking his fifth overall victory by a 1:42 margin over his young co-leader. Hinault knew that he may not have won had LeMond been on a different team; and so, in trying to dissipate any bad feelings that his teammate still held from the incident on the Tourmalet, the Frenchman said on the winners' podium, "Next year, Greg, I'll help you win the Tour."

It was a promise that he didn't exactly keep. The 1986 Tour would be Hinault's last before he retired. The Frenchman would explain away his many attacks in his final Tour by saying he was setting up the race for LeMond. In his actions, though, he did everything he could to become the first six-time winner. The story of how he failed and how LeMond won is in the American's story in chapter 7.

MIGUEL INDURÁIN

This stylish Spanish rider was regarded as unbeatable at the Tour de France, and yet Miguel Induráin took a long time to mature as a potential champion. He abandoned his first Tour after only four stages, and for the following five Tours he rode as a

Induráin's Tour breakthrough came at Luz-Ardiden in 1990 when he followed that year's Tour champion LeMond before racing past the American on the summit finish.

domestique for the leader of his Reynolds team, Pedro Delgado. Induráin had always been a strong time trialist, but he was considered too big to make a Tour winner. At the start of his professional career, the 6-foot-2 rider from Pamplona weighed almost 90 kilos (198 pounds). And it wasn't until he had shed 10 of those kilos (22 pounds), over a number of years, that his inherent power became something he could utilize to ride fast up high mountain passes. His breakthrough came at the 1990 Tour, when on the last mountaintop finish, with Delgado out of contention, Induráin was the only rider able to follow Greg LeMond on the climb to Luz-Ardiden. The Spaniard, then age twenty-six, shadowed LeMond—the overall winner that year—before surging in the last few meters to take the stage.

Induráin almost breezed through his next four Tours, comfortably winning each one. Just like Armstrong today, Induráin was expected to cruise to his fifth victory in 1995, having easily taken his two Tour preparation races, the Midi Libre and Dauphiné Libéré. It didn't exactly work out that way. He did win the 1995 Tour, but Induráin had to fight off a number of determined riders who kept him and his

Banesto team constantly on their toes. Those challengers were the Dane Bjarne Riis, the Swiss Alex Zülle, and the Frenchman Laurent Jalabert.

Perhaps the champion sensed that he was going to be hard-pressed to take a fifth consecutive Tour because he decided to deal a huge psychological blow to his opposition before anyone was expecting it: the day before the first long time trial. On the rolling stage from Charleroi to Liège in Belgium, Induráin shocked everyone with a premeditated attack on the steepest (12 percent) pitch of Mont Theux, the day's second-to-last hill. Describing the move in his book, *Induráin: A Tempered Passion*, Spanish novelist Javier García Sánchez wrote: "It panicked and horrified [his rivals]. Those 30 kilometers to Liège, with Induráin chased by the cream of the international peloton . . . belong to the annals of cycling history. [He] was sealing his fifth Tour win even before the first time-trial stage, even before the first mountain."

Indeed, Induráin did take over the yellow jersey in the next day's time trial and retained it for the rest of that 1995 Tour. But there were many close calls on the way to Paris.

The first was in the time trial itself. In the previous three Tours, Induráin had obliterated the opposition, each time defeating the runner-up by at least 2 minutes. At Luxembourg in 1992, for example, his team manager, Eusebio Unzue, described his rider's performance this way: "Never had I been so ill at ease. I thought Miguel had gone crazy. For the first 20 kilometers, he'd turned his 54x12 at more than 62 kph. If he'd had a 56 chainring, I believe he would have averaged more than 70 kilometers per hour. He was gaining 4 to 5 seconds per kilometer on everyone."

Induráin was almost unbeatable in time trials, especially when he gained almost 4 minutes on all his rivals at the 1992 Tour time trial in Luxembourg.

The picture was vastly different on the hilly route between Huy and Seraing in 1995. Not only did Induráin fail to gain 5 seconds a kilometer, but he was also having trouble gaining that much on Riis over 54 kilometers. In fact, Riis was beating the "unbeatable" until the defending champion surged in the final uphill stretch to win the stage by just 12 seconds.

While resisting Riis was a challenge in his favorite discipline, Induráin's next test came in more unfamiliar territory. It came on the very next stage, on a day of four mountain climbs, following a transfer from Belgium to the French Alps. Zülle, one of the pre-race favorites, crossed to a small breakaway group on the second climb, forcing Induráin and his Banesto team to chase for the rest of the stage. By the foot of the ascent to the finish at La Plagne, Zülle was alone, 4 minutes ahead of Induráin and the other race leaders.

The Spaniard was in danger of losing the yellow jersey. This was perhaps the biggest challenge of his career, one that he needed to respond to unreservedly if he were going to win his fifth Tour. But Induráin was never shy of hard work, as his team director, José-Miguel Echavarri, often pointed out: "Miguel is not a superman. I've seen him stop in a mountain stage, his face twisted in pain. I know that he suffers . . . and that he has exceptional willpower. He knows how to surpass himself."

Induráin surpassed himself on the 12-kilometer climb up to La Plagne. He flew through the sweeping curves of that alpine road, dropping Riis, Marco Pantani, and all the other top climbers by 2 minutes, while closing to within 2 minutes of stage winner Zülle. It was probably the fastest Induráin had climbed a mountain pass in his life.

Normally, his one-man-show into Liège, the time-trial win at Seraing, and this masterly uphill performance to La Plagne would have been enough to cement his grip on the yellow jersey. But another big challenge was on the horizon. This one came from Jalabert, three days later, on a hilly 222-kilometer stage across the Massif Central from St. Étienne to Mende. Then in the first year of a near-five-season reign as the world's No. 1–ranked cyclist, Jalabert was just emerging as a challenger for the grand tours. And on that blazing hot July 14, the French national holiday of Bastille Day, he turned in perhaps the most spectacular ride of his career.

Induráin's Banesto teammates were somewhat sloppy in allowing Jalabert to slip away in an early break, and downright remiss in then letting two of his ONCE teammates to bridge up to him. Over the next several hours, up and down roller-coaster back roads and across wildly beautiful plateaus, Jalabert and his fellow breakaways etched out a near-11-minute lead. That would have been enough to give the

Frenchman the yellow jersey had the lead survived until the day's end; but even though Jalabert eventually took a brilliant solo stage victory, Induráin's men slowly closed the gap, the break eventually split apart, and the race leader put in an impressive defensive effort up the steep climb to the finish to retain his grip on the Tour, and moved up to third on overall classification.

Induráin didn't have to stave off any other big challenges that year, although Riis insisted that he had planned a big attack on the final mountain stage in the Pyrénées—a stage that was neutralized, ridden slowly by the peloton as one big group, in honor of the Italian rider Fabio Casartelli who died in a race crash the previous day. At the time, Riis was criticized for suggesting that the race should have continued normally, and that he should have been given his chance of racing for the yellow jersey.

That chance would come the following year, 1996, when Riis became the man who toppled Induráin from his throne. It was supposed to have been a Tour of triumph for the Spanish champion, a race that the organizers even routed through his hometown on the giant stage 17 through the Pyrénées to Pamplona. But it turned into a Tour of torment for Induráin, whose attempt to take the race for a sixth time fell apart on the very first mountain stage.

Induráin, however, was not shattered by his defeat. His reactions were analyzed by the novelist García Sánchez, whose words perhaps tell us more about what motivated Induráin than any of the praise for his previous successes. After the writer watched his hero fall apart on the alpine climb to Les Arcs, he thought about the week of dreadful wet weather that had preceded that stage, and how Induráin—angry with the wet, cold conditions—had said upon crossing the finish line at Les Arcs, "I had a cloud in front of my eyes."

Then García Sánchez remembered an interview that the five-time Tour winner had once given to a French journalist, who asked if it were true that Induráin had said, "What's the point of climbing mountains if you then have to race down them?"

"Yes," Induráin replied gravely, "maybe there is a philosophy of life in that strength, which takes you beyond your own limits for the entertainment of others. But deep down, if you think about it, you push yourself beyond the bounds of what is reasonable in pursuit of something that is completely intangible."

PART II

North America and the Tour

ONLY IN THE PAST TWO DECADES HAVE
AMERICANS STARTED TO TAKE A TRUE
INTEREST IN THE TOUR DE FRANCE.

───────────⊙───────────

For almost eight decades, the Tour de France was an event that barely existed for North Americans. Perhaps they had heard of it, but it wasn't something that made its way into the news. Not surprisingly, a French Canadian cyclist was the first to take part in the Tour, back in 1937. But perhaps the first time that Americans became more aware of the race was in 1960 when Red Smith, the famed sportswriter of the now defunct *New York Herald Tribune*, followed a half-dozen stages of that year's Tour.

His graphic reports gave his readers a sense of the heroism displayed by the competitors and the spectacular nature of the race. He witnessed several accidents, including one in the Alps, about which he wrote:

> *Coming down a peak called Col de la Colombière yesterday, Martin Van Geneugden, of Belgium, plunged over the side, splitting his head and carving up both arms. "Let me go," he kept sobbing as a doctor bandaged him. He remounted and rode on.*
>
> *Van Geneugden was overtaken in the village below. He seemed to be wearing elbow length gloves. It was dried blood blackening with dust. Along the curb smiles changed to horror as he passed. "It is nothing," he said through a red mask.*

During the 1960s and 1970s, cycling enthusiasts in North America began subscribing to British magazines that reported on the Tour. These included the monthly *Sporting Cyclist*, which was succeeded by *International Cycle Sport*—both of which were edited by the late J. B. Wadley, who first reported on the Tour in 1955. Wadley was a cycling enthusiast and traveler who wrote about the tactics and technical aspects of the race as an insider. He followed the Tour at a time before live television when reporters followed the race on motorcycles or in press cars in the middle of the race, so he could take readers right into the peloton.

This extract from his 1959 Tour report on a stage of blazing heat through the hills of the Massif Central was typical of what he wrote. The chief characters are defending champion Charly Gaul of Luxembourg, three-time Tour winner Louison Bobet of France, and Bobet's young teammate Roger Rivière (the holder of the world hour record on the track). They have just topped the ultra-steep Montsalvy climb, where Gaul and Rivière are in a small lead group with some Belgians, while Bobet has just been left in their wake:

> Along the final straight of that rise, Gaul dropped to the back, with Rivière at the front. Unaccountably, Gaul tailed off a few metres—at first we thought it's just a joke—but then the interval went up to 50 metres. It was then the [French team] manager [Marcel] Bidot raced up alongside Rivière in his car and shouted at the hour-record man something which, obviously we did not know at the time, but learned in the evening of this remarkable day: "Ride, Roger, as hard as you can!"
>
> "But the Belgians, they won't work," Rivière gasped. "If I ride they'll have an armchair ride for the team race."
>
> "Never mind; I say, if you want to win the Tour de France, now is the moment above all to ride and get rid of Gaul."
>
> This was Rivière's first Tour, Bidot's 20th as a rider or manager. Rivière "rode."
>
> And he therefore began to "ride" on the steep descent of Montsalvy, and Gaul, who is never happy on a descent at any time, began to lose ground rapidly.
>
> We were close on his tail on that swish-swush descent through the woods, and again we were looking back for Bobet, who in due course swept by us with [teammate René] Privat close at hand. What would happen, I wondered, when they caught Gaul; what would be their tactics?
>
> We never were able to see, because at the foot of the descent in the village of Junhac, a crowd was surging over the square to the fountain where bicycle No. 1 of the Tour de France was in view with its owner, Charly Gaul, dipping his head in and out of the water.
>
> From Jean Bobet (a journalist who was Louison Bobet's brother) we learned later that Louison and Privat actually saw [Gaul] stopping, and Louison called to his teammate: "We may be cooked, René, but Gaul is beaten!"

Reporting such as this enhanced the legendary qualities of the Tour among the cycling cognoscenti in North America, and this knowledge spread through the years, particularly after *VeloNews* started to devote space to the Tour in the early 1970s. This knowledge in turn enticed a few American amateur racers to go to Europe, perhaps with the dream of competing at the Tour.

The U.S. pioneers were forced to completely integrate themselves into the continental lifestyle to have any hope of getting on a European team. Many returned because of homesickness—this was in the days before e-mail, easy telephone access, and cable TV.

The first American to be signed by a pro team in Europe was Californian Mike Neel, who initially raced in France as an amateur in 1972. "I had no money," said Neel, "so I worked in a bike shop. It was hard working in a bike shop if you didn't speak French."

Living at poverty level was not much different for Neel after he joined the Italian pro squad Magniflex in 1976. He was based at Prato, near Florence. "I stayed in a little apartment near the [Magniflex] mattress factory with the Australian Gary Clively," Neel continued. "I actually worked at the factory. They told me to stop making so many mattresses, as I was making the others look bad."

While in Italy through 1977, Neel helped fellow Californian George Mount join an amateur team in Tuscany, at Castelfranco di Sopra. Mount went on to race as a pro for the Italian pro squads San Giacomo (1980) and Sammontana (1981–82).

Meanwhile, in France, another Californian, Jonathan Boyer, after racing successfully for an amateur team in Paris, turned pro in 1980 for Puch-Sem, and then for a season hooked up with rookie pro Greg LeMond at Renault-Gitane. Riding for Renault, under the team leadership of Tour winner Bernard Hinault, Boyer was the first American to ride the Tour de France, in 1981.

LeMond relocated to Europe that same year. At the beginning, Renault team boss Cyrille Guimard set up the nineteen-year-old LeMond and his new wife, Kathy, with a small house in a village near Nantes in western France; but Kathy felt isolated there, so in 1982 the LeMonds moved to Kortrijk, Belgium, where they would live for the rest of LeMond's racing career. LeMond would make his Tour debut in 1984.

Meanwhile, back in North America, the first U.S. professional team was created in 1985, sponsored by 7-Eleven. It would ride the Tour de France for the first time in 1986, with a roster of eight Americans, a Canadian, and a Mexican. This continent's love affair with the Tour de France had begun.

In total, by the end of the 2003 Tour, thirty-four riders from North America have started the race. Combined, they have won eight Tours, won thirty stages, and worn the yellow jersey for ninety-one days. Here is a rundown on their achievements at the Tour.

CANADIANS

Pierre Gachon

1937 *DNF*

This French Canadian from Québec had been a six-day track rider for seven years when he started the Tour at age twenty-eight as part of a small British team. In his ten six-day starts, Gachon recorded only one top-three performance, coming in 3rd with his partner, Henri Lepage, at Minneapolis in 1931. At the 1937 Tour, Gachon didn't survive the opening stage of 223 kilometers between Paris and Lille. It would be almost fifty years before the next Canadian rode the Tour.

Steve Bauer

1985 *10th*; **1986** *23rd*; **1987** *74th*; **1988** *4th*; **1989** *15th*; **1990** *27th*; **1991** *97th*; **1992** *DNF*; **1993** *101st*; **1994** *DNF*; **1995** *101st*

In eleven appearances at the Tour (a record for a North American), Bauer had one stage win (at Machecoul in 1988), and he wore the yellow jersey for fourteen days (five in 1988, nine in 1990). His best overall performance, 4th overall, came in 1988, when he was the leader of the Swiss-based team, Weinmann–La Suisse.

That year, the Ontario rider won the opening stage with an astounding solo break in the final few kilometers to hold off the whole charging pack by 8 seconds. He lost the lead the same day when his team finished 2nd in the team time trial, 24 seconds

Steve Bauer

behind the winning Panasonic-Isostar squad, whose Teun Van Vliet took over the yellow jersey. But Bauer won it back six days later, at Nancy, and retained the lead for four days until eventual winner Pedro Delgado took over at L'Alpe d'Huez.

In 1990, Bauer again had a hot start to the Tour, this time as a member of the American team, 7-Eleven. After a solid prologue, the Canadian went with a four-man break in the next morning's half-stage at Futuroscope with the Italian Claudio Chiappucci, Frenchman Ronan Pensec, and Dutchman Frans Maassen. The four finished an enormous 10:35 ahead of the peloton, with Bauer taking the yellow jersey by 2 seconds over Maassen. That afternoon, 7-Eleven rode to a strong 6th place in the team time trial, faster than the teams of Maassen, Pensec, and Chiappucci, to keep Bauer in the overall lead. He wore the yellow jersey for the next eight days, before conceding it to Pensec in the Alps.

Alex Stieda
1986 *120th*

This rider from British Columbia was the first North American in Tour history to wear the Tour's yellow jersey. He did it, on July 5, 1986, by making a solo attack on the first stage between Nanterre and Sceaux. Stieda finished in 5th place on the stage, but by winning time bonuses at the intermediate sprints, he took the race lead by 8 seconds over the Belgian Eric Vanderaerden. The Canadian rider's moment of fame quickly ended because in that afternoon's 56-kilometer team time trial, he was dropped by the other members of his 7-Eleven team and fell to nearly last in the overall standings.

AMERICANS
Jonathan Boyer
1981 *32nd;* **1982** *23rd;* **1983** *12th;* **1984** *31st;* **1987** *98th*

This tall, slim Californian (who was born in Utah) was twenty-five years old when the Renault-Gitane team called him up to compete at the Tour—the first-ever American starter. He was only in his second year as a professional, but the previous season, as a member of the Puch-Sem team, he had finished 5th at the world road championship on a mountainous course that cut the field of 107 starters to only fifteen finishers. The winner was the Frenchman Bernard Hinault,

Jonathan Boyer

the Renault team leader who had won the Tour in 1978 and 1979. Renault was also signing the brilliant young Greg LeMond, and team director Cyrille Guimard thought it made sense to sign a second American to make LeMond's transition to pro racing a lot smoother.

As it happened, LeMond and Boyer didn't get on well, and Boyer stayed with Renault for just one year. However, he did ride the Tour (LeMond, twenty, was too young for the Tour and waited until 1984 for his first start). Boyer was a solid 32nd in his debut Tour, and then returned to the Sem team. His top Tour performance came in 1983, when his best quality—endurance—helped him finish the race in 12th overall.

Greg LeMond
1984 *3rd*; 1985 *2nd*; 1986 *1st*; 1989 *1st*; 1990 *1st*; 1991 *7th*; 1992 *DNF*; 1994 *DNF*

History will ask: What would have happened had LeMond not been accidentally shot and almost killed in 1987, a couple of months before he was due to defend his Tour de France title? Before the hunting accident, he had been the world's most dominating rider, a brilliant climber and time trialist who by age twenty-six already had three podium finishes at the Tour. After the accident, he struggled for two years to rediscover a semblance of his pre-1987 form, and almost quit racing at the 1989 Giro d'Italia. Some of his spark then returned, and he won an exciting victory at that year's Tour, and won again in 1990. Surely, the form that he enjoyed in 1986 and before would have carried LeMond to Tour victories in 1987 and 1988. Then he would have been the first American to win five Tours.

In the three years that he did win the Tour, the California native wore the yellow jersey for seventeen days. And in his eight Tours he won five stages: the Lac de Vassivière time trial in 1985; the mountaintop finish at Superbagnères in 1986; and the Dinard-Rennes time trial, Aix-les-Bains mountain stage, and Versailles-Paris time trial in 1989. At 55.545 kilometers per hour, that final stage win remains the fastest long time trial in Tour history, and it brought LeMond the overall win by the smallest-ever margin, 8 seconds, over runner-up Laurent Fignon of France.

Doug Shapiro
1985 *74th*; 1986 *DNF*

This native New Yorker from suburban Long Island remains one of the few Jewish cyclists to have ridden the Tour. After missing the final cut for the U.S. road team at the 1984 Olympics, Shapiro turned professional for the Dutch team Kwantum, led by 1980 Tour winner Joop Zoetemelk. The experience he gained by finishing the 1985 Tour earned him a spot on the 7-Eleven team the following year, the American team's debut. In that Tour, he was sick and pulled out on the twelfth stage through the Pyrénées along with sixteen others.

Andy Hampsten

Andy Hampsten

1986 *4th*; **1987** *16th*; **1988** *15th*; **1989** *22nd*; **1990** *11th*; **1991** *8th*; **1992** *4th*; **1993** *8th*

Hampsten is best remembered as the only American to have won the Giro d'Italia (in 1988), but he also had an outstanding eight years of riding the Tour de France. This slim athlete—who was born in Ohio, grew up in North Dakota, and later moved to Colorado—wasn't a strong time trialist. While this prevented him from being a true contender, four top-ten finishes at the Tour are a testimony to his talent. Hampsten was a gifted climber, and at his first Tour in 1986 he was an invaluable teammate for Greg LeMond at La Vie Claire. It was Hampsten who set the pace on the Superbagnères climb in the Pyrénées and enabled LeMond to race to a stage victory on that mountaintop finish to move within 40 seconds of overall race leader Bernard Hinault. LeMond went on to win the race while Hampsten ended his first Tour in 4th place, becoming the second American to win the white jersey as the best under-25 finisher. Hampsten would finish 4th again in 1992, then with the American team Motorola, after gaining a memorable stage victory at L'Alpe d'Huez.

Bob Roll

1986 *63rd*; **1987** *DNF*; **1990** *132nd*

This Californian had a "wild man" image in the peloton that endeared him to his teammates at 7-Eleven, the first American team to ride the Tour. The other riders in the peloton were wary of Roll, but they grew to respect his work ethic, which helped him finish two of the three Tours he started, despite being a hardworking domestique. He would have finished the other one, too, but for a debilitating bout of gastroenteritis; and Roll would have ridden a fourth Tour (in 1988) had he not crashed in training the day before the start—a New Zealander, Nathan Dahlberg, replaced him on the 7-Eleven team.

Jeff Pierce
1986 *80th*; **1987** *88th*; **1989** *86th*

Recruited at the last minute on the first 7-Eleven squad, this Michigan native was a strong all-rounder who took three middle-of-the-pack finishes at the Tour; but he is remembered most for his win in the prestigious Champs-Élysées stage in 1987. On the last lap around the Champs-Élysées, Pierce attacked from a small breakaway group, which eventually ended the stage 17 seconds ahead of the pack, to win solo. What is rarely remembered is that the runner-up that day was another North American, Steve Bauer, who finished just 1 second behind Pierce.

Ron Kiefel
1986 *96th*; **1987** *82nd*; **1988** *69th*; **1989** *73rd*; **1990** *83rd*; **1991** *138th*; **1992** *DNF*

This native Coloradan was one of the more talented members of the original 7-Eleven team. He was the first American to win a stage of the Giro d'Italia (at Perugia on June 1, 1985), but he could not win a stage at any of the seven Tours he contested. The closest that Kiefel came was at his first Tour, in 1986, when he was in a twelve-man break that sprinted for 1st place on stage 7 from Cher-

Top: Bob Roll **Middle:** Jeff Pierce
Bottom: Ron Kiefel

bourg to St. Hilaire-du-Harcoët in Normandy. Kiefel came in 2nd, just behind Ludo Peeters of Belgium and one place ahead of a certain Miguel Induráin of Spain.

Eric Heiden
1986 *DNF*

The five-time gold medalist in speed skating at the 1980 Winter Olympics was also an accomplished cyclist. He won the first USPRO Championship at Philadelphia in 1985 and tackled the Tour with 7-Eleven the following year. Heiden, from Wisconsin, was bulky for a Tour rider, but he battled commendably through seventeen stages; but on stage 18, he crashed on the descent of the Col du Télégraphe in the Alps, with his injuries forcing him to abandon the race.

Alexi Grewal
1986 *DNF*

The Olympic road champion at the Los Angeles Games was considered a top prospect for the Tour de France when he signed his first pro contract with Panasonic, then one of the world's top teams, in 1985. But Grewal quickly grew homesick for his native Rocky Mountains when he was based in Europe, and he joined 7-Eleven in 1986. He started that year's Tour, but was never happy in the cauldron of the world's biggest race. He is remembered more for his fiery temperament—which led him to throw a water bottle at a CBS camera crew when climbing the Col de Marie-Blanque in the Pyrénées—rather than his brilliant climbing talent. He did ride strongly in the Pyrénées, taking 16th and 12th on the two mountain stages; but he didn't make it through the Alps, pulling out on stage 17 with a throat infection.

A footnote to Grewal's European career (before he returned to racing in the States) came at the end of 1986, when he rode the Tour de l'Avenir (a sort of junior Tour de France) for the French team RMO. On the toughest stage over the legendary Col d'Izoard in the Alps, Grewal made a solo attack and threatened the race leadership of a young Miguel Induráin. The gangly American won the stage, but for the first time Induráin showed the climbing strength that would take him to five Tour de France wins.

Davis Phinney
1986 *DNF;* **1987** *DNF;* **1988** *105th;* **1990** *153rd*

Over the course of his long career—eight years as an amateur, nine as a professional—this native Coloradan scored more than 300 victories, thanks to his impressive

Davis Phinney

sprinting ability. The most prestigious of those wins were the two stages of the Tour he took in 1986 and 1987. In his debut Tour with 7-Eleven, he won stage 3 from Levallois to Lièvin by out-sprinting a nine-strong breakaway group—although he thought he was sprinting for 2nd place. Phinney didn't know until after the finish line that the Spanish rider who had attacked from the break had flatted a couple of kilometers from the stage end.

His other Tour success, the following year, was in stage 12 from Brive to Bordeaux, when he used the bike-handling skills that earned him so many wins in American criterium races to outkick a pack of 178 riders on a finish that had two sharp turns in the final kilometer. He crossed the line ahead of two of the world's fastest sprinters, Jean-Paul Van Poppel of the Netherlands and Malcolm Elliott of Britain, to take what remains the only Tour field sprint won by an American.

Chris Carmichael
1986 *DNF*

For a man who would later become an outstanding coach, guiding Lance Armstrong to his Tour victories, this Florida native did not have a particularly outstanding Tour career. He started just one Tour, 1986, for the pioneer 7-Eleven squad. His best stage placing was 55th on stage 6 at Cherbourg, and he was forced to abandon the Tour on the first day in the mountains, the rugged Bayonne-Pau stage 12 that saw sixteen others pull out, including a young Miguel Induráin.

Jeff Bradley
1987 *DNF*

His blond hair and all-American good looks made Bradley seem more like a tennis player than a Tour rider, and he rarely showed his talent as a cyclist in his brief professional career for 7-Eleven. He chose a tough edition of the Tour to ride, in 1987, and he didn't make it past stage 11—a brutal 7-hour, 255-kilometer trek across the Massif Central between Poitiers and Chaumeil on a day of torrid heat.

Andy Bishop

1988 *135th;* **1990** *116th;* **1991** *126th;* **1992** *DNF*

This rider from Arizona did not win many races as a professional, but he was respected for his work as a team rider, first for the Dutch team PDM, then with 7-Eleven and Motorola.

Roy Knickman

1989 *DNF*

This Southern Californian was heralded as a good prospect for the Tour when he turned pro with Greg LeMond's La Vie Claire team in 1986. And that possibility seemed strong when he held the leader's jersey at that year's Tour de l'Avenir for a week before a stomach virus put him out of the race. Knickman made his Tour debut three years later for 7-Eleven, but he didn't make it past stage 11.

Norman Alvis

1990 *142nd*

This strong California rider was a stalwart on the 7-Eleven and Motorola teams for many years, but he was called up to ride the Tour only once, in 1990. He played a strong team role in defending the yellow jersey of Steve Bauer for the first nine days.

Michael Carter

1991 *DNF*

This native Coloradan was a talented climber who spent most of his career in the United States. He had one season, 1991, with Motorola in Europe, and he was selected to ride the Tour. Unfortunately, Carter was not at his best and he finished the first day in the mountains, stage 11 from Pau to Jaca, in Spain, well behind the pack and was eliminated on time.

Frankie Andreu

1992 *110th;* **1993** *89th;* **1994** *89th;* **1995** *82nd;* **1996** *111th;* **1997** *79th;* **1998** *58th;* **1999** *65th;* **2000** *110th*

This tall Michigander was the last of the crossover American riders, having started his European career with 7-Eleven, moved on to the Motorola team, and ended it with the U.S. Postal Service formation. Andreu was the model team rider—always ready to protect his team leader (who was Lance Armstrong in the Tours of 1993–1996 and 1999–2000). Andreu finished all nine of the Tours he started, a record for an

Frankie Andreu

American rider. The closest he came to a stage win was in 1994, when he was in the winning breakaway on the final day into Paris and finished 2nd to Frenchman Eddy Seigneur.

Lance Armstrong

1993 *DNF;* **1994** *DNF;* **1995** *36th;* **1996** *DNF;* **1999** *1st;* **2000** *1st;* **2001** *1st;* **2002** *1st;* **2003** *1st*

Armstrong was only twenty-one years old when he rode his first Tour in 1993, and he achieved his goal of winning a stage. The Texan helped engineer a six-man breakaway group over the last hill in the Châlons-sur-Marne to Verdun stage 8, and then took the final sprint from Mexican Raúl Alcalá and Frenchman Ronan Pensec, 14 seconds ahead of the pack. Also as planned, Armstrong did not finish either of his first two Tours, completing eleven stages in 1993 and fourteen stages the following year. His goals in year three (still only aged twenty-three) were to finish the Tour and win another stage. He achieved both. After losing a two-man sprint to Ukraine's Sergei Uchakov in Revel after a long breakaway on stage 13, Armstrong was dispirited. Three days later, his Motorola teammate Fabio Casartelli was killed when he fell on a steep descent and collided with a concrete post. Armstrong was distressed by the death of his Italian friend, and another three days later he honored Casartelli's memory by winning stage 18 to Limoges, saying he rode with the strength of two men on his winning solo breakaway. The American finished that Tour in 36th place.

It was expected that Armstrong would improve again in 1996, after he dominated a number of Tour contenders in the East Coast's Tour DuPont, but after an opening week of rainfall at the Tour de France, he abandoned the race on stage 6. Less than three months later he was diagnosed with an advanced form of testicular cancer. Treated by the leading oncologists in their field, Armstrong survived brain surgery and aggressive chemotherapy, and he returned to cycling in 1998. A 4th place that fall in the Vuelta a España inspired the Texan to prepare specifically for the Tour de France in 1999. His return to the race resulted in four stage wins and the overall title; and he has followed that with four more overall titles, along with one stage win in 2000, four in 2001, another four in 2002, and one in 2003. Going into the 2004 Tour, Armstrong had a total of sixteen stage wins and he had worn the yellow jersey for fifty-nine days.

George Hincapie

George Hincapie

1996 *DNF;* **1997** *104th;* **1998** *53rd;* **1999** *78th;*
2000 *65th;* **2001** *71st;* **2002** *59th;* **2003** *47th*

This native New Yorker is the only rider to have been on all five U.S. Postal teams that have carried Lance Armstrong to victory. Hincapie is a tireless team worker who occasionally gets to use his renowned finishing speed to try for a stage win. The closest he came to that goal was in 1998. He was in the winning break on stage 3 from Roscoff to Lorient, but two riders got away from his group in the last few kilometers. He was within seconds of taking over the yellow jersey, and almost took it the next day with a sprint time bonus, but just lost out to Australian Stuart O'Grady. That same Tour, on stage 12, Hincapie felt that he had a good chance of winning the field sprint into Cap d'Agde, but the team botched his lead-out and the stage went to Belgian Tom Steels.

Bobby Julich

1997 *17th;* **1998** *3rd;* **1999** *DNF;* **2000** *48th;*
2001 *18th;* **2002** *37th*

This Coloradan (who was born in Texas) was with Motorola until that team's sponsorship ended, then he signed a contract with the French team Cofidis, which also had signed Lance Armstrong and a few of his other teammates. Julich was hired as a team worker, but he quickly emerged as a leader after Armstrong went down with cancer and, at the 1997 Tour, Cofidis's veteran team leader, Tony Rominger, crashed out of the race on stage 3. Later in his debut Tour, Julich climbed with the best in the Alps and

Bobby Julich

finished 17th overall. In 1998, he emerged as one of the main contenders by taking a top-three place at the first long time trial, and then climbing brilliantly in the Pyrénées to move into 2nd overall behind German Jan Ullrich, the defending champion. Julich held strong, taking 2nd to Ullrich on the last long time trial, to place 3rd overall in Paris. He was only the second American to finish on the Tour podium. A nasty crash eliminated him from the 1999 Tour in the time trial at Metz—where Armstrong took over the yellow jersey on his way to becoming the third American on the podium (and its second Tour winner). Julich wasn't able to rediscover his top form with Cofidis in 2000 and then moved on to the Telekom team as a domestique for Ullrich.

Kevin Livingston

Kevin Livingston

1997 *38th;* **1998** *17th;* **1999** *36th;* **2000** *37th;* **2001** *43rd;* **2002** *56th*

This Missouri native was an invaluable teammate for Bobby Julich at Cofidis in 1997 and 1998, and then used his climbing skills at U.S. Postal to help Lance Armstrong win the Tours of 1999 and 2000. Perhaps Livingston's greatest performance was in 1999, when he set the pace for Armstrong all the way up the Col du Galibier (in the Alps) and the Col du Tourmalet (in the Pyrénées), the Tour's two highest climbs. Livingston finished his Tour career with two years of riding for Jan Ullrich at Telekom.

Tyler Hamilton

1997 *69th;* **1998** *51st;* **1999** *13th;* **2000** *25th;* **2001** *94th;* **2002** *15th;* **2003** *4th*

An original member of the U.S. Postal team, this Massachusetts rider first showed a hint of his abilities at his second Tour, in 1998. On the stage 7 time trial at Corrèze, Hamilton came in 2nd; unfortunately, two days later, a bout of gastroenteritis saw him dropped by the peloton on the rolling stage to Pau. He gamely finished the stage within the time limit, then showed similar courage the following two days of racing in the Pyrénées. Hamilton was a tireless team worker for Lance Armstrong the following three years, before he transferred to the Danish squad, CSC, in 2002. His 2nd place overall at the Giro d'Italia, most of which he rode with a broken bone in his shoulder, emphasized Hamilton's grit; and despite not being fully recovered going into the 2002 Tour, he still managed to place 15th.

Tyler Hamilton

Marty Jemison
1997 *96th;* **1998** *48th*

This Utah native put in solid rides at the two Tours he rode for the U.S. Postal team, helping to establish the team in Europe prior to Lance Armstrong's becoming a yellow jersey contender. Jemison came close to winning a stage in 1998, when he was sprinting for the win in a small breakaway group in stage 13 at Carpentras, but was beaten by the Italian Daniele Nardello.

Christian Vande Velde

Christian Vande Velde
1999 *85th;* **2001** *DNF*

One of the most talented riders of the new generation, this rider from Illinois has yet to show his full potential at the Tour. Vande Velde showed signs of that all-around talent at his first Tour, at age twenty-three, in 1999, when he finished 85th. The following year, he was stopped from riding the Tour at the last minute by an infected spider bite. Then, in 2001, he was providing Armstrong strong support until he crashed (bringing down

Roberto Heras) on a rain-slick road near the end of the team time trial. His Tour ended three days later when he collided with a lamppost.

Jonathan Vaughters
1999 *DNF*; **2000** *DNF*; **2001** *DNF*; **2002** *DNF*

This native Coloradan might be the only rider in history to have started four Tours and be forced to abandon all four of them. It could have been five. In 1998, a crash a couple of weeks before the Tour prevented Vaughters from even starting the race. In 1999, he was out by stage 2 after crashing in the pileup on the infamous Passage du Gois causeway. In 2000, he crashed out again, this time on the first mountain stage of the Tour. And in 2001, it looked like Vaughters was finally out of the woods when he made it through all of the Tour's mountains, but a freak accident—an allergic reaction to a wasp sting—put him out before the finish. His luck was no better in 2002, when he pulled out of the Tour on the first mountain stage in the Pyrénées, same as he did two years earlier.

Fred Rodriguez

Fred Rodriguez
2000 *86th*; **2001** *DNF*; **2002** *DNF*; **2003** *DNF*

This fast California rider made a strong Tour debut for the Mapei team in 2000. He was key in setting up then teammates Tom Steels and Stefano Zanini for stage wins, and came close to winning two himself: on stage 8 to Villeneuve-sur-Lot, when he was the fastest finisher in the winning break but couldn't control a late attack that gave Dutchman Erik Dekker the win; and stage 17 to Lausanne, when Dekker again made a late break to win, while Rodriguez just lost the sprint for 2nd to German Erik Zabel. In 2001, Rodriguez struggled with aftereffects of a stomach virus, eventually dropping out on stage 13. In 2002, he had two top-ten stage finishes in the opening week, but was never comfortable on the mountain stages and eventually finished outside the time limit on the alpine stage 17 to La Plagne.

Chann McRae
2000 *DNF*

This Texan emerged as a top amateur cyclist at the same time as Lance Armstrong, but as a professional he didn't follow the same path. His first real chance at the big time didn't come until 1999, when at age twenty-eight he rode both the Giro d'Italia and the Vuelta a España with the famed Mapei team. McRae finished 19th overall at the Vuelta after working as a team worker for his Russian teammate Pavel Tonkov. The following year McRae made his Tour de France debut with Mapei, but he arrived at the start exhausted after he was called up late in the game to ride the Giro in May. He abandoned the Tour after a crash on stage 12.

Levi Leipheimer
2002 *8th;* **2003** *DNF*

This rider from Montana made a stunning grand-tour debut at age twenty-seven in the 2001 Vuelta a España, where he finished 3rd overall, behind Spaniards Angel Casero and Oscar Sevilla, and outrode his U.S. Postal team leader, Roberto Heras. The Dutch squad Rabobank was quick to sign him, and Leipheimer made his Tour debut as its team leader in 2002. He rode a strong race, particularly on the mountain stages of the final ten days to finish 8th overall.

Floyd Landis
2002 *61st;* **2003** *77th*

With a background in mountain bike racing, this Pennsylvania rider came late to road racing, but he soon showed that he had an aptitude for long stage races. He earned his place on the U.S. Postal team at the 2002 Tour with a strong ride at the preceding Dauphiné Libéré race in the French Alps, placing 2nd overall behind team leader Lance Armstrong. At the Tour, Landis proved that he could ride day after day at the head of the peloton, on the flats, or in the mountains.

MEXICANS
Raúl Alcalá
1986 *114th;* **1987** *9th;* **1988** *20th;* **1989** *8th;* **1990** *8th;* **1991** *DNF;* **1992** *21st;* **1993** *27th*

With a better training program and a greater focus, this Mexican from Monterrey could have gone even further in his Tour de France career. In only his second Tour, while with the pioneering 7-Eleven team, Alcalá finished 9th overall, won the white jersey as the top under-25 rider, and finished 3rd in the King of the Mountains competition. He finished top ten again in both 1989 and 1990 for the Dutch team PDM, winning a stage each year. His 1989 win came on stage 3, from Luxembourg to the Spa-Francorchamps motor-racing circuit in Belgium: Alcalá broke clear of a six-man breakaway group on the hilly finishing circuit for a solo win. The following year, he

Raúl Alcalá

scored a stunning victory on the 61.5-kilometer stage 7 time trial from Vittel to Épinal: On a wet day on a hilly course, the Mexican defeated runner-up Miguel Induráin by 1:24, with Italy's Giro champion Gianni Bugno in 3rd, and defending Tour champion Greg LeMond in 5th, 2:11 back.

Miguel Arroyo
1994 *48th;* **1995** *61st;* **1997** *76th*

After spells with the ADR, Z, MG-Bianchi, and Subaru teams, this little climber from Taxcala finally rode the Tour for the small French team Chazal. In his three Tours, Arroyo was solid, but never made a true impact on the race.

--------------- ---------------

When one considers that more French and Italian riders take part in the Tour every year than the total number of North Americans who have started the Tour in race history, then their success rate can be seen as nothing less than remarkable. With eight overall victories in the eighteen Tours between 1986 and 2003, the United States has been the dominant force, with Greg LeMond and Lance Armstrong becoming household names around the world. During the same two decades, American interest in the Tour has grown from the presence of one or two U.S. reporters at the race to dozens of journalists covering the event, along with daily live television coverage. The pioneering sportswriter Red Smith would be astounded that forty years after his initial dispatches from France not only are Americans winning the Tour, but they are also watching the Tour on the big screens of sports bars all across America.

First American Winner

GREG LEMOND OVERCAME THE ODDS,
PARTICULARLY IN 1986, TO WIN THREE TOURS.

———————◉———————

When the Tour de France began in the suburbs of Paris in 1986, Greg LeMond couldn't help but think back a year to the words his French teammate Bernard Hinault had said to him from the winner's dais on the Champs-Élysées: "Next year, Greg, I'll help *you* win the Tour."

This would be Hinault's last Tour—he had already announced he was to retire after his thirty-second birthday that year—and he was determined to enjoy himself. When asked recently about that 1986 Tour, Hinault said he wanted to have fun, to make the race spectacular. He was true to his word, even if his aggression made life difficult (some would say impossible) for LeMond, his co-leader at La Vie Claire.

Partway through that Tour, their team soon became divided on partisan lines. The majority, the French riders Jean-François Bernard, Charly Bérard, Philippe Leleu, and Alain Vigneron, rode for Hinault; the minority, the North Americans Andy Hampsten and Steve Bauer, rode for LeMond; while, as could be expected, the Swiss Niki Rüttimann and Guido Winterberg were largely neutral.

Hinault didn't wait for the mountains to start having "fun." On stage 6 across the pastoral plains of Normandy, from Villers-sur-Mer to Cherbourg, Hinault attacked after taking 3rd place in an intermediate sprint. He was soon joined by ten others, including Irishman Stephen Roche, who was one of the men on LeMond's danger list. "I was just behind the sprint and when I saw there was a strong crosswind, I called up three [Carrera] teammates and told them to ride hard," said Roche. "We rode flat out for about 5 kilometers, by which time the lead was over a minute. I then spoke to Hinault and asked if he would ride with us. He said he would."

Was the Frenchman's almost shocking reply a short-term decision, because a successful break would have given him the yellow jersey the next day when the Tour rolled through his native Brittany? Or was it long term, putting him on course to win his sixth Tour? Whatever it was, he worked hard with Roche and his teammates to grow the gap to a minute and a half before most of the peloton knew what was happened.

The other teams had to make some quick decisions. Clearly, LeMond couldn't ask his La Vie Claire "Anglos" to chase, even if he perhaps saw "his" Tour slipping away down the roller-coaster road. The Panasonic team of the then race leader Johan van der Velde had two men in the break so it was quite happy to see the move succeed. That left the onus with the other race favorite, Laurent Fignon, the 1983 and 1984 Tour winner, who had a Système U teammate in the break, Christophe Lavainne. Système U director Cyrille Guimard first ordered Lavainne back to the bunch to help lead the chase; but though the pack began to cut into the lead, things were going too slowly for Fignon. The impetuous Frenchman then decided to take charge and he made a strong attack on a hill leaving the town of St. Lô. Fignon's lieutenant, Charly Mottet, went with him, while LeMond, Bauer, and six others quickly joined the chase group. For the next 60-or-so kilometers, the Hinault-Roche group was chased by the Fignon-Mottet group until both were finally absorbed by the peloton.

In retrospect, Hinault's attack could have been interpreted as helping LeMond, because the American was able to comfortably follow wheels the whole day. But if Fignon hadn't sparked that chase, and Hinault had ridden away to, say, a 5-minute gain, would the mood have remained mellow in the La Vie Claire camp?

The answer to that possibility would come six days later on the first day in the mountains, when Hinault went on the rampage on a torrid, 6-hour stage through the Basque part of the Pyrénées between Bayonne and Pau. Once again, an intermediate sprint saw the defending champion make his move. But this time the circumstances were vastly different. This particular sprint came at Lanne-en-Baretous, a tiny village tucked into a deep, green valley about 90 kilometers from Pau. By that point in the stage, Hinault was one of six La Vie Claire riders in a twenty-three-man front group that had left the rest of the field in their dust on the preceding Col de Burdincurutcheta. Importantly, both Roche and Fignon had been dropped on the long, steep climb. Therefore, Hinault and LeMond's teammates Bauer, Hampsten, Bernard, and Rüttimann were riding hard to prevent the two dropped favorites from catching back. But did Hinault see LeMond as his true rival, and not Fignon or Roche? That appeared to be the case at Lanne-en-Baretous when the other "Frenchie" in the group, Bernard, sprinted for the time bonus with his leader Hinault right on his wheel. Only one of the other twenty-one riders in the group joined them: Spanish climber Pedro Delgado.

LeMond climbs strongly to win the stage at Superbagnères in 1986, putting himself back in contention for the yellow jersey.

LeMond, when asked what he would have done if he had been on another team, later said, "I would have never let him go. That's why I could never understand the attitude of [Urs] Zimmermann and [Robert] Millar. Going for a victory, how could they let Hinault just walk away like that? They just sat there. I was peeing in my pants that they were just sitting there."

That was the last they would see of Hinault that day until they crossed the finish line in Pau where the French superstar was awarded the yellow jersey. For a little more than 2 hours of racing over viciously steep climbs like the Col de Marie-Blanque, Hinault gave his supporters a devastating sample of his panache. Pushing a big gear, his shoulders rocking, his legs dropping like lead weights on the pedals, he pounded toward glory. He was making sure that people were going to remember his last Tour de France.

His young teammate, Bernard, rode as hard as he could before he was left behind by Delgado and Hinault—who arrived together in Pau 4:37 ahead of 3rd finisher LeMond, while Roche finished almost 20 minutes back, and Fignon pulled out completely. LeMond and the rest had been dealt a body blow by Hinault, who appeared to be well on his way to Tour victory No. 6. So what was LeMond's reaction to the reality of conceding 5 minutes to his teammate on one stage? He shrugged his shoulders and said, "That's life. I guess I'm going to finish 2nd in the Tour de France again."

As for Hinault, he said, "I've done what I wanted. I've put my rivals 5 minutes behind me." He then added, perhaps trying to mollify his American teammate, "But Greg will be able to do the same tomorrow."

Now in the yellow jersey, Hinault was where he wanted to be, and for LeMond to attempt an attack the next day would certainly look like treachery. Such a move by the American also would likely elicit the anger of team owner Bernard Tapie, the showboating French businessman who had brought LeMond to La Vie Claire as Hinault's successor at a then record million-dollar, three-year salary—but he would much rather see his beloved Hinault win the Tour. Just as he had been in 1985, LeMond was being shackled by team tactics.

As for him "doing a Hinault," LeMond's situation appeared not to improve but to worsen the next day, when Hinault attacked again! This time, he broke away from a front group of seventeen riders, descending from stage 13's highest peak, the Tourmalet. After being at the head of the race for 90 kilometers through the mountains the day before, the race leader was setting off an almost identical caper. Tackling the Tourmalet's endless downhill at the very edge of credibility, hitting 100 kilometers per hour on the straightaways, Hinault gained 1:40 by the valley; and within another 30 kilometers, after crossing the Col d'Aspin, his lead was almost 3 minutes. Was Hinault delivering the knockout blow?

"I risked it alone," he said, "telling myself that if things went well, I would win, and if I failed I would at least have made my opponents do some work—which Greg could profit from. I was lucky because the chasers didn't know how to descend."

While Hinault was thinking of winning, LeMond was again feeling frustrated. "If [Hinault] had gone all the way to the finish," the American said later, "he would have been 8 minutes in the lead. And that would have been it."

But while LeMond was playing the role of a real-life Robin, "Batman" Hinault finally showed he was mortal. Going up the day's next-to-last climb, the Peyresourde, the red-faced race leader visibly wilted. In cycling parlance, he had bonked, and his 3-minute lead evaporated to just 25 seconds by the summit. "I took some glucose," Hinault said, "but you have to wait 15 minutes before it takes effect."

By then, racing through the town of Luchon before the final 17-kilometer haul to the mountaintop finish at Superbagnères, the leader was caught and a new battle began. This one pitted LeMond (aided by Hampsten) against Zimmermann (now the leader of Roche's Carrera squad), Millar (the Scottish climber with Panasonic), and the Colombian climbing star Luis Herrera, while Hinault steadily lost ground despite the help of teammate Rüttimann. After much infighting, Hampsten counterattacked, LeMond jumped across to him, and the two Americans flew toward the summit.

This time, finally, LeMond was able to show his true strength and, after Hampsten dropped back, he won the stage alone by 1:12 over Millar and Zimmermann, while Hinault crossed the line in 11th place, 4:39 behind. The Frenchman had saved his yellow jersey by 40 seconds—the margin of his stage 8 time-trial win over LeMond—but it seemed that Hinault's belligerence had finally been halted. It was time for the younger man to claim his rightful place.

Three days later, though, on the stage preceding the Tour's arrival in the Alps, Hinault was off the front again, "having fun." This time, his aggressive move came on a short climb midway into a fearfully long stage—almost 8 hours in the saddle—between Nîmes and Gap. The problem was not so much that Hinault attacked, but that he took the dangerous Zimmermann with him, probably the one man who could challenge for the yellow jersey in the coming days.

"I felt like pulling out of the race," said LeMond. "I think that everything Hinault has done in this race has been for himself, not for me. It's the same every day. I never know what to expect, so I'm always riding under this psychological pressure."

That pressure showed when Hinault and Zimmermann were eventually reeled in after a chase by Millar's Panasonic team. "[Greg] came at me very angrily," Hinault said. "I told him to calm himself, that I would explain it all at the hotel in the evening. He complained about my riding with Zimmermann and throwing away our chances. [Greg] really panicked and I told him he needed to steady his nerves."

LeMond, even if he felt like pulling out, needed to control himself because the next day would see perhaps the most demanding stage of this very demanding and, yes, spectacular 1986 Tour. On the day's agenda were the legendary 7,000-foot Col de Vars and Col d'Izoard before the final climb to a bleak mountaintop, the Col du Granon, which, at 7,916 feet elevation, remains the highest stage finish in Tour de France history.

As it happened, Hinault wasn't having a good day. "It was a strained [knee] muscle, because I had raced too hard and put too much pressure on it," he admitted. It wasn't a huge problem, but it explained why Hinault lost a minute or so to the Zimmermann-Millar-LeMond group up the Vars, before catching back on the descent. He was again gapped on the Izoard, but this time he wasn't able to make up his 2-minute deficit because LeMond descended like a kamikaze and only Zimmerman could keep up. Millar's chase group conceded 44 seconds by the time they reached the valley at Briançon, where Hinault was fighting a rearguard action.

Then came the savagely beautiful 11-kilometer Granon ascent. LeMond and Zimmermann made the narrow, steep climb look like any other mountain pass, but after finishing the stage, the tall, blond Swiss champion spent many minutes straddled over his bike before he found the strength to speak with a group of Swiss reporters. Hampsten, 7th on the stage, was sitting on the gravel shoulder a few yards from Zimmermann, in a similar state of sublime exhaustion. Millar, whose stage ended in tatters after he ran out of fuel, was doubled over his handlebars, clinging to a metal barrier, spitting up phlegm before he was helped out of his sweat-drenched polka-dot climbers' jersey and sponged down by his *soigneur*. And a French rider, Joël Pelier, who reached the mountaintop almost 30 minutes after LeMond, collapsed on the road and was carried to an ambulance with an oxygen mask over his mouth, having forced his body too far at that high elevation. Meanwhile, in the center of a mob of media reporters, a joyous LeMond was saying, "I feel very proud to be the first American to wear the yellow jersey."

He *had* taken the overall lead—with Zimmermann in 2nd and Hinault 3rd—but LeMond still had six stages to survive before he could claim the victory. First up was the last alpine stage over the Galibier and Croix de Fer passes to L'Alpe d'Huez, followed by a rolling stage to St. Étienne, where there would be a long time trial, and then a final mountaintop finish, on the Puy de Dôme.

Hinault was upset at dropping below Zimmermann in the standings, and he vowed to get rid of the Swiss rider on the Alpe d'Huez stage. He didn't wait long before trying. On reaching the Galibier summit with a small group, Hinault decided to break away on the long, swashbuckling descent. Bauer, also a great descender, chased and joined his team leader while LeMond eventually caught up with Zimmermann and a Spanish rider, Pello Ruiz Cabestany. Right away, Hinault attacked again, this time taking a 24-second lead on the short climb to the Col du Télégraphe before the downhill continued for another 10 kilometers. LeMond was not going to wait around like he did in the Pyrénées; he went after his teammate, using his bike-handling skills to great effect on the Télégraphe's technical switchbacks. Bauer and Cabestany managed to hang on, but Zimmermann misjudged one of the tight turns, almost fell, and lost 50 meters. By the time the tall Swiss reached the valley in a group of eight, he was already 1:39 behind LeMond, when he, Bauer, and Cabestany pulled alongside Hinault.

Bauer buried himself with long, hard pulls into a strong head wind on the valley road before he dropped back at the beginning of the Croix de Fer, where the gap was up to 2:49. Cabestany was soon dropped on the near-30-kilometer climb, leaving Hinault and LeMond to continue together for the remaining 80 kilometers. Giving the appearance of being the best of friends, despite their stormy relationship of the previous two weeks, the two waltzed up the remaining two climbs, hurtled down the descents, hitting a mind-boggling 110 kilometers an hour at times, to arrive at L'Alpe d'Huez a massive 5:15 ahead of 3rd-place Zimmermann.

At Hinault's request, the two linked hands as they cruised across the finish line, in what would become the enduring (if fictitious) image of that 1986 Tour. A few days later, LeMond confided, "I agreed to it [linking hands] because I felt I'd won the Tour and I didn't really care if he won the stage. There had been a lot of tension between us and I felt that it would clear everything up. [But] immediately after the finish on [the live TV show] *Chacun à Son Tour*, [presenter] Jacques Chancel said to Hinault, 'Well, that means you still might attack him?' And Hinault said, 'Possibly. It's not over until the time trial.' The whole pressure started again. I was a little disappointed that he didn't just let up."

In turn, Hinault later admitted, "I had decided to harass Greg for [another] two days, to engage him in psychological warfare to see if he could hold up. It's his first yellow jersey; he might have cracked."

But LeMond did not crack. On the stage to St. Étienne, he followed Hinault almost everywhere, and then came the time trial.

The French media and public still thought that Hinault could pull back his deficit of more than 2 minutes in the time trial's 58 kilometers. As for LeMond, he would start with Hinault's statement at L'Alpe d'Huez ringing in his ears: "The time trial at St. Étienne will decide. After that there will be no more racing between Greg and me."

On merit, the two were just about equal in the time trials that year—LeMond's 40-second defeat at the first time trial was caused mainly by a flat tire and a switch to a non-aerodynamic bike. This time, it seemed, other forces were at work. Witness the words of LeMond's wife, Kathy, in this 1995 interview with the late freelance writer Matthew Mantell. When asked about the 1986 Tour, Kathy LeMond said, "It was awful . . . awful. I couldn't stand Hinault because of his deception. [Tour race director] Jacques Goddet came up to Greg the night before the final time trial and said, 'I'll try to protect you in the race tomorrow. I know Hinault has something planned for you. Be careful.' And Greg's bike was messed with. That's why he went down in the corner in the time trial."

(A few minutes after falling heavily on a sharp turn midway through the stage, picking himself up and continuing on the same bike, LeMond was forced to stop. "I thought everything was all right," he said, "but my front brake was hanging on the wheel." Was it sabotage?)

Kathy LeMond continued, "Maurice Le Guilloux, the assistant manager on La Vie Claire, came out and said that [the bike was messed with] in *L'Équipe* three or four years ago. And he hasn't had a job since. The team made sure that Greg's bike wasn't working right."

She then added, "Greg took a camera into dope control to photograph his vials—to be sure they weren't tampered with."

Maybe LeMond was overreacting, but it was clear that Hinault's "psychological warfare" had worked. Yet the American came through, and despite the crash and eventual bike change he still placed 2nd in the time trial, only 25 seconds slower than his boss. He then put time into Hinault on the Puy de Dôme, and finished the Tour in Paris the overall winner by 3:10.

It took a while for the first American to start a Tour de France, but only five years later the Tour had its first American winner.

After Hinault retired at the end of 1986, LeMond was expected to have a much easier time winning the Tour in the following few years. But then came the devastating hunting accident that almost cost him his life on April 20, 1987. In his absence, the Tour that year went to Roche, while the 1988 race was taken by Delgado—both men that LeMond had dominated in 1986. He most likely would have won those two Tours, to bring him to 1989 with three Tours under his belt. Instead, in the late spring of that year, LeMond was in bad shape. He hadn't won a race of any note for almost three years; the European press said that he would never recover fully from his accident; and even his fans started to drift away when he performed without luster at the 1989 Tour de Trump in the United States.

Matters worsened in the ensuing weeks, at the Giro d'Italia, where the 1986 Tour de France winner was languishing around 50th place after twelve days of racing.

"I was dying on the smallest hill and had no recuperation. It didn't make sense," said a puzzled LeMond. "I was contemplating looking for another job." His concerns reached desperation point on June 2, the day that the Giro entered the mountains, with a giant climb to the famed Tre Cime di Lavaredo summit, 7,874 feet up in the Dolomites. It was a cool, overcast day at the start in Padua, and LeMond knew he was in for a hiding. Yet, being the dedicated professional that he is, he also knew that he would have to struggle through this 207-kilometer stage—and the following three days in the mountains—if he were to stand any chance of being competitive at the following month's Tour de France.

The Tre Cime climb—where many champions have become unstuck in the past—proved a terrible ordeal for LeMond. Instead of being in his accustomed place at the head of the race, he was among the first riders to be dropped on the 20-kilometer climb. Heavy rain started to fall as he anonymously pedaled upward through a forest of dripping pine trees to the mountain resort of Misurina. And by the time the rain-jacketed American reached the rugged finale—4.4 kilometers at an average grade of almost 18 percent—Colombian mountain goat Herrera had already won the stage.

LeMond could have easily quit, as the course passed his team's hotel, the Sorapiss at Misurina. Instead, he gritted his teeth and fought his way upward on that wicked climb, feeling his way through the pouring rain and freezing mist, ignoring the catcalls of the spectators, as he focused on one goal: finishing. At the top, he struggled from his bike and disappeared into his awaiting team car as fast as possible.

That night, LeMond and his personal *soigneur*, Otto Jacome, searched for answers to Greg's incapacity to compete at his expected level. His legs were fit, but he was still dying on the hills. A blood test revealed a lack of iron, and—for the first time in his life—LeMond was given an iron injection. Was this the answer? If not, the racer would probably have quit—except that his wife, Kathy, and two sons, Geoffrey and Scott, would be waiting to greet him at the end of the next stage, in Corvara.

So, on June 3, LeMond was at the start line in Misurina, looking anxious and cold on a morning of 30-degree temperatures. He survived the day, over four mountain passes, in rain and snow, and was in his hotel room with his family when a journalist knocked on the door that evening. Sounds of a travel-weary child emanated when the door opened, and, after saying a few words to Kathy, LeMond emerged. He sat on the stairs outside his room for a half hour, talking about the past days and the recent weeks of ignominy. But this was a smiling and joking LeMond: The crisis had

LeMond reacts to winning the 1989 Tour in the very last meters of the time trial in Paris.

passed. Seven weeks later, Greg LeMond came from 50 seconds behind on the final day to beat Giro victor Laurent Fignon by 8 seconds at the Tour de France. LeMond had overcome the odds against a proud Frenchman, just as he did in 1986. He would go on to win another Tour, overcoming a 10-minute deficit at the start of the race to beat the Italian Claudio Chiappucci.

So LeMond won "only" three Tours. It could have been five, or if one considers his restraint in finishing a supportive runner-up to Hinault in 1985, it might even have been six. But it was what it was. And if LeMond had won only that spectacular 1986 edition, then he would have already carved his place into cycling history as the first American, indeed the first non-European, to win the Tour de France.

There was relief in LeMond's smile on reaching Paris in 1986 as the Tour's first American winner.

Lest We Forget

ARMSTRONG'S COMEBACK FROM
CANCER DESERVES THE RETELLING.

———————————◉———————————

When we watch Lance Armstrong propel his aerodynamic bike at 55 kilometers per hour in a time trial or spin a 39x21 gear up a mountain at a pedal cadence of more than 100 revolutions a minute, it's easy to forget that doctors were fighting for his life in the fall of 1996. On October 2 that year, after coughing up blood in the kitchen sink at his Austin, Texas, home, Armstrong made an appointment to see his doctor. After going through a series of tests, he couldn't believe the words his doctor was saying: "You have cancer." It wasn't what America's top professional cyclist had expected to hear. On learning of the diagnosis that he was in an advanced stage of testicular cancer, which had spread to his abdomen and lungs, Armstrong's response was "complete denial. I thought, 'It can't be. I'm only twenty-five. Why should I have cancer?'"

But there wasn't much time for denial. The next day, the young Texan entered the hospital for surgery to remove a malignant testicle. What followed were months of aggressive chemotherapy—including one of the scariest things of all: brain surgery to remove two lesions.

When he spoke about the cancer a week after the first operation, Armstrong said, "There are moments when I cry all the time. Days are up and down." The doctors had told him there was a strong possibility that he would die.

What made the prognosis so shocking was the fact that Armstrong had just completed his fourth year as a professional cyclist and was ranked No. 7 in the world, after what he termed his "best year ever." Now, he realizes that he achieved some of his best results—including a 6th-place finish in the time trial at Atlanta's Olympic Games in late July 1996—while suffering from testicular cancer.

Armstrong wore the U.S. professional champion's jersey in his debut at the Tour de France in 1993.

Before cancer, Armstrong weighed a highly muscular 175 pounds, which, given his height of 5 feet 10 inches, was a little on the heavy side for a top cyclist. But that didn't stop him from becoming the first American since Greg LeMond to win the world professional road race championship (in 1993), or from winning two stages of the Tour de France (in 1993 and 1995).

Commenting on the rigors—and health risks—of his chosen sport, Armstrong said, "What athletes do may not be that healthy, the way we push our bodies completely over the edge to degrees that are not human. I've said all along I will not live as long as the average person. The Tour de France is not a 'human' event—but it doesn't give you cancer at twenty-five."

Despite the prognosis, Armstrong said in the early days of his cancer treatment, "I don't want to sound too confident, [but] I intend to beat this disease and, further, I intend to ride again as a professional cyclist."

These were bold statements. But those close to Armstrong knew that if determination alone could defeat cancer, then his words would come true. Still, even his friends had doubts when they visited him in the hospital during an early round of chemotherapy. One friend confided: "I'm afraid Lance is going to die."

Looking back on that difficult period, Armstrong said, "I had a lot of support. The well-wishers and the cards and the messages helped a lot; I was very motivated by that." He received thousands of get-well cards, letters, faxes, e-mails, and phone calls, all encouraging him in his fight against cancer. "But at the same time," Armstrong continued, "I think that the same desire I had on the bike—to be a champion, to try and win races, or work hard—is the same desire that helped me when I was sick: 'This is something I want. I want to get better.' And you can't be taught that. . . . Maybe you can be pushed in a certain direction, but it's a unique quality that you have to be born with."

Besides that inner strength, Armstrong pointed out that he also had unusual physical and mental strength. "I think the training, both physically and mentally, helped me tremendously. When I was diagnosed [with cancer], physically I was in great shape. And mentally, having been a professional cyclist—which I consider to be a hard life—the *grind* of a cyclist helped. I was able to set goals for myself with cancer like I had in the past. The doctors also set objectives for me, for my progression."

The chemotherapy may have taken its toll, but Armstrong continued to amaze the doctors by always beating their objectives with his resilience, spirit, and determination. Within two months, the cancer was in remission. At that time, he even attended a gala banquet in Los Angeles, where he received the *VeloNews* 1996 North

American Cyclist of the Year award. In his acceptance speech, Armstrong candidly removed a black beret to reveal his shiny pate.

By this point in his battle, and with his doctors' blessing, Armstrong was already going on daily 90-minute bike rides—although at a pace and strength at a fraction of what he had been doing a few months before. By March 1997, his hair had started to grow back, his tan was returning, and he was strong enough to take part in the Ride for the Roses—a 100-mile charity bike ride through the Texas Hill Country that kicked off fundraising for the just-started Lance Armstrong Foundation. Armstrong explained that since testicular cancer accounts for less than 4 percent of all cancers—7,000 cases a year, all of them in young men—his foundation wanted to broaden its scope. "So we went with urological cancers," he said, "which is testicular, prostate, renal, and bladder. We focus on educational awareness and research."

Armstrong continued with his training, knowing that he still had a long way to go if he were ever going to ride the Tour de France again. With summer 1997 approaching, he was riding 2 hours a day and slowly building up his strength. But if he were to return to the top of what is regarded as the most physically demanding of sports, he would be navigating uncharted territory. No professional cyclist had returned from cancer; indeed, very few had made successful comebacks from even a year away from the sport after injury.

The months of treatment had dropped Armstrong's weight by more than 10 pounds, which, ironically, became an asset in his quest to regain his position among the cycling elite. Being lighter would help him to climb better in the high mountains, like those that decide the outcome at the Tour de France. And for that reason, the Texan was committed to keeping his weight down.

"I eat healthy because of the weight issue. My main motivation for eating well is not because I had cancer. It's because I don't want to be fat and get dropped on the climbs," Armstrong confirmed. "If there's evidence that eating poorly causes cancer—which I'm sure it does some of the time—in my situation I don't think testicular cancer is related to hamburgers and margaritas."

Avoiding such junk food, the young Texan continued to make progress through the latter half of 1997; the monthly tests confirmed that his cancer was in remission. So, in agreement with his cycling coach, Chris Carmichael, Armstrong decided to begin a more vigorous training program. His goal was to return to European cycling in February 1998.

It was a highly ambitious target, but Armstrong is a highly ambitious guy. Throughout that winter, he followed Carmichael's strict schedule, which included some days of riding hard for 6 hours. In February 1998, Armstrong was one of the strongest riders at the California training camp of his new team, sponsored by the U.S. Postal Service. He duly made his return to racing at Spain's five-day Ruta del Sol in mid-February. And he did strikingly well, finishing in the top fifteen out of 200 starters.

The pressure of returning so quickly from cancer at such a high level, and the subsequent mass publicity in Europe—where cycling is followed as fervently as baseball is in the United States—even got to Armstrong. In his next big race, the weeklong Paris-Nice, the cancer survivor quit early on the second day. His friends said that Armstrong would never race again.

He went home to Austin, where his bike remained in its travel case for four weeks. And it would probably have stayed there, if there hadn't been another commitment: He needed to prepare himself for his foundation's second annual Ride for the Roses weekend, scheduled for early May. He couldn't let down the thousands of cancer patients who now regarded Armstrong as their inspiration and role model.

"I eventually unpacked the bike," he said, "stopped playing so much golf, stopped drinking too much beer, and then started to *slowly* train, just for fun, just with friends, for 2 hours a day at the most."

Carmichael encouraged Armstrong to do a training camp to see if he still had the desire to ride hard. He accepted the challenge and went to Boone, North Carolina, for a week with just his coach and a former Motorola teammate, Bob Roll, for company. It rained every day, but the two riders covered hundreds of miles in the hilly terrain.

"I said, 'We're going for a training camp. I'm going to train and see if we can get going again. To see if I want to do it, to see if I have fun, to see if I love the bike,'" Armstrong recalled. "And I think I discovered there that I *do* love the bike and that I can get through conditions that are just terrible. I left there a different person."

A couple of weeks later, Armstrong took part in the Ride for the Roses weekend, which opened with a 2-hour-long circuit race in the heart of Austin. There, even though he was far from top shape, Armstrong came in first—his first victory on a bike for almost two years. It was just the encouragement he needed to make one more attempt at a comeback in Europe. This time, it was for real. Armstrong returned to the Continent in June, and he promptly won two multiday races, the Tour of Luxembourg and Germany's Lower-Saxony tour. He wasn't yet ready for the Tour de France, but in September 1998, the Texan came in an improbable 4th at the mountainous, three-week Tour of Spain, and he went on to finish 4th in the top road race and time trial at October's world championships. With those encouraging performances behind him, Armstrong was persuaded that he could do well at the Tour de France in 1999. Did anyone doubt that he would do something special?

Most Europeans watching Armstrong apparently toying with his opposition on the climb up to Sestriere at the end of the first mountain stage of the 1999 Tour could not believe what their eyes were telling them. In order to describe the insolent manner in which the Texan first rode away from his main rival Alex Zülle, then closed down an attack by ace climbers Fernando Escartin and Ivan Gotti, and finally rode away from them all to score a superb stage victory, they had to search their memory banks. They could remember similar rides by great Tour winners like Miguel Induráin, Bernard Hinault, Greg LeMond, and Eddy Merckx. But how was such a performance possible, they asked, from a rider who had just recovered from cancer and, before that, had always floundered in the Tour's high mountains?

Those European observers were entitled to their views. After all, the last time they had seen him at the Tour de France, in 1996, Armstrong abandoned the race the day before it even reached the Alps. Midway through the hilly stage to Aix-les-Bains

Armstrong did not know that cancer was already developing in his body when he quit the 1996 Tour in a rainstorm.

on a day of apocalyptic rainfall, he pulled over at the foot of a climb after being dropped by the main pack. "I'm bummed," he said that day. "I had no power . . . couldn't breathe." He thought it was a throat infection, but in hindsight it was probably the cancer starting to show itself.

In previous years, Armstrong's best effort, the critics remembered, was his finishing the 1995 Tour in 36th place, more than an hour behind winner Induráin. What they didn't recall, or didn't want to, was how Armstrong always possessed explosive strength on the uphills. One can think back to his first full season as a professional cyclist in 1993 when a twenty-one-year-old Armstrong took solo victories in the world's and nationals, each time making his winning move on a steep climb. It was also his climbing strength that earned him a World Cup win in San Sebastian and a Tour stage victory at Limoges in 1995, and won him the Flèche Wallonne classic in 1996.

And the Europeans probably never knew about Armstrong's phenomenal climbing demonstrations in mountain stages at the Tour DuPont, most notably on North Carolina's rugged Beech Mountain. Those successes, like the ones in Europe, came prior to Armstrong's fight with cancer, at a time when he was much heavier.

Then came the cancer that threatened his life, but from which Armstrong emerged, in his own words, as "a better rider than I was before." With a body now weighing closer to 160 than 180 pounds, he had automatically gained almost 10 percent in his power-to-weight ratio—and that's not taking into account his improved training methods, and a focus on climbing, which both helped to increase his power output.

Despite all these factors, the U.S. Postal Service leader still had to translate the theory into practice. He still had to defend the Tour yellow jersey he had won in the previous stage's time trial in the mountains for the first time in his life, and do it in what some considered to be the race's most challenging stage.

Its *pièce de résistance* was the Col du Galibier, the legendary 8,677-foot peak on whose slopes the Tour was played out in 1998, when Marco Pantani attacked to drop Jan Ullrich and Bobby Julich on the stage to Les Deux-Alpes. That finish was only 43 kilometers (including one climb) from the Galibier summit; in 1999, some 68 kilometers (and two climbs) separated the Galibier from Sestriere, giving rise to very different tactics.

One similarity was heavy rain in the closing part of the stage, but thankfully the worst of the conditions didn't arrive until well after the Galibier, which was climbed on mainly dry roads, after a menacing thunderstorm only skirted the mighty mountain pass. Because of the more distant finish, this Sestriere stage was tactically much different. Instead of deciding the whole race, the Galibier became a climb that filtered out the weaker riders.

Found lacking was Spanish favorite Abraham Olano, who was dropped by Armstrong's group 8 kilometers from the top, when U.S. Postal's Kevin Livingston was leading a successful chase for the yellow jersey to catch a potentially dangerous attack by Richard Virenque and the two Kelme climbers, Escartin and José Castelblanco. By the summit, Olano was about a minute behind the ten-strong Armstrong group, a situation that would dictate the tactics for the rest of the stage.

First over the Galibier was Spaniard José-Luis Arrieta of Banesto, who had been sent ahead by his team leader, Zülle, in a five-man break that gained 6:15 by the foot of the Col du Télégraphe. This, in effect, is also the foot of the Galibier because only 5 kilometers separate the top of the Télégraphe from the start of the Galibier. Starting a combined 30 kilometers of climbing in about 90 minutes, Arrieta soon left behind the rest of the break and managed to keep a lead of 1:40 over the Galibier.

On this first major obstacle of the Tour, Armstrong's Postal team rode impressively: Frankie Andreu pulled for the first 10 kilometers of the Télégraphe, before sitting up and letting George Hincapie take over. Then, on the Galibier, according to Armstrong, "Kevin [Livingston] pulled for 19.5 of the 20 kilometers."

Once at the top, Arrieta stopped to don a rain jacket, then waited for the chasers, who shed Castelblanco on the fast descent, while Livingston also dropped back when the rain jacket he had been handed got tangled in a wheel. The resultant nine-man lead group was comprised of Banesto's Zülle, Arrieta, and Manuel Beltran; Polti's Virenque and Gotti; Kelme's Escartin and Carlos Contreras; Saeco's Laurent Dufaux; and race leader Armstrong.

"It wasn't a good situation for me, with a couple of Banestos, a couple of Kelmes, a couple of Poltis [in the group]," Armstrong later said. "But they were very anxious in getting away from Olano, so they worked, and I was able to ride easy."

Indeed, a minute back, a chase group of twenty-seven had come together, led down the valley road by four ONCE riders, trying desperately to keep their team leader, Olano, in the top three overall. It proved to be a classic chase, with most of the work ahead being done by Zülle's lieutenants, Arrieta and Beltran—who sat up when they reached the short hill up into Briançon, with the gap up to 1:20.

Now came the Cat. II Montgenèvre climb, opening with a false flat and culminating with 7 kilometers of steep switchbacks. Overhead, menacing clouds were about to unleash a rainstorm that would increase in intensity for the next couple of hours—and would most affect the *gruppetto*, the big group of back markers, a half hour back, and the last man on the road, Aussie Jay Sweet, who had been riding alone since the early slopes of the Télégraphe.

While Sweet was just starting the Galibier descent, the eight-strong lead group was fighting a gusting headwind on the early slopes of the Montgenèvre; and it looked like Olano's men might succeed in catching them when the gap was cut to 54 seconds. But then the grade steepened, and Beltran went to work for Zülle, along with Escartin and Gotti, to reestablish their 1:25 lead.

All this played in favor of Armstrong, who was able simply to follow the others, without digging deep. "On the Galibier I was comfortable but I didn't feel super," he said, "but I always ride good in these cold, wet conditions and on a day like this you automatically eliminate 50 percent of the opposition. . . ." Armstrong then said he looked at his rivals' faces, and "it looked like they were suffering a little bit."

Suffering or not, Gotti and Escartin sped clear of the other six leaders on the steep, curving descent of the Montgenèvre. They were not taking too many risks, as the heavy rain was making conditions treacherous.

This was confirmed when there was a crash in the big chase group. Among those who came down were Pavel Tonkov and two Postal climbers, Tyler Hamilton and Livingston.

"It was a left turn . . . a little off camber . . . I was following Olano," Livingston reported. "We got in the turn, and I thought, 'This looks slick.' And the next thing my front wheel slid out. My bike went to the right, and I went out sliding headfirst. . . . I couldn't believe how fast I was going. I saw the guardrail coming, with the pillars— and I actually changed my direction [to go] in between 'em, under the rail.

"I didn't hit my head, I was lucky. I was thinking, 'You idiot, you don't have your helmet on.' I'd taken it off just before."

Hamilton later described his own fall: "One guy goes down . . . you touch your brakes . . . I just slid forever, and then crashed into the barricades. Kevin went down, too, so I thought, 'Do I wait [for him]?' But we were only a minute behind Lance . . . so I just got on my bike as fast as possible and went. I thought it was important to still ride just in case there was a problem [for] Lance."

Armstrong, however, said he was having "good feelings on the last climb." So 2 kilometers into the 11-kilometer ascent to the finish in the Italian ski resort of Sestriere, with the two leaders 32 seconds ahead of Armstrong's group, the American decided, "I didn't want Gotti and Escartin to go too far."

Impressively, Armstrong smoothly crossed the gap, chased at a distance by Zülle. On reaching the lead pair, the race leader quickly countered a smart attack by Gotti—the former Giro winner who was hoping to score a stage victory on home

As Escartin struggles behind, Armstrong starts the attack that earned him the 1999 stage win at Sestriere.

soil. Armstrong then went to the front to control the pace, and when he saw Zülle latching on to the break just inside 7 kilometers to go, the Postal leader accelerated.

"I wasn't trying to attack," Armstrong said. "Johan [Bruyneel] told me on the radio that I had a gap, so I rode a little faster tempo. Then he told me the gap was bigger, so I tried to go. . . ."

So, on a flatter part of the stepped climb, Armstrong shifted onto his fifty-three-tooth big ring and went hard, out of the saddle, to create a 12-second gap. Twelve seconds became 30 seconds at the 5 kilometers-to-go point, and 43 seconds a kilometer later. Riding through the icy rain, his yellow jersey blackened by tire spray, Armstrong kept up the pressure, looking invincible. But Zülle was slowly closing in on him, cutting the gap to 37 seconds with 3 kilometers left.

The Texan later said that his move "was too early in hindsight, because the last three kilometers I was suffering. . . . It was just exhaustion. I was running out of fuel. It gets hard after 220 kilometers, with a finish at 2000 meters [elevation]."

Zülle chased all the way to the line, finishing with his mouth wide open, 31 seconds after Armstrong. It was another minute before Escartin and Gotti appeared, and 2:27 until Beltran arrived with Virenque and Contreras. Olano lost more than 3 minutes, Dufaux 3 minutes and 30 seconds, and Tonkov—who chased hard after his crash—a solid 5 minutes.

Armstrong's demonstration surprised the world, but for him his beautiful victory was a just reward for the many months of hard work preparing for this moment. But he wasn't boastful of his feat. After saying that his team was "superb," he told a packed press room in Sestriere, "I'm still nervous and still don't think the race is over. The others will be back and they will be better than they were today. They're all scrappers and they will make life hard for us. I respect all of them 100 percent."

Armstrong has been a champion since he began his cycling career. On this rainy summit, he simply reached another step in his ascendancy. He went on to win that Tour, and the next one, then another, and the one after that.

Armstrong's story is about one man's battle with a sickness that helped make him a better, more rounded human being. He still feels the way he did after that Sestriere breakthrough, the day he turned the Tour on its head and demonstrated to a skeptical public that he was an athlete who could climb mountains as well as win one-day classics and time trials. "Cycling is still very much a part of my life," he said. "It's the thing I do every day. But it's not as big a part as it was before [cancer]. If it leaves tomorrow, or for some reason I can't race again, it's okay—whereas in the past, I didn't feel that way.

"I like to think that I represent what's good in the sport. At least a good story. Somebody that has come back from near-death, that is incredibly healthy. I think that the story is good for the sport."

It's also good for the rest of us.

PART III

PARIS
ÎLE-DE-FRANCE

CHARLEVILLE-MÉZIÈRES
MONDAY 7
SEDAN
TUESDAY 8
MEAUX
SAINT-DENIS
LA FERTÉ-SOUS-JOUARRE
SAINT-DIZIER
SUNDAY 27
TROYES
SATURDAY 5
SUNDAY 6
JOINVILLE
VILLE-D'AVRAY
MONTGERON
WEDNESDAY 9
THURSDAY 10
NANTES
PORNIC
SATURDAY 26
NEVERS
FRIDAY 11
MORZINE
SAINT-MAIXENT-L'ECOLE
SALLANCHES
FRIDAY 25
SATURDAY 12
LYON
SUNDAY 13
L'ALPE-D'HUEZ
BORDEAUX
LE BOURG-D'OISANS
MONDAY 14
THURSDAY 24
GAP
DAX
GAILLAC
CAP' DÉCOUVERTE
TUESDAY 15
PAU
FRIDAY 18
BAGNÈRES-DE-BIGORRE
TOULOUSE
MARSEILLE
BAYONNE
THURSDAY 17
SAINT-GIRONS
TUESDAY 22
WEDNESDAY 23
MONDAY 21
WEDNESDAY 16
LUZ-ARDIDEN
NARBONNE
LOUDENVIELLE
SUNDAY 20
SATURDAY 19
AX - 3 DOMAINES

Start
Finish
Stage start
Stage finish
Stage start and finish
Rest day/start
Individual time trial
Team time trial

Copyright Société du Tour de France

2003 Tour de France Team Rosters

U.S. POSTAL–BERRY FLOOR
1. ARMSTRONG Lance, USA
2. HERAS Roberto, Spain
3. BELTRAN Manuel, Spain
4. EKIMOV Viatcheslav, Russia
5. HINCAPIE George, USA
6. LANDIS Floyd, USA
7. PADRNOS Pavel, Czech Republic
8. PEÑA Victor Hugo, Colombia
9. RUBIERA José Luis, Spain

ONCE-EROSKI
11. BELOKI Joseba, Spain
12. ANDRLE René, Czech Republic
13. AZEVEDO José, Portugal
14. GONZALEZ DE GALDEANO Alvaro, Spain
15. JAKSCHE Jörg, Germany
16. NOZAL Isidro, Spain
17. ZARRABEITIA Mikel, Spain
18. SERRANO Marcos, Spain
19. VICIOSO Angel, Spain

TELEKOM
21. BOTERO Santiago, Colombia
22. AERTS Mario, Belgium
23. ALDAG Rolf, Germany
24. GUERINI Giuseppe, Italy
25. KESSLER Matthias, Germany
26. KLÖDEN Andreas, Germany
27. NARDELLO Daniele, Italy
28. VINOKOUROV Alex, Kazakhstan
29. ZABEL Erik, Germany

IBANESTO.COM
31. MANCEBO Francisco, Spain
32. FLECHA Juan Antonio, Spain
33. GARCIA ACOSTA José Vicente, Spain
34. KARPETS Vladimir, Russia
35. LASTRAS Pablo, Spain
36. MENCHOV Denis, Russia
37. MERCADO Juan Miguel, Spain
38. PETROV Evgueni, Russia
39. ZANDIO Xabier, Spain

RABOBANK
41. LEIPHEIMER Levi, USA
42. BOOGERD Michael, Netherlands
43. DE GROOT Bram, Netherlands
44. FREIRE Oscar, Spain
45. HUNTER Robert, South Africa
46. LOTZ Marc, Netherlands
47. NIERMANN Grischa, Germany
48. WAUTERS Marc, Belguim
49. WIELINGA Remmert, Netherlands

SAECO
51. SIMONI Gilberto, Italy
52. BERTAGNOLLI Leonardo, Italy
53. COMMESSO Salvatore, Italy
54. DI LUCA Danilo, Italy
55. FORNACIARI Paolo, Italy
56. GLOMSER Gerrit, Austria
57. LUDEWIG Jörg, Germany
58. SACCHI Fabio, Italy
59. ZANINI Stefano, Italy

COFIDIS
61. MILLAR David, Great Britain
62. CLAIN Médéric, France
63. CUESTA Iñigo, Spain
64. GAUMONT Philippe, France
65. LELLI Massimiliano, Italy
66. MONCOUTIÉ David, France
67. PEERS Chris, Belgium
68. TRENTIN Guido, Italy
69. VASSEUR Cédric, France

CSC
71. HAMILTON Tyler, USA
72. BLAUDZUN Michaël, Denmark
73. JALABERT Nicolas, France
74. CHRISTENSEN Bekim, Denmark
75. LUTTENBERGER Peter, Austria
76. PERON Andrea, Italy
77. PIIL Jakob, Denmark
78. SASTRE Carlos, Spain
79. SÖRENSEN Nicki, Denmark

FASSA BORTOLO
81. BASSO Ivan, Italy
82. BRUSEGHIN Marzio, Italy
83. CIONI Dario, Italy
84. GONZALEZ Aïtor, Spain
85. GUSTOV Volodymir, Ukraine
86. LODA Nicola, Italy
87. MONTGOMERY Sven, Switzerland
88. PETACCHI Alessandro, Italy
89. VELO Marco, Italy

FDJEUX.COM
91. CASAR Sandy, France
92. CASPER Jimmy, France
93. COOKE Baden, Australia
94. DA CRUZ Carlos, France
95. FRITSCH Nicolas, France
96. McGEE Bradley, Australia
97. MENGIN Christophe, France
98. VOGONDY Nicolas, France
99. WILSON Matthew, Australia

KELME–COSTA BLANCA
101. GUTIERREZ Ignacio, Spain
102. GUTIERREZ José Enrique, Spain
103. LATASA David, Spain
104. MANZANO Jesús Maria, Spain
105. MUÑOZ David, Spain
106. PARRA Ivan, Colombia
107. PASCUAL LLORENTE Javier, Spain
108. TAULER Antonio, Spain
109. USANO Julian, Spain

QUICK STEP–DAVITAMON
111. BETTINI Paolo, Italy
112. BODROGI Laszlo, Hungary
113. BRAMATI Davide, Italy
114. CAÑADA David, Spain
115. KNAVEN Servais, Netherlands
116. PAOLINI Luca, Italy
117. ROGERS Michael, Australia
118. VAN DE WOUWER Kurt, Belgium
119. VIRENQUE Richard, France

CRÉDIT AGRICOLE
121. MOREAU Christophe, France
122. AUGÉ Stéphane, France
123. FEDRIGO Pierrick, France
124. HINAULT Sébastien, France
125. HUSHOVD Thor, Norway
126. JEGOU Lilian, France
127. O'GRADY Stuart, Australia
128. POILVET Benoît, France
129. VOIGT Jens, Germany

BIANCHI
131. ULLRICH Jan, Germany
132. BECKE Daniel, Germany
133. CASERO Angel, Spain
134. GARCIA Felix, Spain
135. GARMENDIA Aitor, Spain
136. GUIDI Fabrizio, Italy
137. LIESE Thomas, Germany
138. PLAZA David, Spain,
139. STEINHAUSER Tobias, Germany

LOTTO-DOMO
141. McEWEN Robbie, Australia
142. BAGUET Serge, Belgium
143. BRANDT Christophe, Belgium
144. DE CLERCQ Hans, Belgium
145. GATES Nick, Australia
146. MERCKX Axel, Belgium
147. MOERENHOUT Koos, Netherlands
148. VAN BON Leon, Netherlands
149. VERBRUGGHE Rik, Belgium

AG2R PRÉVOYANCE
151. BROCHARD Laurent, France
152. ASTARLOZA Mikel, Spain
153. BOTCHAROV Alexandre, Russia
154. CHAURREAU Iñigo, Spain
155. FLICKINGER Andy, France
156. KIRSIPUU Jaan, Estonia
157. ORIOL Christophe, France
158. PORTAL Nicolas, France
159. TURPIN Ludovic, France

VINI CALDIROLA–SO.DI
161. GARZELLI Stefano, Italy
162. ANDRIOTTO Dario, Italy
163. BOSSONI Paulo, Italy
164. HAUPTMAN Andrej, Slovania
165. MAZZOLENI Eddy, Italy
166. MILESI Marco, Itay
167. RODRIGUEZ Fred, USA
168. VAINSTEINS Romans, Latvia
169. ZAMPIERI Steve, Switzerland

EUSKALTEL-EUSKADI
171. MAYO Iban, Spain
172. ARTETXE Mikel, Spain
173. ETXEBARRIA David, Spain
174. ETXEBARRIA Unai, Venezuela
175. LAISEKA Roberto, Spain
176. LANDALUZE Iñigo, Spain
177. LOPEZ DE MUNAIN Alberto, Spain
178. SANCHEZ Samuel, Spain
179. ZUBELDIA Haimar, Spain

BRIOCHES LA BOULANGÈRE
181. ROUS Didier, France
182. BENETEAU Walter, France
183. CHAVANEL Sylvain, France
184. GESLIN Anthony, France
185. HARY Maryan, France
186. NAZON Damien, France
187. PINEAU Jérôme, France
188. RENIER Franck, France
189. VOECKLER Thomas, France

GEROLSTEINER
191. REBELLIN Davide, Italy
192. BÖLTS Udo, Germany
193. HASELBACHER René, Austria
194. PESCHEL Uwe, Germany
195. POLLACK Olaf, Germany
196. RICH Michael, Germany
197. SCHMIDT Torsten, Germany
198. TOTSCHNIG Georg, Austria
199. ZBERG Markus, Switzerland

ALESSIO
201. DUFAUX Laurent, Switzerland
202. BALDATO Fabio, Italy
203. BERTOLINI Alessandro, Italy
204. CAUCCHIOLI Pietro, Italy
205. FERRARA Raffaele, Italy
206. FURLAN Angelo, Italy
207. MIHOJLEVIC Vladimir, Croatia
208. NOÈ Andrea, Italy
209. PELLIZOTTI Franco, Italy

JEAN DELATOUR
211. HALGAND Patrice, France
212. BOURQUENOUD Pierre, Switzerland
213. DUMOULIN Samuel, France
214. EDALEINE Christian, France
215. FINOT Frédéric, France
216. GOUBERT Stéphane, France
217. KRIVTSOV Yuriy, Ukraine
218. LEFÈVRE Laurent, France
219. NAZON Jean-Patrick, France

Week 1: Into Battle

THE CENTENNIAL TOUR HAS A
DRAMA-FILLED OPENING OF CRASHES,
CASUALTIES, AND CRAZY SPRINTS.

———————◈———————

Contenders for the Tour de France spend many months preparing their minds and bodies for the three weeks of intense competition in July. Every minute of every day is focused on bringing their fitness and form to optimum levels. Some of them weigh everything they eat so that their power-to-weight ratio is perfect for the climbs. They hold training camps in the mountains to scout the more difficult stages they will race at the Tour. And they have to meticulously plan their season racing schedules so they are not only race-hardened but also well rested for their biggest challenge of the year.

Then, in a split second, their hopes and aspirations can come tumbling down.

That split second at this centennial Tour came at 4:59 p.m. on July 6, exactly 425 meters from the finish line of the 168-kilometer stage 1 from Montgeron to Meaux. A frightening high-speed crash sent dozens of riders tumbling to the tarmac, forced American hope Levi Leipheimer out of the race, and gave his compatriot Tyler Hamilton a broken collarbone that jeopardized his continuation in the Tour.

It wasn't the defining moment of this opening week that the organizers were hoping for. They thought it would be the spectacular prologue around the grand boulevards of Paris circling the Eiffel Tower; or perhaps the reenactment of the 1903 Tour's start outside the Réveil Matin café at Montgeron; or even stage 4's team time trial between Joinville and St. Dizier, not far from the birthplace of the man who invented the Tour, sportswriter Géo Lefèvre.

But there was little time for nostalgia. The prologue did produce a drama-filled finish, with the victory of Australian Brad McGee of fdjeux.com by eight-hundredths of a second over unlucky Brit David Millar of Cofidis. The Montgeron start was a nice gesture, no more than that, especially as the Victorian-era café has been renamed the Hacienda Reveil Matin with an upscale menu of "traditional and Tex-Mex" cuisine. And well before the team time trial won by Lance Armstrong's U.S. Postal Service team, this ninetieth Tour de France took its dramatic turn on the streets of Meaux in a massive pileup that drastically altered its expected balance of power.

But, first, let's return to Paris on a weekend of mild temperatures and a sense of expectation in the air. All week there had been celebrations around the capital: the inauguration of a sports facility in the name of 1903 Tour winner Maurice Garin, the opening of the photo exhibit *100 Years of the Tour* at the city hall, and the unveiling of a plaque to commemorate the start of the first Tour at Montgeron. There was even a little controversy when a former district mayor, Jean-François Pernin, placed a wreath in the Paris street named for the father of the Tour, Henri Desgrange, who Pernin claimed was the forgotten figure of the week's various ceremonies. Tour director Jean-Marie Leblanc testily reminded the local official that Desgrange had not been forgotten. He pointed out that Desgrange's initials, HD, would appear on the shoulders of every yellow jersey; Desgrange's tomb had been restored at Grimaud in the south of France; and a ceremony would take place on stage 8 at the Desgrange memorial on the Col du Galibier. Leblanc added that negotiations were taking place with the city council to affix a commemorative plaque on the building where Desgrange was born on the Boulevard Magenta in the northeast part of Paris.

It was on the other side of the capital, in the unglamorous Porte de la Plaine neighborhood, that all of the official pre-race preparations took place in the capacious, but somewhat run-down, Paris Expo center. Besides the stickering of the hundreds of official vehicles, the accreditation of the thousands of race personnel, and the dressing of the publicity caravan floats, both Lance Armstrong and Jan Ullrich held news conferences for the media.

Neither of the Tour protagonists said much beyond the expected, but their physical appearance and moods were the subject of endless discussions among the reporters. There was agreement that Ullrich looked relaxed and was ready to race; but the verdict on Armstrong was mixed, some saying he looked sharp when the thirty-one-year-old Texan stepped into his press conference wearing a tight-fitting gray Postal team T-shirt and a broad smile. Others said that the defending champion looked more strained than usual, as though he had a lot on his mind.

Just about the only significant question asked of him at the July 3 event was this one: Have you had any surprises in your lead-up to the Tour? Armstrong answered,

"Hurrah for the 100 years of the Tour," reads this family's placard.

"The worst surprise came as a result of my crash at the Dauphiné. I had a hard time recuperating. I had to take antibiotics and that's never a good thing."

Perhaps there was significance in the date of his high-speed fall at the Dauphiné Libéré, twenty days before this conference: Friday the 13th. Armstrong, wearing the leader's yellow-and-blue jersey he donned after winning the stage-3 time trial, crashed 14 kilometers into stage 5 between Morzine and Chambéry in the Savoy Alps. The peloton was moving at 70 kilometers per hour on a sweeping descent across an open hillside toward the village of Taninges when the Texan's rear wheel locked up entering a turn, sending him sprawling. The damage was limited to two stitches in his right elbow and road rash on his right side, but he also was hopping mad at Frenchman Patrice Halgand of Jean Delatour, who attacked just as Armstrong crashed. In referring to Halgand—who claimed he didn't know the race leader had crashed—the American told reporters at the stage finish, "That f—ing guy can say what he likes now. Only an amateur would attack a leader who's on the deck."

Armstrong's adrenaline was flowing for a different reason the next day when Spanish challenger Iban Mayo of Euskaltel-Euskadi attacked on the mighty Col du Galibier and gained 25 seconds. The race leader had to make a furious solo chase on the descent to catch his rival. Armstrong fought off several other attacks, but he went on to win the Dauphiné, just as he had done on 2002. The victory confirmed that his Tour preparations were on target, but he wasn't in good shape coming out of the eight-day race, saying he didn't "feel right" on the bike. So when, just before the Tour, he went to a high-altitude training camp at St. Moritz, Switzerland, he had treatment for his ailing back from an Italian specialist, Gianluca Carretta. Carretta is somewhat of a celebrity in Italy, being the osteopath of the famed Parma soccer club and fiancé of the European women's marathon champion, Maria Guida.

After St. Moritz, Armstrong returned to his European base in Gerona, Spain, for some time with his family before the Tour. Unfortunately, it wasn't a perfect homecoming. "I had very bad diarrhea, very bad stomach problems that almost prevented me from making the trip [to Paris] on time," he later revealed. "Then [came] this problem with trying out new shoes and the cleats, and tendinitis in the hip."

He was reluctant to add to the list of problems that made his start to the Tour less than perfect. "It's not really my style to complain and make excuses about things," he said, thereby echoing some words from his autobiography, *It's Not About the Bike,* in which he wrote: "When my right testicle became slightly swollen that winter [1995–96], I told myself to live with it." He was diagnosed with testicular cancer nine months later.

Having coped with the often-dreadful suffering and indignities of chemotherapy, Armstrong was certainly not going to make a big deal about a stomach virus or some muscle pain. But little things can add up. As he pointed out, "There were enough physical problems that prevented me from feeling normal on the bike."

So it seemed that those journalists who perceived Armstrong as being somewhat distracted were perhaps right. There were no such concerns about Ullrich, Armstrong's perennial rival, who showed up for his news conference the following day. The twenty-nine-year-old German, wearing a baseball cap, was bronzed, smiled a lot, and took over the Bianchi team news conference, unlike the waiflike personality who faced the media at earlier Tours—such as in 1997, the year he won the Tour. At a rest-day press conference in St. Étienne that year, Ullrich barely said a word, leaving the talking to his then senior teammate Bjarne Riis (who currently runs the Danish-based team CSC). In Paris six years later, Ullrich was in charge, and his actions confirmed his declarations that he was a "new man." In the two years since his last Tour appearance, he had undergone two knee surgeries; been convicted of drunk driving; been suspended by the cycling authorities for testing positive for an amphetamine-laced leisure drug, ecstasy, at an out-of-competition control; moved with his companion, Gaby Weiss, to a new house overlooking Lake Constance in Switzerland; and become the father of a baby girl, Sarah Maria, the previous weekend.

Ullrich returned to cycling only three months before the Tour, after a tumultuous fourteen months out of the sport. The return started well. Just two weeks into his comeback, he scored a solo victory at the Tour of Cologne single-day race in front of thousands of adoring German fans. Then things soured. In May, the sponsor of his team, Coast, went bankrupt, and there were many anxious moments before the squad reemerged as Team Bianchi after the Italian bicycle manufacturer stepped up its investment. Under his new colors, Ullrich successfully completed his Tour preparations by finishing 5th at the Tour of Germany and 7th overall at the Tour of Switzerland—his first racing in high mountains since the Tour de France of 2001.

When asked what he felt about being named by Armstrong as one of the major contenders for the Tour, Ullrich was gracious. "It's an honor to be named by Lance," he said. "In three weeks' time we'll find out whether he's right. I've come here with very good preparation." Indeed, between the Tours of Germany and Switzerland in mid-June, he went to the Alps with some of his Bianchi teammates for a special training camp, similar to one that Armstrong did in mid-May with his U.S. Postal teammates.

Armstrong versus Ullrich was the match that the media was hoping for. Twice before they'd faced each other as Tour contenders, and each time the American had come out on top: by 6:02 in 2000 and by 6:44 in 2001. At both of those Tours, the third man on the podium was Joseba Beloki, who stepped up to 2nd place in Ullrich's absence in 2002. Beloki was the forgotten man of pre-race hype, but his ONCE-Eroski team looked as strong as ever, and Beloki himself was so confident of his form that after winning the final stage of the Bicicleta Basca race in late May he decided not to race again until the Tour. "I'm not going to settle for 2nd or 3rd place this year," he said. "I'm racing the Tour to win." They were strong words, but only a month short of his thirtieth birthday, Beloki knew that it was time to shoot for the yellow jersey.

CSC's Hamilton was in a similar position. Already thirty-two, the "other" American was quietly confident of his chances. He had established himself as one of the top riders of the season by winning the Liège-Bastogne-Liège classic in April, followed by overall victory at the mountainous Tour de Romandie in Switzerland—where he slaughtered the opposition in a difficult closing time trial that was held on a definite power rider's course. Hamilton later rode the Dauphiné as training after going into it with a stomach virus. But he examined the difficult stages of the Tour perhaps even more thoroughly than Armstrong, his former boss at Postal, did, and his final month of training brought Hamilton to Paris in peak condition.

Another name that appeared on Armstrong's pre-race list of favorites was Giro d'Italia winner Gilberto Simoni of Saeco, who was hoping to repeat the feat of his countryman Marco Pantani in 1998 by winning the Tour after dominating the Giro with his climbing ability. It had been five weeks since Simoni won the Giro for a second time, and but for an easy victory in a time trial up the Mottarone mountain in the Italian Lake District, he barely raced in June. Yet Simoni had been focused on the Tour and on preparing himself to challenge Armstrong. He told the French newspaper *L'Équipe* on July 4: "I won the Giro and I know that few riders have gone on to win the Tour. But I've already said that I believe in the impossible."

Also confident of success was Alex Vinokourov, Ullrich's former lieutenant at Telekom who was having his best-ever season, with wins at Paris-Nice, the Amstel Gold Race, and the Tour of Switzerland. This solidly built rider from Kazakhstan thought he could finish on the podium. Finally, there was much talk about the young Basque rider Mayo who had pushed Armstrong so closely at the Dauphiné. Mayo earlier won the prestigious Tour of the Basque Country, over Hamilton, and followed that with 2nd place (behind Hamilton) at Liège-Bastogne-Liège. After finishing a close 2nd to Armstrong at the Dauphiné, Mayo, twenty-five years old, said that a stage win was his highest priority at the Tour and that he didn't think he was ready to challenge the defending champion.

But all this speculation was just that. It was time to put a stop to the talk . . . and for the racing to begin.

Prologue: Central Paris

Performances—even those in an event as short as the prologue time trial—count for something. The original idea of a prologue was to simply determine who would wear the yellow jersey on the Tour's first road stage. It has since become not only a showcase for the short-distance speedsters but also a good barometer of the form of the overall contenders. So it was no coincidence that in the previous four years Armstrong had finished top three every time in the opening time trial. Looking at the four Tours he had won, here is how each year's eventual podium finishers performed:

1999 (PUY-DU-FOU): 1. Armstrong; 2. Zülle; 107. Escartin
2000 (FUTUROSCOPE): 2. Armstrong; 4. Ullrich; 12. Beloki
2001 (DUNKIRK): 3. Armstrong; 4. Ullrich; 7. Beloki
2002 (LUXEMBOURG): 1. Armstrong; 3. Rumsas; 9. Beloki

As can be seen, Armstrong was the best of the favorites each time, while the only podium finisher not to do well in the prologue was the Spanish climber Fernando Escartin in 1999. Escartin wasn't discouraged by his poor time trial because he knew that the only way he would challenge the top favorites was on *his* terrain: the mountains.

Like Escartin, Giro winner Simoni knew he wouldn't be too close to Armstrong in the prologue—although he was hoping to be closer than the 51 seconds that Escartin conceded to the Texan in 1999. For the Italian climber, the Paris prologue would give him a first assessment of his ability to be a contender at the Tour.

What then could be interpreted from Simoni conceding only 6 seconds to Armstrong, who in turn lost 7 seconds to prologue winner McGee? For Armstrong's army of fans, his 7th place in the 6.5-kilometer prologue time trial around the center of Paris was cause for concern. Maybe that stomach bug was to blame. Indeed, prologue winner McGee revealed to a journalist that Armstrong told him he had to go to the bathroom four times right before the start. And it wasn't due to nervousness.

So was it time to hit the panic button?

"No, no panic; absolutely none whatsoever," said Armstrong's personal coach, Chris Carmichael, who noted that his client started too slow and was only 13th fastest at half-distance, before a more solid second half took him to a 7:33 finish, 7 seconds behind McGee.

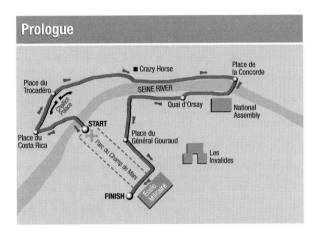

But did his rider's slow start surprise Carmichael?

He replied, "I was with George [Hincapie] and Lance in the bus when George just finished [in 7:37]. He said, 'The hardest part is the beginning. You've gotta start hard.'"

Instead, unlike his aggressive winning rides at Le Puy-du-Fou in 1999 and Luxembourg in 2002, Armstrong didn't truly attack the initial 500-meter-long hill that climbed away from the Seine River at the Paris prologue. Rather, he cruised on the uphill and then seemed undergeared on the ensuing gradual downhill over smooth cobblestones back toward the river. He was spinning rather than windmilling. A heavier gear would have been more appropriate.

Carmichael agreed. "Especially on the cobbles," he noted, "you need some of that beef under you, because you bounce around, and there's some traction working the wheel."

Along this same section of the course, the world pursuit track champion McGee was churning a 54x11 gear that took him to the halfway point, down on the Right Bank of the Seine, in a time of 3:46 (see inset), 4 seconds faster than Armstrong.

The Texan would concede another 3 seconds to McGee on the second, flatter half; but what was most worrisome for Armstrong was that in that opening 3.2 kilometers (just 2 miles), he was a whopping 9 seconds slower than Millar of Cofidis. And that was huge

when you remember that in 2000, when Millar won the Tour's opening time trial at Futuroscope, he beat Armstrong by just 2 seconds over a distance of 16.5 kilometers.

In Paris, though, the big Brit gambled on using a single chainring for the prologue, rather than the usual two-ring setup. It proved to be a bad decision by the Cofidis team. Before Millar started, three of his teammates had problems with the chain jumping off the single chainwheel because there was no front shifter to keep it in place.

This spelled disaster for Millar, who was looking like the winner, still 4 seconds ahead of McGee, when he approached the 1-kilometer-to-go mark along the Avenue Rapp. Rattling over more of those little cobblestones, his chain bounced off the chainring and forced him to stop pedaling. Millar then calmly reached down and lifted the chain back into place. The incident cost him at least 4 seconds, probably more, when you factor in his lost momentum.

Three minutes ahead of Millar, McGee was having a little trouble of his own when his rear tire slowly lost air on the finishing straight before he stopped the digital timer at 6:26:16. This was the best time of the bright, calm evening, 2 seconds faster than the previous best time set by Haimar Zubeldia of Euskaltel-Euskadi, who was the 93rd of the 198 starters.

Zubeldia was the forgotten man of Spanish cycling. The Basque rider was one of Spain's big hopes in 2000, when at age twenty-three, he placed 2nd at the Dauphiné— between winner Hamilton and 3rd-placed Armstrong! A series of illnesses and injuries kept Zubeldia from fulfilling that promise, but his prologue ride in Paris showed that this tall, slim athlete was probably going to be a force in this 2003 Tour.

The only other riders who had come close to McGee's time had been Armstrong's Colombian teammate Victor Hugo Peña (the winner of a Giro time trial back in 2000), who recorded 7:32, and Ullrich. The German was impressive as he powered down to the line in his celeste green Bianchi skinsuit and helmet to finish in 7:26:20, after consistent 3rd-fastest splits for both the first and second halves.

It was a ride that easily eclipsed the times of the two men who took over the Telekom team leadership after Ullrich left: Vinokourov (whose 7:51 was good enough for only 71st place) and 2002 world time trial champion Santiago Botero (7:35 for 9th

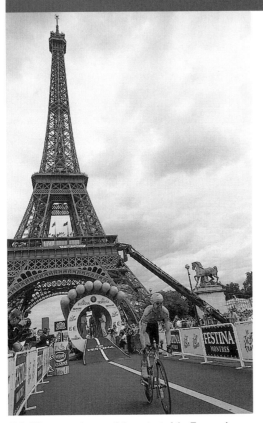

Zubeldia savors the prestigious start of the Tour prologue.

place), while 2002 Vuelta a España winner Aïtor Gonzalez of Fassa Bortolo recorded a disappointing 7:50.

Following McGee, who was the tenth-to-last starter, Fassa Bortolo's other leader, Ivan Basso, the winner of the best young rider competition in 2002, finished with a disastrous time of 7:57. Then came Hamilton. The New Englander said he had ridden the course three times in the morning, he had then checked into a downtown hotel instead of returning to CSC's overnight accommodations near the airport to avoid the traffic, and prior to his prologue he warmed up for an hour on a wind trainer near the start by the Eiffel Tower. The preparations paid off, as Hamilton gained his best prologue result in his seven years of Tour starts, recording a 7:32, which was eventually the 6th-best performance.

Right behind the relaxed Hamilton came a very angry Millar. Trying to make up for his lost time, he furiously pedaled down the last straightaway before turning his head to see his not-quite-good-enough-to-beat-McGee time of 6:26:24 flashing from the finish gantry in the shadows of the grandiose eighteenth-century École Militaire—where Napoleon Bonaparte received his military training 220 years ago.

Napoleon's teachers said he "will go far in the right circumstances." The same could be said about Millar, twenty-six, and McGee, twenty-seven. They are prologue specialists, for sure, but each of them has much higher ambitions. Even as high as knocking the "emperor," Armstrong, from his pedestal. For now, though, the Aussie was in yellow, Millar's mood was black, and Armstrong had a touch of the blues.

PROLOGUE: PARIS TT
1. Brad McGee (Aus), fdjeux.com, 6.5 km in 7:26:16 (52.466 kph); 2. David Millar (GB), Cofidis, 7:26:24; 3. Haimar Zubeldia (Sp), Euskaltel-Euskadi, 7:28:20; 4. Jan Ullrich (G), Bianchi, 7:28:20; 5. Victor Hugo Peña (Col), U.S. Postal–Berry Floor, 7:32; **6. Tyler Hamilton (USA), CSC, 7:32; 7. Lance Armstrong (USA), U.S. Postal–Berry Floor, 7:33**; 8. Joseba Beloki (Sp), ONCE-Eroski, 7:35; 9. Santiago Botero (Col), Telekom, 7:35; 10. Viatcheslav Ekimov (Rus), U.S. Postal–Berry Floor, 7:37.

STAGE 1

Montgeron to Meaux

Before (and just after) the massive pileup in Meaux, stage 1 provided a classic opening for the centennial Tour. Hundreds of thousands of spectators lined the scenic route through the greenbelt valleys and hills, towns and villages of the Île de France. Three Frenchmen—one wearing red (Walter Beneteau of Brioches la Boulangère), one white (Christophe Mengin of fdjeux.com), and one blue (Andy Flickinger of ag2r)—conducted a break of 137 kilometers that ended just 10 kilometers from Meaux. And then Alessandro Petacchi scored a convincing stage win.

Petacchi's Fassa Bortolo team had been smart in scouting the finish, with its controversial S-curve in the last kilometer, before the Tour started, taking a short ride from their hotel on the northern outskirts of Paris. And what they saw caused them to get to the front before that curve, to lead out their enormously improved sprinter with a long charge.

The Vini Caldirola team of former world champion Romans Vainsteins had similar ideas, but as his teammate Fred Rodriguez explained, exercising their plan wasn't as easy as thinking it up. "I was leading out with about a kilometer to go," said the American. "We thought we had it all wired. But we made a mistake coming in, maybe a little too anxious, and we got swung to the front a little bit too quick on the downhill [with 2 kilometers to go].

"We need more practice, I think. We haven't done too much, not like Petacchi's team. To lead out Romans, we were lacking a couple of guys. Next time we'll get it better."

As for Petacchi, he said, "My teammate [Nicola] Loda went down [in the crash]; he was the last rider before [Marco] Velo to lead me out for the sprint. So we were lucky."

About 120 riders involved in the pileup were not so lucky. It was a crash that was perhaps inevitable, given the uncompromising nature of modern cycling that virtually

Stage 1

S Sprint
4 Cat. 4 Climb

Meaux
St. Denis
PARIS
Coulommiers
Mauperthius
Montgeron
Corbeil- Essonnes
Mormant
Côte de Champcueil
Côte de Barbeau
Fontainebleau
Avon
Côte de Boutigny-sur-Essonne

Just as they did in July 1903, the Tour starters gather outside the Réveil Matin café in Montgeron.

precludes successful breakaways in the Tour's opening days and brings the peloton together by each stage end.

Coming into Meaux after crossing the Marne River near the center of town, all 198 riders entered the last 2 kilometers together. They then headed east on a straight, wide road, moving at 60 kilometers per hour before hitting a short uphill inside the final kilometer. Then, with 500 meters to go, the road began a fairly tight right-handed curve as it dropped toward a final left curve leading into the finish.

Because of the contours and the metal barriers that narrowed the roadway to about 20 feet, it was virtually impossible for riders midpack to see what was happening ahead around the bend. And with the Fassa Bortolo lead-out men for Petacchi gaining speed on the slight downhill, the pack was moving at a conservative 70 kilometers per hour.

Then, only six rows back in the fast-moving serpent, two men suddenly lost their balance: Parisian rider Médéric Clain of Cofidis, who was hoping for a good result in front of his local fans, and José Enrique Gutierrez of Kelme–Costa Blanca, a Spanish sprinter riding his third Tour. The Spaniard, whose carbon-fiber bars snapped in the impact, said that a rider from behind him bumped into his back tire. But whatever started the resultant chain-reaction pileup, the root cause of the crash was the organizers' choice to include the now infamous chicane in the final half-kilometer.

Once two riders were down, row after row of those behind, not having time to react because of the restricted sight lines, smashed into them. Rabobank's Levi Leipheimer later recalled that riders and bikes seemed to be falling on him for half a minute. It wasn't that long, of course, but the volatile mixture of frantic speed, proximity of the riders, narrowness of the roadway, and lack of visibility led to the monstrous, mind-jarring wreck.

After the clatter of machines hitting the pavement and the thud of bodies falling on bodies had subsided, and after a handful of sprinters had contested the 2003 Tour's first sprint finish, won by Petacchi from Robbie McEwen of Lotto-Domo and Erik Zabel of Telekom, a strange silence hung in the heavy air of the warm July afternoon. The quietness was soon broken by the sinister sound of sirens as ambulances began transporting riders to Meaux's *centre hospitalier*, just a mile across town.

It took awhile for everyone to cross the line, except for a stunned Jimmy Casper of fdjeux.com, who badly sprained his neck and went straight to the hospital. Tour rules allow a rider who crashes in the final kilometer to remain in the race, even if he doesn't cross the line, while being given the same G.C. time as the first rider in the group.

Armstrong was a bit player in the pileup drama, having emerged with minimal contusions. After crossing the line on a teammate's bike, the defending champion hustled past a small group of reporters extracting quotes from the main players in the day's final sprint. Armstrong, grim-faced, a white towel around his neck, was spinning a low gear as he rode off toward his U.S. Postal–Berry Floor team's big blue bus. He quickly dried off, and within 8 minutes of falling, he was in a tinted-window station wagon, heading for his team's Radisson about half an hour away across the open countryside northeast of Paris.

After the big pileup in Meaux, only a handful of riders are left to contest the stage 1 finish, which Petacchi took from McEwen and Zabel.

Another to come through with minor injuries from the Meaux pileup was Giro winner Simoni. Twenty-four minutes after the crash, though, he was still sitting in the back seat of a Saeco team car, his racing jersey off and his bib shorts hanging loose, his bare feet propped up on the driver's seat, as he spoke to a French camera crew. In France, Simoni still lacks the star status afforded to Armstrong. But the crowds would probably soon get to know him when the Alps arrived, especially after his exceptional prologue time trial in which he conceded only 6 seconds to the Texan. Another to come through unscathed was Beloki, who placed his traditional top ten in the prologue, and who looked relaxed and happy on his return to his yellow team bus in Meaux. As for Armstrong's other rivals, Ullrich was the only one who avoided the crash altogether, crossing the line in 27th place.

The first rider to be declared out of the Tour was Rabobank's solid Dutch domestique Marc Lotz. He had drilled headfirst into the pavement, and a ragged incision split his face from chin to eyebrow. His team leader Leipheimer appeared to be luckier, at first. The American had ridden from the blood-spattered crash scene with fellow faller George Hincapie of Postal. Leipheimer told his former teammate Frankie Andreu, now a Tour correspondent for the Outdoor Life Network, that he was feeling some back pain and was hoping that nothing was broken.

The X rays revealed otherwise. A fractured tailbone meant that last year's 8th-place finisher—who was looking good to improve on that after a move from 18th to 12th in the prologue, an exercise he doesn't enjoy—would be on a plane the next morning, on his way to his summer base at Gerona, Spain. His Tour aspirations would have to wait another twelve months.

It also looked as though Hamilton would be out of the race. The CSC leader is used to overcoming pain and suffering, but perhaps no cyclist has braved such misfortune as he did in this Tour's opening. Although he crossed the finish line at Meaux under his own steam, he went straight to medical for treatment, and then had to report to the antidoping trailer for a random test. His right arm hung down from his shoulder, which was giving him considerable pain, so his next stop was the hospital.

Hamilton spoke about the crash a few hours later at his team hotel, the Millennium, near Paris's Charles de Gaulle airport, where his CSC team doctor showed a few reporters the X ray of Hamilton's fractured right collarbone—the same one he broke when he collided with an opening car door as he warmed up for Belgium's Eddy Merckx Grand Prix in August 2002.

"I was right with [race leader] Brad McGee [heading into the finish]," said a distraught Hamilton. "I was in the position I needed to be in, particularly the first

MEAUX-ED DOWN

Tour organizers under fire for dangerous finish.

THE "UNAVOIDABLE" CRASH at the end of stage 1, which eliminated Levi Leipheimer from the Tour de France and put Tyler Hamilton's chances of winning on hold, called into question the competence of race organizers who include highly dangerous finishes at big races. One of the most vociferous critics of race director Jean-Marie Leblanc after the high-speed pileup at Meaux was American sprinter Fred Rodriguez of Vini Caldirola–So.Di, who was leading the peloton as it headed into the final kilometer. While Leblanc was hoping for a weekend of uninterrupted celebrations for the centennial Tour, he received a mouthful of abuse from the two-time U.S. pro champion.

"This is the Tour de France, you know. We're asked to wear helmets—Leblanc preaches that we're trying to have a safer Tour—and then they put in a finish like that. It's completely unprofessional. That's ridiculous," Rodriguez said. "I mean, I was doing 60K an hour, and it wasn't the lead out yet. So they were gonna do like 65K an hour going around that corner. The crash was unavoidable.

"You can't realize it until you go into it. You know it's a chicane, but we're thinking we're coming into a big city, maybe four lanes wide, and they put in about a lane and a half? That was an unavoidable crash. And that's completely on Leblanc's shoulders."

Rodriguez's complaints were echoed by many others, including stage winner Alessandro Petacchi of Fassa Bortolo, along with crash victim Hamilton and his CSC team director, Bjarne Riis. "I was frightened on every stage at the Giro, and it's the same here," said Petacchi. "I didn't see the crash because it happened behind me . . . but when you arrive at 70 kilometers an hour in the last bend . . . They ask us to wear helmets, but to have to take such a dangerous bend so close to the finish in a race as important as the Tour de France, on the first stage, it shouldn't have been on the course."

Even Hamilton, the most polite of professionals, was critical. "I don't think the finish today was a very good finish for the start of a Tour de France. A hundred and ninety-eight riders, everybody's fresh, everybody's ready to give it a go, and for a lot of these guys, you know, their only opportunity is the first week to really do something. And you throw in an S-turn with 500 meters to go, and with the road becoming more narrow . . . It's just . . .

"I feel like we [the sport of cycling] have learned our lesson over the years [with] the many big crashes in the finale because of crazy finishes. And here we go again! I think we need those wide boulevard straights for at least 1 or 2 K, for the first few stages. Okay, when the peloton gets a little smaller, you can have something like today."

When Riis was asked to comment on what the organizers presented to the riders at the Meaux finish, he replied, "I don't know. This is the race, this is the game, but …there should be a rule, at least in big races like this. Like Tyler said, every [one of the] 200 riders is fresh, they're sprinting like hell, and there's just one S-curve 500 meters from the finish line. It's crazy, it's stupid.

"When [they] build in ten curves, then you have the peloton spread out, then it's less dangerous. Just one curve, and then— everybody knows the peloton is big—500 meters from the finish line the road's gonna be small and more narrow, then of course they're gonna crash."

Asked if he thought that he and the other team managers should protest the dangerous finish to prevent a repetition of the Meaux pileup, Riis replied, "Let's sleep on it. . . . Let's talk about that another day. We can't do anything about that now."

The criticism was cavalierly dismissed by the Tour's course designer, Jean-François Pescheux, who said, "The finish was absolutely worthy of the Tour de France, the obstacles [such as traffic islands] had been removed. Above all, I think that even if we put the finishes on auto routes during the first week, there would still be crashes."

Crashes, maybe, but not of the calamitous magnitude of the pileup at Meaux. ■

[stage]. In years past, I finished 70th, 80th, 90th on the first stage, and this year I said I had to be smarter about it, more at the front, to avoid the bullshit crashes. What happens at the front, happens at the front. You know, the way Lance has ridden over the years, he's always in the top thirty or forty guys in these big field sprints, and he always stays out of trouble."

But Hamilton's smart riding didn't help on this occasion. "There was a body lying right in front of me, a fdjeux.com rider. I think it might have been Jimmy Casper." He continued, "I really had no time to react. Before I knew it I was on the pavement. I landed on my head, and my back first. All the abrasions I have are on my back . . . but my collarbone's broken at the front. I think I hit my shoulder and my head at the exact same time. Good thing I had my helmet on.

"I knew there was a problem right away, because when I got up I couldn't really lift my arm. I broke the same collarbone ten months ago and I kind of had the same feeling over it. And when I rode to the finish I couldn't really hold my hand to the handlebar."

While detailing his own misfortune, the New Englander unselfishly spoke about the experience of men he hoped to be challenging for the yellow jersey. In fact,

Hamilton, expecting that he wouldn't be able to continue, said he had been deter-mined to challenge for the podium in Paris; and he felt that he would have had a very good chance. "This is my year," he said.

As for Hamilton's competitors, he said about the crash, "It's too bad. There're a lot of other guys who have paid the price today, too. Levi Leipheimer, you know. I think Lance is okay, but what if it happened to Lance? If this happened to Lance, and just ruined his chance of No. 5, that would be just awful."

As for his own chances of continuing, Hamilton said, "We won't make the final decision until the morning, but it's gonna be very difficult. It's not a pretty fracture. It's actually two fractures, sort of in a V. Quite painful now, and that's actually with a little painkiller, so . . . I think when I wake up, it'll be a lot more painful."

STAGE 1: MONTGERON TO MEAUX
1. Alessandro Petacchi (I), Fassa Bortolo, 168 km in 3:44:33 (44.890 kph); 2. Robbie McEwen (Aus), Lotto-Domo; 3. Erik Zabel (G), Telekom; 4. Paolo Bettini (I), Quick Step–Davitamon; 5. Baden Cooke (Aus), fdjeux.com, all s.t.
Overall: 1. McGee, 3:51:55; 2. Millar, at 0:04; 3. Zubeldia, at 0:06.

STAGE 2
La Ferté-sous-Jouarre to Sedan

Hamilton slept only four hours the night after he broke his clavicle, partly because his team physiotherapist Ole Kaere Føli had to work on the shoulder for several hours. The Danish healer—who helped Hamilton get through the 2002 Giro d'Italia to finish 2nd overall after he fractured the humerus bone in his other shoulder—did another 90 minutes of kneading in the morning. The shoulder was braced with bandaging, his bars were padded with three rolls of absorbent gel tape, his tires were slightly deflated for extra cushioning, and only an hour before the stage-2 start Hamilton decided to risk racing. "I feel a bit stiff," he said after finishing the stage. "My goal is to get to the team time trial, to repay Carlos Sastre, to help him gain some time for the G.C."

Following stage 1's calamitous final-kilometer crash, there were fears that the mayhem would be repeated on the run-in to Sedan, where there was a similar S-curve as that at Meaux 1,200 meters from the line. But this time the peloton was split up 5 kilometers from the finish by an uncategorized, but by no means insignificant, climb in this outlying region of the Ardennes. "I wasn't at red-line, but it was going," Vini Caldirola's Rodriguez said about the speed on the uphill. "It was hard, a lot of sprint-ers got dropped. Petacchi got dropped, [Alessio's Angelo] Furlan got dropped."

The blitz on the climb was partly in response to an attack by the frisky Millar. "I feel better today," the Brit said before the start, having been upset since losing

the prologue because of what he regarded as his Cofidis team's poorly chosen equipment. His attack also indicated that he was planning to play an important role in this year's Tour. Millar's acceleration on the climb, which was preceded by a pileup that delayed a half-dozen others, meant that the typical lead-out trains didn't happen.

This opened up the final sprint to several riders whose teams didn't have the power to match Petacchi's Fassa Bortolo squad. One such man was Rodriguez, who described the windup to the sprint: "I was up there with the French team, La Boulangère, and ONCE. I thought I had a good lead out from them. But they didn't have the speed to lead it out, and we got swarmed from behind."

Coming off the S-curve, race leader McGee surged to the front for the final kilometer-long finish straight, with fdjeux.com teammate Baden Cooke on his wheel. As the pace picked up, riders were jumping to the left and right, to set up what Rodriguez called a chaotic sprint.

McGee soon left Cooke to find his own way through, which was not a daunting task for a young rider reared on handicap races back home at the Northcote velodrome in Melbourne, Australia. In such events, the fastest riders have to make up "handicaps" of 100 or more meters, with the idea being that everyone arrives together for the sprint. Cooke talked about touching shoulders with other racers while battling through a small pack to contest the sprint.

"Obviously, in a finish, I don't give up my place very easily, that's just a part of being a sprinter. And that's the same with respected sprinters like Erik Zabel and Robbie McEwen," said the rider who was accused of causing a pileup in the sprint that ended stage 1 of June's Dauphiné Libéré.

In this wild finish on Sedan's Avenue Philippoteaux, though, McEwen was shut out and Zabel mistimed his final charge. The sprint was late in being launched, a situation that suited Jean-Patrick Nazon, the Jean Delatour rider who had been contesting the intermediate-sprint points left by the day's two breakaway riders: his teammate Frédéric Finot (who was caught 2.5 kilometers from the finish) and Crédit Agricole's Lilian Jegou.

Into the final 50 meters, Nazon was a length clear of the veteran Jaan Kirsipuu of ag2r, when Cooke shot through from 3rd position to pass both of them for a narrow, but hard-earned, stage win. It earned him the white jersey of best young rider, while the 20-second time bonus he received deprived Nazon of taking the yellow jersey from teammate McGee.

Cooke's win was impressive, but perhaps the day's most remarkable ride was Hamilton's. To not only start the stage with a broken collarbone, but also to finish the five hours of racing with the pack, over terrain that resembled the hilly Amstel Gold Race, was nothing short of remarkable. During a mob scene at the CSC team bus in Sedan, as TV, radio, and press reporters jostled to get a quote or two from the heroic Hamilton, his team boss, Riis, said in admiration, "It is amazing what he can do. He can suffer, that guy."

STAGE 2: LA FERTÉ-SOUS-JOUARRE TO SEDAN
1. Cooke, 204.5 km in 5:06:33 (40.026 kph); 2. Jean-Patrick Nazon (F), Jean Delatour; 3. Jaan Kirsipuu (Est), ag2r; 4. Zabel; 5. Thor Hushovd (N), Crédit Agricole, all s.t.
Overall: 1. McGee, 8:58:28; 2. Millar, at 0:04; 3. Cooke, s.t.

STAGE 3
Charleville-Mézières to St. Dizier

Both Petacchi and Nazon woke up on the morning of stage 3 in low spirits. "My morale was at zero," said the big Italian, "after I got dropped on the hill yesterday." As for the slim Frenchman, he said, "I was so upset at missing the yellow jersey in Sedan, I'll have to try something today."

Nazon knew that taking the race leadership was a possibility for him, particularly as he would be racing through his home territory, being from nearby Épinal. He also knew that the day's three intermediate sprints were all flat and straight, and perfectly suited to his greyhound-type sprint. And he duly went for them, just losing the first to Kirsipuu (for a 2nd-place, 4-second time bonus), winning the second from McEwen (for another 6 seconds), and at the third, 23 kilometers from home, taking the sprint from Kirsipuu, a minute or so behind longtime breakaway rider Anthony Geslin of La Boulangère.

"We decided to go for the last sprint instead of trying to win the stage," said Nazon. And those 14 total bonus seconds did take him to the yellow jersey. Nazon was almost not a pro cyclist in 2003, because after five mixed seasons at fdjeux.com, he was discarded by team manager Marc Madiot, who was banking on his Aussie dis-

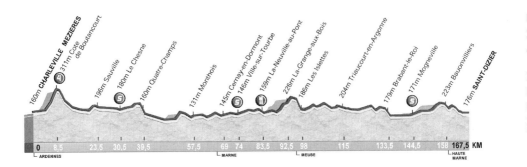

covery, Cooke. Nazon was eventually picked up by lowly Jean Delatour—and now he was leading the Tour de France.

The locals were ecstatic, and Nazon himself was practically speechless when French TV crews interviewed him. As for Cooke, he could have taken yellow if he'd beaten Petacchi in the mass-sprint finish at St. Dizier. But during a rambunctious sprint, the twenty-four-year-old Aussie got stuck in a dangerous place, between the curb and McEwen, and he had to stop pedaling when the Austrian René Haselbacher of Gerolsteiner almost fell into him. McEwen managed to stay upright to take 5th place, but there was no denying Petacchi, who took his second stage win with a long, long sprint that held off two former world champions, Vainsteins and Oscar Freire of Rabobank.

The day's other story was the continuing saga of the injured Hamilton, who achieved his initial goal of getting to the stage-4 team time trial, despite the many hills and high speeds of this stage across the Champagne district. And word from the CSC camp was that its Danish physiotherapist, Kaere Føli, indicated the American might even go farther, much farther.

STAGE 3: CHARLEVILLE-MÉZIÈRES TO ST. DIZIER
1. Petacchi, 167.5 km in 3:27:39 (48.399 kph); 2. Romans Vainsteins (Lat), Vini Caldirola–So.Di; 3. Oscar Freire (Sp), Rabobank; 4. Zabel; 5. McEwen, all s.t.
Overall: 1. Nazon, 12:25:59; 2. McGee, at 0:08; 3. Millar, at 0:12.

STAGE 4

Joinville to St. Dizier Team Time Trial

For a Tour de France cyclist, few experiences can match the thrill of winning a team time trial. And if you were a U.S. Postal rider on July 8, that thrill was very, very special. Because your team started last, you knew that you'd won the stage even before finishing. At that moment, you and your eight teammates were on an adrenaline high, fresh from taking your 60-kilometer-per-hour pulls and knowing that at a time check 10 kilometers from the finish, your biggest rival was almost 20 seconds slower.

No wonder Lance Armstrong and his buddies were whooping with joy even before they crossed the line in this 69-kilometer stage from Joinville to St. Dizier. The Postal men continued pumping their fists as they skidded their bikes to a halt on the Avenue du Belle Forêt and frantically hugged each other to celebrate their triumph.

What was even more special for team member Peña was the yellow jersey he'd just earned—the first by a Colombian in Tour history. Almost as happy as the smiling Peña were the two Colombian radio reporters who exuberantly commentated on the team time trial, stressing what a great ride Peña and his team were having.

"We put it all on the line, and it went just perfectly," confirmed an elated George Hincapie as he walked back toward the podium for the stage winners' presentation. "We didn't want to go to dinner tonight and say we could have done this, we could have done that. We didn't want any excuses."

Hincapie should know. The native New Yorker had been alongside Armstrong every year of his first four Tour victories, and in two of them their Postal team was runner-up to ONCE-Eroski in the team time trial—losing by 46 seconds on the Nantes–St. Nazaire stage in 2000 and by 16 seconds between Épernay and Château-Thierry in 2002.

For Armstrong, his fight to win a Tour team time trial goes back even farther. On his debut in 1993, the Texan was one of the strongest riders in the Motorola team that finished 3rd to the then all-powerful MG-GB squad at Avranches. And the following year, Motorola lost by only 6 seconds, taking 2nd place behind MG-GB, on a windswept course between Calais and Eurotunnel.

Stage 4

To come so close, but to be denied so many times, is a bad feeling, one that can only be expunged by finally winning. Because of this history, it was obvious that Armstrong was just as excited by the St. Dizier victory as his teammates—even though he had won fifteen individual stages since suffering that first team time trial loss ten years ago. His pride at achieving a long-held goal was reflected in his words: "Some days when you win, you get to the finish line and say, 'Shit, that was easy.'

Today was not one of those days. It was a full effort for everybody."

Postal had the confidence to make a full effort because the preparations for this team time trial were meticulous: a visit by assistant directeur sportif Dirk Demol in May to make an initial review of the course; a brilliant effort to place three riders in the prologue top ten to ensure their last-place start in the team time trial; a detailed reconnais-

> **SPLITS**
>
> **FIRST 18 km:** 1. Telekom, 21:25 (50.428 kph); 2. Crédit Agricole, 21:26; 3. ibanesto.com, 21:32; 4. Vini Caldirola, s.t.; 5. ONCE-Eroski, 21:33. (7. U.S. Postal–Berry Floor, 21:39).
> **NEXT 26.5 km:** 1. ONCE, 29:26 (54.020 kph); 2. U.S. Postal, 29:29; 3. Bianchi, 29:37; 4. ibanesto.com, 29:39; 5. Gerolsteiner, 29:51.
> **NEXT 14.5 km:** 1. U.S. Postal, 16:19 (53.319 kph); 2. Bianchi, 16:41; 3. ONCE, 16:45; 4. ibanesto.com, 16:51; 5. Gerolsteiner, 16:55.
> **LAST 10 km:** 1. U.S. Postal, 11:00 (54.545 kph); 2. Bianchi, 11:11; 3. ONCE, 11:13; 4. fdjeux.com, 11:17; 5. Telekom, 11:21.

sance the day before the stage by team director Johan Bruyneel, making note of every turn; and on the morning of the stage, a collective ride by the whole team— the first half in the car, the last 35 kilometers by bike.

As a result, all nine riders knew that the 3-kilometer-long, 5 percent climb, starting in the sun-splashed streets of little Joinville, needed to be taken steadily, before the course emerged from a forest onto an exposed plateau where a strong side wind was blowing from the right. "It wasn't strong enough to blow us off line," said Hincapie, "but it was a factor."

The wind was certainly a factor in the times recorded at the first split, at 18 kilometers, after a long, straight, roller-coaster road that followed the initial hill. The fastest four teams to this point—Telekom, Crédit Agricole, ibanesto.com, and Vini Caldirola— started one after the other in the seventh to tenth starting slots, an hour before Postal lined up in Joinville. The wind was gusting and changing directions, and the time splits showed that the conditions on that opening stretch were far less favorable for Postal.

That didn't bother the American team, because it based its progress on the intermediate times of ONCE—which started 25 minutes before Postal. "We knew we were on track when we heard that ONCE was only 6 seconds faster than us at the first split," said Hincapie. "We knew it was a hard start and almost a 70-kilometer time trial, so the ending is where you can make up the most time."

That the final kilometers would be the most important was emphasized by the wind being favorable on the 26.5-kilometer-long section after kilometer 18. Pushing their 55x11 gears, Postal was second best on this stretch, only 3 seconds slower than ONCE—which had taken the lead by the 44.5-kilometer point. Now it was time for Postal, with only 9 seconds to make up, to "put it on the line."

Bruyneel said that his team followed the suggested strategy perfectly. "We reserved our strongest guys to take the longest turns in the last 20 kilometers, when we could make the difference," stated Bruyneel. "Five riders—Lance, George,

Team time trial victory is sweet for Postal riders (left to right) Rubiera, Heras, Landis, Armstrong, Padrnos, Ekimov, Hincapie, and Beltran. (The ninth rider, Peña, is missing from this shot.)

Victor, Floyd [Landis], and [Viatcheslav] Ekimov—were the real motors of the team who took very long pulls."

But the headwind over the final 25 kilometers, which was also the flattest part of the course, somewhat modified the plans. The five riders Bruyneel mentioned *did* do the driving, but their efforts weren't quite as simple as it sounded. "In the end, we were intending to take long pulls," said Armstrong. "But we were taking these 10-second pulls—we were empty."

Empty or not, Postal rode as impressively as any of the great teams of the past, like Panasonic in the 1970s and 1980s, and GB-MG in the 1990s. The well-disciplined American squad pulverized the opposition in the final stretch, to take 39 seconds out of ONCE in 25 kilometers. Just as phenomenal was the fact that over the last 10 kilometers, into a head wind, Postal averaged almost 55 kilometers per hour—the fastest split of the day.

In terms of all-time records, the Postal riders' overall speed of 52.772 kilometers per hour was the third fastest in Tour history; but the two past record performances were both ridden on courses shorter than this year's.

Besides the team's historic victory and Peña's yellow jersey, this was also the first joyful experience of a grand tour stage win for Hincapie, Landis, Manuel Beltran, and Pavel Padrnos; and for Armstrong, it was an emphatic confirmation that he was right on track to win his fifth consecutive Tour.

Besides taking 30 seconds from ONCE's Beloki, Armstrong gained 43 seconds on Bianchi's Ullrich, 1:30 on Telekom's Vinokourov, 1:45 on CSC's Hamilton, 3:02 on Saeco's Simoni, and 3:22 on Euskaltel's Mayo and Zubeldia. The importance of those time gaps would become very apparent in week two.

STAGE 4: JOINVILLE TO ST. DIZIER TTT
1. U.S. Postal–Berry Floor (USA), 69 km in 1:18:27 (52.772 kph); 2. ONCE-Eroski (Sp), 1:18:57; 3. Bianchi (G), 1:19:10; 4. ibanesto.com (Sp), 1:19:32; 5. Quick Step–Davitamon (B), 1:19:50.
Overall: 1. Victor Hugo Peña (Col), U.S. Postal–Berry Floor, 13:44:44; **2. Lance Armstrong (USA), U.S. Postal–Berry Floor, at 0:01**; 3. Viatcheslav Ekimov (Rus), U.S. Postal–Berry Floor, at 0:05.

STAGE 5

Troyes to Nevers

Whatever the weather, whatever the terrain, the peloton in this baking-hot Tour seemed determined to race fast and hard every day. The first attack of stage 5 came only 4 kilometers out of Troyes; and by 14 kilometers, as the race left the wide valleys of the Champagne region for the rolling hills of Burgundy, fourteen men were clear.

It was a big break that included Italian champion Paolo Bettini and his Quick Step–Davitamon teammate Laszlo Bodrogi and Crédit Agricole's Jens Voigt, along with the usual flotilla of French riders hoping for a miracle. The U.S. Postal team recognized the break's potential danger and sent along Armstrong's lieutenant, Roberto Heras, to police the attack.

That was a smart decision by team director Bruyneel, rather than making his riders, somewhat wearied by their team time trial win, chase down the break so early in the day. Other teams closed the gap from 35 to 20 seconds before five men split from the front: Voigt, Bodrogi, and the French riders Frédéric Finot of Jean Delatour, Nicolas Jalabert of CSC, and Ludovic Turpin of ag2r.

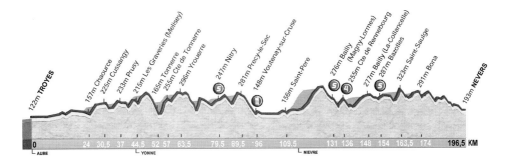

Through the 90-degree heat, and with a gusting tailwind, the five men looked determined to go all the way; but despite getting a lead of 3:20 by the feed zone, that was their maximum gap. Finot, who displaced fdjeux.com's Christophe Mengin from the polka-dot jersey on the stage, extended the break on his own, as he did on stage 2, but he was reeled in 19 kilometers from Nevers.

Then, on a short uphill, curving past a green meadow into some woods, Bettini, Telekom's Vinokourov, and Crédit Agricole's Sébastien Hinault made a dashing counterattack. They soon gained 15 seconds, eliciting a sharp response from Postal that quickly reeled in the dangerous Vinokourov.

So another stage was going to end in a sprint. Petacchi had hung tough in the hills this time, but it looked as though fdjeux.com was going to repeat its stage-2 win at Sedan. An impressive McGee, still on the form that won him the Paris prologue, had Cooke safely on his wheel as they rounded the tight left turn into the final 700 meters that curved slowly to the right.

Lining up behind the two Aussies were Petacchi, Vini Caldirola's Rodriguez, and ag2r's Jaan Kirsipuu.

"I was actually on Petacchi coming around the last corner," said Rodriguez, "but I lost his wheel to Kirsipuu. And when Petacchi and Kirsipuu went, I lost the gap, bumped into somebody, and lost momentum."

Petacchi, meanwhile, was scenting victory, and when he made his move with about 250 meters to go (with Kirsipuu still glued to his wheel), he was in a different gear than the others and powered to the win. Commenting on the Italian's powerful finish, 3rd-placed Cooke said, "I think you saw that when Brad [McGee] was doing the lead out, [Petacchi] jumped and went straight past, and he was able to hold it. I think he's generally getting the best lead outs and he's generally the fastest—if he can get up the hills."

STAGE 5: TROYES TO NEVERS
1. Petacchi, 196.5 km in 4:09:47 (47.201 kph); 2. Kirsipuu; 3. Cooke; 4. Zabel; 5. McEwen, all s.t.
Overall: No change.

STAGE 6

Nevers to Lyon

In this first week of the Tour, it seemed that you only had to point Petacchi in the right direction and he would find a way to win the stage. The big, wavy-haired Italian didn't even feel up to contesting the sprint into Lyon, but he took it anyway—though it wasn't quite as straightforward as it looked.

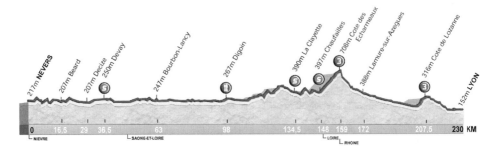

First of all, there was the small matter of catching the day's long, long breakaway by Crédit Agricole's Australian champion Stuart O'Grady and the second-year French pro Anthony Geslin of La Boulangère. After attacking only 34 kilometers into the 230-kilometer stage, just before the first intermediate sprint, O'Grady and Geslin worked well together to establish a maximum lead of 18:05 over a disinterested peloton.

"We really needed 20 minutes," said O'Grady, who has multiple experiences of marathon moves like this one. Back in 1998, he was part of the nine-man, stage-3 break across Brittany to Lorient that netted him the yellow jersey the following day; that same Tour he took a stage win at Grenoble after driving a six-man move for most of a long, hot day through the Alps; and two years ago, he was part of that thirteen-rider breakaway group that raced through torrential rain to gain more than half an hour on the main pack into Pontarlier, a move that also netted the freckle-faced Aussie the yellow jersey.

A two-man break is different, though, especially on a day of 90-degree temperatures along wide, straight rolling roads when all the sprinters' teams have their last chance of a stage win before the mountains. Cooke's fdjeux.com team and Kirsipuu's ag2r men began the chase soon after the 18-minute gap was announced, and they worked steadily to cut the gap to 12 minutes with 100 kilometers to go, and 8 minutes with 50 kilometers left. Those 50 kilometers would be raced in exactly 1 hour even though they included a Cat. IV hill—where O'Grady tried unsuccessfully to drop Geslin.

Petacchi's Fassa Bortolo team eventually joined in the chase, and the two leaders entered Lyon, with 11 kilometers to go, with less than 2 minutes in hand. It was an impressive trip through the city where the first Tour de France stage finished in 1903. Coincidentally, there were two men together 100 years ago, but after riding the 467 kilometers of stage 1 from Montgeron at 26.3 kilometers per hour, Maurice Garin and Emile Pagie arrived in Lyon almost 3 hours ahead of their opposition. They weren't being pursued by a 150-strong pack swishing along the elegant quays of the Saône and Rhône Rivers at 60 kilometers per hour.

The Australian champion O'Grady (right) and Frenchman Geslin conduct a 195-kilometer breakaway that falls 500 meters short of success in Lyon.

On one of the right-angle turns with 5 kilometers to go, several riders went down, including the top two sprinters of the 2002 Tour, McEwen and Zabel. "There must have been something on the road, oil maybe," said McEwen, "because we were going around the corner normally, not touching the brakes. Two riders fell right in front of me [when] their wheels just slid out."

The elimination of McEwen and Zabel from the picture certainly improved the chances of the other sprinters. Petacchi, though, wasn't feeling well and told his teammates that he wasn't planning to contest the finish. They and their Fassa Bortolo team boss, Giancarlo Ferretti, didn't agree.

Luckily for the Italians, the *arrivée* sign was at the end of a wide, flat boulevard, more than 2 kilometers long—where the fdjeux.com and ag2r teams completed the job of catching O'Grady and Geslin. While that near-200-kilometer adventure was ending, the Fassa Bortolo riders had time to literally drag Petacchi to the head of the pack just as Vini Caldirola, Crédit Agricole, and the other teams launched their sprinters. For a moment, it looked as though Cooke would be rewarded for all the hard work done by his teammates, but then Petacchi came hurtling through the middle to complete a Cipollini-like week: four sprints, four wins.

While Petacchi's victories lifted the spirits of his Fassa Bortolo teammates, a visit to the team staging area in Lyon showed that the combination of heat-wave temperatures, record stage speeds, and frequent crashes was eating at the morale of most. Many of the sweaty riders, their jerseys open to the waist, couldn't find their team buses in the crowded streets near the Palais des Sports. And all they wanted was to be out of the baking sunshine and into the air-conditioned haven of their hotels.

In seven days, only four of the twenty-two teams had won a stage, and the majority knew that they were not going to get a chance to improve their success rate in the mountain stages that lay ahead. Indeed, if they looked east from their hotel rooms that evening they'd be able to see the Alps awaiting them on the horizon.

STAGE 6: NEVERS TO LYON
1. Petacchi, 230 km in 5:08:35 (44.720 kph); 2. Cooke; 3. Fabrizio Guidi (I), Bianchi; 4. Hushovd; 5. Vainsteins, all s.t.
Overall: No change.

STAGE 7

Lyon to Morzine

If you had watched the beginning of this longest stage of the Tour you'd have thought that it was just another flat one getting under way. There was an attack from the start by four riders, who averaged 50.2 kilometers per hour for the first 40 kilometers on roads, swinging through crowded villages and past lush fields of corn and potatoes.

In the front were French Tour rookies Benoît Poilvet of Crédit Agricole and Médéric Clain of Cofidis, along with the German veteran Rolf Aldag of Telekom and the ever-aggressive Bettini of Quick Step. "When the gap stayed at 15 seconds for a long time, I thought we'd be caught," said Poilvet, "and my day would be over."

It was only just beginning, though, because when a big pileup slowed the pack after 32 kilometers, the gap quickly opened to 5 minutes. A dozen riders went down, including points competition protagonists Cooke and McEwen, along with

G.C. contender Basso of Fassa Bortolo—who needed two bike changes before reaching the day's first climb, the surprisingly difficult Col de Portes.

The first mountain of the Tour always sends dread through the peloton, as it marks the brutal change from big-ring churning to small-ring spinning. Not everyone feels that way, of course.

That morning, in the Quick Step team's Mercure hotel southeast of Lyon, five-time Tour King of the Mountains Richard Virenque told his young Aussie teammate Michael Rogers that he was going to attack on the first climb. The Swiss-based Frenchman was as good as his word.

On the opening 10-percent stretch of the Col de Portes, which angles across a grassy hillside and opens up wide vistas over the meandering Rhône River and its wide valley, Virenque spurted ahead. With him went the Spanish climber Jesús Manzano, who was the Kelme–Costa Blanca team's big hope for the Tour in the absence of regular leader Oscar Sevilla. As Virenque and Manzano raced away from the pack, two others, both sprinters, dropped behind. One was Gerolsteiner's Olaf Pollack, the other, points leader Petacchi. Both quit before the top of the hill.

Given the organizers' decision not to invite world champion Mario Cipollini to the Tour, it was an embarrassment that the new green jersey should quit so quickly, especially when he was followed into retirement by ag2r's Kirsipuu. These two sprinters were a big part of their teams' relevance and by their quitting so soon they made Tour boss Leblanc's reasons to turn away Cipollini look even flimsier.

Meanwhile, Virenque was on a mission. After leaving behind the promising Manzano—who collapsed from heatstroke on the Portes climb and was rushed to a hospital—the Frenchman caught Clain, who had fallen back from the leaders. This pair eventually bridged to the front group after Bettini was told by his team director to wait for teammate Virenque.

"There were five of us, so it wasn't hard to ride," said Poilvet, twenty-six, of his first experience in a big Tour breakaway. "But Virenque made it hard [on the climbs] and my back was a little stiff. It was a lot of fun to be at the front, though."

While the five leaders (four after they dropped Clain on the very steep Mont des Princes climb) moved to a maximum lead of 9 minutes, the Postal domestiques were having their first real test of riding tempo on difficult terrain. "The team was riding strong," said Hincapie. "We didn't want to kill ourselves to keep the jersey today. . . . It was a tough day, but it was hard for everybody. The roads were up and down and windy."

Indeed, it was a testing course, and 5 hours of riding were already behind them when the main pack of 100 riders reached the foot of the day's prime obstacle, the

Virenque (right) and Aldag battle for the stage win up the Col de la Ramaz.

Cat. I Col de la Ramaz. This was where many questions would be answered. Which of the pre-race favorites would crack? Could Hamilton be a factor with his broken collarbone? Did Armstrong and his Spanish teammates have the form to dictate the race?

First, though, there was the battle for the stage win. Virenque was the clear favorite, especially after his teammate Bettini had ridden hard in the last valley to keep the four leaders 7 minutes clear going into the Ramaz. The recently crowned Italian champion gave some last strong pulls at the base of the 14-kilometer ascent before leaving Virenque to do battle with his last opponent, the surprising Aldag.

The tall German, thirty-four years old, was initially dropped, then came back and actually rode away from Virenque at one point; but he eventually "died" 5 kilometers from the top. Virenque, who has had no positive doping results since his admitted use of the blood-boosting drug EPO during his Festina years, went on to win the sixth Tour stage of his career and took the yellow jersey for the first time since his race debut in 1992. Virenque finished in Morzine—where he also won in 2000—2:29 ahead of Aldag and 4 minutes ahead of a forty-strong peloton that regrouped in the 22 kilometers after the Ramaz.

The big climb, though, did provide some answers about the overall picture. Five potential race contenders couldn't stay with the pace on the Ramaz: Saeco's Simoni and Telekom's Botero conceded 6 minutes to Armstrong; Fassa Bortolo's Gonzalez and Bianchi's Angel Casero lost 4 minutes; and Gerolsteiner's Davide Rebellin finished almost 2 minutes back.

Hamilton, however, rode through his pain to match the top contenders, even on the stiffest 10-percent pitches. And Postal's Beltran, Heras, and José Luis Rubiera all went over the Ramaz summit with Armstrong. But perhaps the most relevant action of the day was a staggering acceleration by Vinokourov about 5 kilometers from the top. When the blond rider from Kazakhstan attacked, looking both fast and strong, no one even tried to follow him. And although he subsequently weakened and temporarily fell back on the climb's last 2 kilometers, Vinokourov seemed to be saying that he was going to be a big factor in this centennial Tour.

STAGE 7: LYON TO MORZINE
1. Richard Virenque (F), Quick Step–Davitamon, 230.5 km in 6:06:03 (37.782 kph); 2. Rolf Aldag (G), Telekom, at 2:29; 3. Sylvain Chavanel (F), La Boulangère, at 3:45; 4. Michael Rogers (Aus), Quick Step–Davitamon, at 4:03; 5. Stefano Garzelli (I), Vini Caldirola–So.Di, at 4:06; 6. Christophe Moreau (F), Crédit Agricole; 7. Laurent Dufaux (Swi), Alessio; 8. Millar; 9. Georg Totschnig (A), Gerolsteiner; 10. Alex Vinokourov (Kaz), Telekom, all s.t.
Overall: 1. Virenque, 29:10:39; **2. Armstrong, at 2:37**; 3. Aldag, at 2:48.

SATURDAY, JULY 5

PARIS—*After a long week of getting ready and all of the pre-race hype, the centennial Tour de France got under way today. There usually comes a point when I'm anxious to get rolling, because, believe it or not, things almost always calm down after the race begins.*

This will be my seventh Tour de France, which is no small detail with my wife. Seven is her favorite number. She also likes that my race number is 71, which is the year I was born. I wouldn't be surprised if she high-fived herself when she heard my start time for the prologue was 7 p.m. **sharp**. *I'm waiting for her to remind me that July is the seventh month of the year.*

We arrived in Paris on Tuesday night and drove out to preview the course for the team time trial on Wednesday morning. It was a good opportunity to practice the route and ride together in a relaxed environment. Everyone on the team looked strong and seems ready to work hard here at the Tour.

Thursday was hectic with medical checkups and media interviews. Friday was also busy with the team presentations in the heart of Paris. It feels kind of funny being in the city at the start of the race. Traditionally, the goal is to get to Paris. This year I guess it will have to be to get back to Paris.

I went as hard as I could in today's prologue, but my crash in last year's Giro d'Italia prologue is still a pretty fresh memory, so I didn't want to get overexcited, or take too many risks. In addition, cobblestones don't generally suit me too well. I don't have enough body mass to keep from getting bounced around. But all in all, I'm happy with today's effort. It was really the first race where I've had some pressure on me since the Tour de Romandie.

Behind the Scenes

Since many of you wrote to tell me you liked hearing about how many water bottles a team consumes on hot days, I've decided to add a section to my Tour journals that gives you a little more insight about the team, the riders, the staff, and the equipment.

Some generic stats to start things off: This year's CSC Tour team has 9 riders, 3 directors, 3 mechanics, 4 soigneurs, 2 physiotherapists, 1 chef, 2 press agents, 2 doctors, 1 team consultant, 1 sponsor liaison, 1 large bus, 1 camper, 7 team cars, and 1 mechanic's truck. Multiply all this by 22 teams and you pretty much get the picture: It's the French equivalent of a traveling circus. Which is about the best way to describe this race, I guess.

WEDNESDAY, JULY 9

ST. DIZIER—*Sorry for the delay in getting this update out. The last 72 hours have been quite a roller-coaster ride. Not surprisingly, there have been some mixed reports about my health and status in this year's Tour de France, so with a couple of minutes of downtime, I'll try to get my version of all that's transpired typed out.*

I've probably talked a thousand times about how hard it is to get ready for a Tour de France. It's not something you do in a week, or add to your annual list of objectives at the last minute. It really takes the better part of a year to get yourself to the point where you can be bold enough to say you are able to lead a team at the Tour. If you added up every sacrifice, every hour of training, and every moment the race is on your mind in an eleven-month period, it would be easy to conclude that preparing for the Tour de France can just about take over your life.

But even if you are fortunate to have your lead up to July go just about perfectly, as it did for me this year, there are still a fair amount of things that can change everything.

The first week of the Tour is always fast and nervous. Traditionally, there are a number of crashes throughout the early stages. But not always at the level we encountered in stage 1. As pileups go, this was one of the worst I've ever been in. I can't really describe the crash to you; because it happened so fast, I didn't even see or hear it coming. All I knew was that I was where I was supposed to be when heading into a sprint—behind the guys going for the win, but close enough to the front to stay out of trouble. Normally, if a crash occurs near the finish or the field splits in the final kilometers, the repercussions are the worst for the guys at the back.

*But Sunday was fairly unique, because the crash occurred close to the front and spread rapid-fire across the peloton. A rider on my left slid into me and I hit the ground hard with the right side of my back and head. I was able to get right up and continue on to the finish. My teammates stopped and rode in around me. I think I was so stunned I didn't have time to absorb that I was actually hurt when I got back on my bike. But as soon as I crossed the finish line, I knew there was **something** wrong with my shoulder. It took a fair amount of mental and physical strength not to panic. This was, after all, only stage 1.*

As I crossed the line I found out that, regardless of my condition, my number had been pulled to do a random drug control. So I had to go there immediately after the race ended. I saw Levi Leipheimer on my way to the control. He had also gone down hard, but was probably still feeling the effects of adrenaline when I saw him, because he was more concerned with me and why I was holding my shoulder than he was for himself.

After the control, I traveled by ambulance to a nearby hospital to have an X ray. The pain was getting worse, but I was still hoping nothing was broken. They took me right away, and they had the results as soon as I got redressed. I could tell by the look on Bjarne's face it wasn't good. Then he made a hand gesture to say the collarbone was broken. I didn't quite know how to react. It felt like someone had sucked all the air out of the room. There were two fractures to my right collarbone that met at the base of the bone to form a "V." At that moment, the Tour was over.

On my way out of the hospital I bumped into Levi. He had just been told he had a broken tailbone. I felt like I was walking through a nightmare. There were cyclists all over the place waiting to be examined. I called my wife from the car and gave her the update. I don't know if we said more than five words. We were both in shock.

I don't know when we actually started to think about my continuing on with the race. But by about 8:30 p.m. Sunday evening, the team had decided to hold a press conference to share my X rays and confirm the rumor I had broken my collarbone. The funny part was that I think I was supposed to announce that I was retiring from the race—but neither Bjarne nor I wanted to say those words.

Maybe we couldn't come to grips with the reality of the situation in such a short span of time. Who knows? But I went to bed that night thinking that I would at least try to ride my bike in the morning. For some reason it wasn't enough for someone to say, "It's time to quit." I had to prove to myself that I couldn't ride.

I didn't sleep much during the night. My mind was racing with all that had happened and the pain in my shoulder was pretty bad. Our physiotherapist, Ole, spent a large portion of the evening working on me. With my neck, back, and collarbone all in rough shape, Ole put in extra hours even through the middle of the night. He sat next to my bed and applied pressure where he could to try and alleviate some of the pain.

When we arrived at the start of stage 2 there was a mob of cameras and reporters. After one step forward from the bus I was swarmed. And, believe it or not, I took a hit from a camera lens right on my broken collarbone.

Luckily, I was taped up pretty good beneath my jersey, so no additional harm was done. Even Bjarne got knocked above the eye by a camera. It was insane. So before I could go from the bus to sign in, I had to explain exactly what I thought I was doing continuing on in my condition. All we could say was that we were giving it a try. At the time, I didn't know if I'd make it 1 km or 10 km. We were prepared for the fact that this effort might not fly. My race bag was going to be waiting for me at the feed zone, in the event things weren't going well.

My teammates never left my side during the stage. We stayed at the back and just took it kilometer by kilometer. Luckily, it wasn't a super difficult day, since a lot of riders were feeling the effects of the crash. The speeds stayed at a manageable pace for me. But when the race was over I was exhausted. I can't remember the last time I felt that tired.

Haven, my wife, and Tugboat, our dog, drove 1,100 km from our home in Spain to the finish in Sedan, but I didn't get to see them until we arrived at our team hotel. Regardless of how the day unfolded, they wanted to be around when the stage ended.

Stage 3 was a little more difficult for me because there were a lot of accelerations in the peloton. And just like the day before, I stayed toward the back. This got us into a little trouble at one point when crosswinds split the peloton into two groups. We had to work pretty hard to get back with the front group. And the extra effort took its toll on me. I was in a lot more pain last night than the night before.

If I had one goal after deciding to stay in the race, you could say it was to make it to the team time trial. There is no telling how long I am going to be able to keep going, but today was a critical day for the team. With Carlos [Sastre] carrying the weight of our G.C. hopes, we didn't want him to lose too much time. Everyone put in a good effort, and I was happy to be able to do my part. But it was pretty gritty out there. There may be a few more trips to the dentist in my future after today.

Behind the Scenes
After stage 1, our mechanics were busy late into the evening gluing tires. Every rider on the team flatted his rear wheel from braking so hard to avoid the crash.

FRIDAY, JULY 11
LYON—We've made it through six stages—about five more than I thought I would see last Sunday.

We're still taking things day-by-day here at Camp Collarbone. I had a second set of X rays taken last night. The good news was there was no further displacement, or injury. The bad news was there was no evidence of any healing. We've chosen to focus on the good news, so I started today's stage from Nevers with the same mind-set I've had all week, which has basically been "Let's see what we can do."

I'm completely amazed with all the attention my situation is getting. I've been riding my bike for several years and have endured more ups and downs than I can count along the way. But no success or setback of mine has ever been so closely followed.

I've finished six Tours in my career so far, so I don't feel like I have to prove that I can make it to Paris. I guess my primary reason for being here up until now has been to see if I can hang on and lend support to my good friend Carlos Sastre.

He has done so much for me over the last year and a half that I feel like I should make the most of every opportunity to repay him. I wanted to be a contributing factor in the team time trial for him, and tomorrow we will see if I still have what it takes to do some work for him in the mountains.

I'm a little concerned about whether or not I will be able to stand up on the bike. I'm only riding with about 50 percent of my full strength on my right side. So, it hasn't been that easy to keep pace with the accelerations in the peloton over the last few days. To stay with the first group, you really have to be able to pull on the handlebars when the speeds heat up on the climbs.

Ole has been hard at work on my collarbone, neck, and back all week. To complement his efforts, Bjarne invited a doctor from Denmark who specializes in atmospheric ionic therapy to come see me tonight. He gave me about an hour's worth of treatment that is meant to help promote healing to my fractures. I don't know much about the treatment, but at this point, I'm keeping an open mind.

Behind the Scenes

My wife and dog arrived at the race Monday night thinking they were coming to take me home after my accident. But their mission has changed a bit. Now they are following the Tour, which is no small feat for a 90-pound golden retriever. For luck, I've been packing one of Tugboat's favorite tennis balls in my race bag every morning, which is in addition to carrying a small vial of salt in my jersey pocket sent to me from a good-vibe guru who's a friend of one of our team's mechanics.

And now you know why I've made it this far. Thanks for reading.

Tyler Hamilton

SATURDAY, JULY 5

PARIS—*The Tour de France is the biggest race in the world. Everyone knows that. But today, as it celebrated the start of its centennial edition, I really found out firsthand how big it is.*

First off, there's the organization and number of people. Although when you're racing, you can't really hear them. I saw them, but I was in my zone.

The number of media here is another thing altogether. In the days leading up to the start there are so many interviews, so many questions. It all takes a bit out of you.

It is clear to anyone who races the Tour how winning a stage can change your life, with the result being so important to your team and sponsors.

So I did have a real go today in the prologue. Obviously, by finishing 19th at 13 seconds to Brad McGee, I'll have to rest up, take stock of the experience, and then wait for another chance to try again.

The course was hard, with the hill straight from the start. I rode as well I could and felt pretty good, but then the last 2 km were like riding into a cement wall.

Was the pressure of being a Tour debutant and billed as one of the winning hopes too much? No . . . I don't think so. I've had really good legs for two months, winning the Tours of Belgium and Germany and then the Route du Sud, so I was named as a favorite.

It is also true that I have been basing my whole year around this prologue. I made no secret of that, nor do I regret it.

Sure, I was a bit nervous before the start. I had a really good warm-up, and my thoughts were positive. My preparation today was down pat. I slept well on Friday night, sharing the hotel room with my Italian teammate Davide Bramati. Then this morning I rode three or four laps of the course before reminding myself that if I have a good ride, everything changes from here.

I just pushed the biggest gear I was most comfortable in and went as hard as I could. It would have been nice to go better today. But there are still 19 or 20 days to go, so what I have to do now is get some rest and hope for the best.

SUNDAY, JULY 6

MEAUX—*I've got one big hope for tomorrow: I hope that the peloton relaxes a bit. Then again, maybe I'm dreaming.*

The ground is pretty hard, as the massive crash in today's finish at Meaux showed. If riders keep racing like they did today, I think **everyone** *is going to go down at some point this Tour.*

Me? I was right in the middle of the spill, at about 30th wheel. I don't know what happened, except one important fact: I didn't go down. I was just lucky I didn't. I'm still not sure why, but I managed to avoid the worst of it, while riders were falling and crashing everywhere around me.

The bunch was so nervous it wasn't funny. They say it is like this in the first stage of a Tour every year. But for a first-timer like me, that doesn't stop the flighty nature of the pack from having some impact. And don't think it was just in the last kilometers after the daylong break was finally reeled in that the nerves ran high. It was that way from the very start. As people got more and more tired, it became more and more dangerous.

The speed, which today averaged 44.890 kph, may be a tiny bit quicker than other races, but it wasn't the speed, it was the nervousness within the pack at that speed that made it dangerous.

TUESDAY, JULY 8

ST. DIZIER—*For everything you learn in a single day of racing in the Tour de France, one of the biggest lessons for a rookie like me has nothing to do with performance on the bike. It is how to spend your time off it and, most importantly, try to recover for another day in the saddle in between each stage.*

Like every other team in the Tour, mine—Quick Step–Davitamon—is equipped with an army of personnel who do their best to make sure your recovery is as swift as possible. But as my roommate, Davide Bramati, has taught me, there is only so much that others can do for you. In the end, when it comes to rest, the responsibility is yours.

Davide, 34, one of the oldest in the race, is in his 14th year as a professional. With 17 finishes in the three-week tours of France, Italy, and Spain, he knows what he is talking about.

This Tour may only be four days old, but he is always on at me for something I am not doing right. But his experience counts for a lot and is really helpful.

The main message is clear: Rest is as important to a Tour rider as fitness and preparation. He says every moment you can, you have to try and save energy. If you get an extra hour's sleep each day, after 21 days you have almost two nights more sleep.

I used to be an early riser, but now I am becoming a late riser. Over the last couple of years I have learned the benefits of that. Now that we are in the Tour, it's paying off.

Before today's stage 3 got underway, I didn't get up until 10 a.m. We usually eat three hours before any event. So with today's 167.5-km stage starting at 1 p.m., we tried to sleep in as much as we could to do what Davide preaches: expend as little as possible.

It is the same after a stage. When we go to the team hotel rooms to shower, we often eat a snack and try to get in half an hour of sleep before our massage. Then we watch television in our rooms before dinner. After eating we return to our beds to watch more television until we fall asleep—who does first reaps the maximum gain, as it's the other fella who has to get out of bed and turn off the lights!

On the Tour, the day follows a basic routine: race, eat, sleep, massage, lie around until dinner, and then lie around again until you fall asleep again. After stages like today's, sleeping is never a problem. What a fast race it was. You wouldn't think this is a three-week event. After an hour and a half, I looked down at my computer and saw we still had a 51-kph average!

And again the peloton was jittery, helped by the slight crosswind that blew for most of the day, which could easily have splintered the pack into echelons. At one point, the wind **did** *split the whole group in two, but then, to my relief, it came back.*

THURSDAY, JULY 10

NEVERS—The Tour de France learning curve steepens dramatically after tomorrow's stage 6—literally and metaphorically—when we hit the Alps. A lot of people have been asking how I hope to go. I can see why there are some expectations after I defended my lead at the Route du Sud in the last Pyrenean stage.

It's great knowing that after five stages I am feeling better than I did when we began in Paris last Saturday. Today's stage 5 to Nevers was the best I felt the whole race.

You don't have to be a rocket scientist to know that if you are going to have any chance of riding strongly in the mountains—good form, health, and a strong mind are musts. So, hopefully, I can just continue on and rest by hiding in the bunch as much as possible and then see what I can do in the mountains. I just don't know.

The Pyrenean stage of the Route du Sud also taught me to have confidence in my own ability, and not to measure how I race against the way others may do it. In that stage, two danger men attacked on the final climb. It would have been easy to try and go with them (although harder to **stay** with them). But instead I stuck by my game plan and rode my own tempo. In the end, the overall victory was still mine.

The lesson learned was that I am not the kind of rider to accelerate repeatedly, but I am better at keeping my one speed and milking my strength and turn of pace to the maximum. This plan worked, providing a major boost in my self-confidence. I am still learning about my limits in these kinds of races. And by Saturday I am sure I will have learned more.

Italian Luca Paolini is the only team rider on the Tour who was with me at the Route du Sud. On the Tour where we have a cosmopolitan mix of riders from seven countries, Kurt Van de Wouwer is the only Belgian riding with us.

But, there is still much experience to draw on for advice and support. As I said, I have been talking to Richard Virenque quite a bit. He's been telling me about the mountains we will pass in the Alps on Saturday, Sunday, and Monday as I haven't ridden any of them—even though I have trained on other climbs in the region.

I may regret saying it, but talking about it gets my blood pumping—even after finishing another hot and fiery 4 hours in the saddle at an average speed of 47 kph on stage 5.

SATURDAY, JULY 12

MORZINE—*What a day stage 7 into the Alps turned out to be! To finish with my Quick Step teammate Richard Virenque taking the first mountain stage and the yellow jersey—and me "passing" my first test in the Alps—it couldn't have been better.*

First, a few words about Richard: I said the other day he has given me a fair bit of advice and inside knowledge about the mountains. He proved today that his word is good. He told me this morning at breakfast that he was going to go for the stage win. He said he was going to attack on the first kilometer of the first climb, the Col de Portes. And that is exactly what he did. He was pretty keen all right. And he soon showed everyone else how.

Today also showed we can be effective in not only the one-day races and smaller stage events where we have made our name as a team this year, but also in the major tours. My Italian teammate Paolo Bettini, who won Milan–San Remo, did a terrific job getting into that early break before Virenque went away to chase them. He rode his heart out for Richard. But the two of them . . . they rode like animals. It was really inspirational.

As for me? Well, 4th place, 4:03 behind Richard, on my first alpine stage was a really pleasing result. As I've said, I have never raced in the Alps and today I only had recent good form and the advice of teammates like Richard to go on.

For me, they were big climbs too. But I kept to my goal of trying to stick with the main group led by Lance Armstrong's U.S. Postal Service team, which I succeeded in doing until just before the top of the second-to-last climb, the Col de la Ramaz.

I have to admit it was pretty tough for me. It was hard at the start. They fired, fired, and fired (with the pace), and while I was riding a 39x23 gear they eventually dropped me. But as I did in the Route du Sud stage in the Pyrénées, I just settled into my own pace and, after losing 30 seconds at the summit, I managed to get back on to the group on the descent.

After the descent, Armstrong's team was still driving. But for me the pace was good—comfortable, in fact. It also stopped all the attacks. But as I was no threat to Lance's overall plans, I knew he wouldn't chase me if I had a go and attacked. There was no benefit in chasing me. That I got 4th place after Richard's success gave the team a double boost, as we have the lead in the team competition in addition to the yellow jersey.

I'd be lying if I said I wasn't starting to feel the effects of what has already been a hard season. Mentally I'm a bit tired; but I managed to push myself today and still got a good result. It is good for the morale to know I can do that. So while I spent a lot of cookies today, I just hope I can recover well tonight and hold on for another effort tomorrow.

Michael Rogers

Week 2: On a Knife's Edge

ARMSTRONG WEARS THE YELLOW JERSEY,
BUT IT HANGS BY A THREAD AFTER A
SECOND DRAMATIC WEEK.

———————⊙———————

The centennial Tour's fourteenth stage finished just an hour before a brief, but heavy, thundershower fell upon Loudenvielle-Le Louron. It was a welcome rain that would end the suffocating heat wave that had gripped France ever since the race left Paris two weeks earlier. It was also a rain that Lance Armstrong had been craving in the two days following the Tour's first long time trial, when dehydration almost ended his bid to become the fifth five-time winner. Perhaps he also found solace in the fact that it was here, in the lush Louron valley ensconced in the green folds of the central Pyrénées, that in 1991 Miguel Induráin ended a long breakaway through the mountains with the Italian Claudio Chiappucci to begin his reign of five consecutive Tour victories.

Like Induráin, Armstrong established his dominance at the Tour by winning the long time trials and being as strong (or stronger) than the best climbers. But this year was different. When the American came across the line in the little village of Loudenvielle in 11th place—1:24 behind stage winner Gilberto Simoni of Saeco and, more importantly, 43 seconds after Telekom's Alex Vinokourov—only 18 seconds covered Armstrong, Jan Ullrich, and Vinokourov, the top three riders in the overall standings. That's as close as any Tour has been poised a week before the finish. Back in 1977, 25 seconds covered Bernard Thévenet, Didi Thurau, and Eddy Merckx after stage 15.

Armstrong was brutally honest in assessing the unexpected tightness of the race when he spoke at a brief press conference shortly before the rain fell on Loudenvielle. "As I said in Paris, I knew it was going to be close. I probably didn't expect it to come down to the last few decisive stages, the last two mountain stages and the time trial at Nantes," he said. "This is perhaps a bit of a surprise, but okay, as I said, something's not going right, and there's nothing I can do about that now. All I can do is wake up every morning and do my best, and that's what I'm doing. And if we get to Nantes and I have 15 seconds, and I lose by 16, then it'll go down as the closest Tour de France in history. And I'll go home and have a cold beer and come back next year. So I'm not gonna cry and whine. I'm just gonna do my best."

As he sat there speculating, Armstrong could feel proud that, despite a string of physical and mechanical setbacks, along with some bad karma and the luck of Houdini, he was wearing the yellow jersey for the seventh night in a row—ever since he claimed the race lead in L'Alpe d'Huez. Reflecting on the up-and-down week he had just lived through, Armstrong said, "It's obvious I'm not riding as well as I have in years past. I can't exactly say why. This is a sport where you cannot only look at the difference between other riders, but you can look at the times on certain climbs, and you look at the times of Alpe d'Huez—[for me] to ride about 4 minutes slower—it doesn't take a rocket scientist to figure out that that rider wasn't as strong as he was two years ago. So something's not clicking."

The numbers don't lie: Armstrong rode the Alpe in 41:20, compared with the 38:01 he took to climb the 14-kilometer mountain road in his solo victory of 2001. Those times compare with the 39:06 of 2003 stage winner Iban Mayo of Euskaltel-Euskadi and Marco Pantani's 1997 record of 37:35.

Armstrong was clearly not at 100 percent on the climb to L'Alpe d'Huez, but that doesn't entirely explain the much slower times. The Texan said later that a rubbing brake pad had tired him earlier that day, and that the tactics employed by his rivals then contributed to the malaise. In fact, despite not feeling perfect, Armstrong saw L'Alpe d'Huez as a missed opportunity to put time on Ullrich, who fell back as soon as U.S. Postal's Manuel Beltran applied pressure at the foot of the climb. "I think that the ones in the front should have taken advantage of a dropped Ullrich and not have been [negative]," he said, referring to those who rode with him on the climb, Joseba Beloki of ONCE-Eroski, Tyler Hamilton of CSC, Ivan Basso of Fassa Bortolo, and Francisco Mancebo of ibanesto.com. "There were times on Alpe d'Huez when it was almost a track stand. At the end of the day, we only had a minute and a half on [Ullrich] when easily we could have put 3 minutes into him."

Besides the various problems he suffered, Armstrong and the rest had to deal with the daily demands of riding through a heat wave. It wasn't uncommon for one rider to get through 20 half-liter bottles of water each stage. The near-100-degree temperatures melted tar on many of the back roads, and that was a factor in Beloki's stage-9 fall near Gap that eliminated the three-time Tour podium finisher from the race.

Armstrong was extremely lucky not to have crashed with Beloki that day, and also lucky not to have Beloki as yet another adversary as the Tour reached its most critical stages. However, after Vinokourov jumped into the picture with his solo stage win at Gap, Armstrong had three relatively quiet days. He rode in the pack on the long, hot, and fast stage 10 across Provence to Marseille, enjoyed the first rest day at Montpellier with his family, and rode with the pack again on the short, fast stage to Toulouse. The Postal leader, though, was somewhat spooked by "the incident with [Czech teammate] Pavel Padrnos on the stage into Marseille," when, Armstrong noted, "the front wheel was completely loose and just came out." Was the U.S. Postal leader intimating that his team was the subject of sabotage, was it just technical sloppiness, or were the Postal riders simply cursed?

After all, when team director Johan Bruyneel had his dress suit soiled by a bird through the open sunroof of the Postal bus before the team presentation in Paris, hadn't the burly Padrnos said that this was "the beginning of what could be a damned Tour"? Damned or not, Armstrong was about to suffer his worst day at the Tour since running out of fuel on the Joux-Plane climb in 2000. This time, in the Gaillac–Cap'Découverte time trial on July 18, it wasn't the bonk that caused Armstrong's sudden bad patch, but dehydration. The result was pretty much the same, though: a loss of 1:36 to Ullrich, compared with 1:37 on the alpine stage into Morzine in 2000.

Ullrich, too, said he had a heat-related crisis in the time trial, but he recovered quickly. Not Armstrong. The next day, the race entered the Pyrénées on another baking-hot stage that had a summit finish in Ax-3 Domaines. After again losing time to Ullrich, Armstrong crossed the line with his head bowed. That was his nadir, though, because Armstrong's form appeared to improve on the six-climb stage to Loudenvielle; he was more in control, although still not 100 percent. And when Vinokourov made a spectacular attack on the last of the day's six climbs, the Peyresourde, Armstrong decided not to chase, leaving that duty to Ullrich. It was a calculating attitude that the Texan had not shown in previous Tours. But by conserving his energy and gaining another day toward recovery from the time trial, Armstrong appeared ready for the crucial final week of a Tour that still hung in the balance.

As a second rain shower pelted the waters of Loudenvielle's lovely lake that Sunday evening, breaking up the reflections of a steep, green mountainside and an ancient church steeple, we speculated whether Ullrich or Vinokourov—or even Mayo or Hamilton—would be strong enough to squash the defending champion.

STAGE 8

Sallanches to L'Alpe d'Huez

With his gold earrings, bronzed, eaglelike face, and swashbuckling climbing style, Iban Mayo was a hero waiting to break out. That affirmation came on the final 7.3 kilometers of the climb to L'Alpe d'Huez on July 13. On a solo break that took him to this citadel of cycling more than 2 minutes ahead of the four-time defending champion, the twenty-five-year-old Basque bombshell found consecration from a swirling, pulsating mass of a half-million fans that lined the famous twenty-one-turn climb from the first vicious ramp out of the Romanche valley to the finish between the deep-roofed chalets and stark modern hotels of the "sunniest ski resort in France."

Mayo had challenged Armstrong a month earlier at the Dauphiné Libéré, but this was the Tour, the global event that can transform a simple cyclist into an international icon. Mayo was today's story, today's star. When asked by a journalist why he wasted time in celebrating his stage win over the final 500 meters, instead of gaining a few extra, possibly precious, seconds for the overall standings, Mayo replied, "I wanted to savor this moment. I've been through some hard times, and a moment like this may not come to me again."

Mayo later joined most of the former Alpe d'Huez stage winners, including Armstrong, on the podium for a historic photo opportunity. While Mayo's memory was very fresh, Armstrong perhaps recalled his spectacular win here just two years before. It was different this time.

We saw two Lance Armstrongs on what was the most important stage so far of the nineteeth Tour de France. There was the cool, confident Armstrong before the stage 8 start in Sallanches. And there was the Armstrong 6 hours later who arrived at L'Alpe d'Huez behind two dangerous rivals and in the company of five others. This Armstrong, even though he had taken the yellow jersey, was somewhat flustered and less sure of himself. He said he "didn't have the greatest legs," he was critical of other riders' tactics, and he admitted that his team had made some mistakes.

The Texan knew before the start in Paris that trying to take a fifth Tour was going to be more difficult than winning the previous four, but he didn't know that it was going to be this hard.

In Sallanches, the alpine town where a year before he gave a celebratory press conference with his fourth victory in the bag, Armstrong was unmistakably confident. "We'll try to make the race as hard as we can," he said. "It's a big opportunity and there are not many days like this. So if you expect to win then you better start doing it today."

Clearly, he expected that he would be the one doing the winning, especially when he said about the finish on L'Alpe d'Huez, "I feel good, and I know the mountain well . . . and I love the mountain, so I'll give it my best. In conjunction with the Galibier, it's an epic day, two of the most legendary mountains in the Tour. And then, it's [a] hard . . . long day, hot day." But even when you anticipate a hard stage, unexpected developments can make it even harder.

Indeed, most of the peloton was expecting Armstrong to dominate on L'Alpe d'Huez in the same fashion he did in 2001—when he gave Ullrich the famous "look" and began his drive toward the yellow jersey. That year, the Texan didn't have too many teammates left with him after the opening Col de la Madeleine, and he feigned fatigue on the Col du Glandon, the climb preceding the Alpe, to make his opponents think he was vulnerable. Then, led out by a surging José Luis Rubiera, he applied the killer punch, to put 2 minutes into runner-up Ullrich and the rest.

This year, the circumstances were different. After some initial short climbs out of Sallanches, the peloton regrouped on the long, flat run up the Maurienne valley to the Télégraphe-Galibier combo climb. These 30 kilometers of uphill work can be destructive, and it's where Mayo attacked and dropped Armstrong (temporarily) in June's Dauphiné Libéré. On this second Sunday in July, the Texan was again not at his best.

"I could tell I was not [having] a great day on the Galibier," said Armstrong. Because of his fatigue, he changed his game plan. "It was my decision at that time to just ride a conservative race. If you're realistic and you have the experience to know that, 'Hey, it's not a great day,' you don't need to make a show."

The show on the Galibier was instead provided by Vini Caldirola's Stefano Garzelli, the former Giro d'Italia champion, who spurted ahead at the lofty summit to take the $5,000 Henri Desgrange Memorial prime. The Italian—who was having stomach problems—wouldn't have been in contention for the prize if there had been a true battle on this Tour's highest peak. Instead, Postal was able to ride a smooth tempo that left about thirty riders together instead of a handful.

Another thirty or so managed to chase back on the almost 50 kilometers of descending roads before the Alpe. Postal's Hincapie and Landis were among the first to latch back on, and soon they were towing the peloton down the mountain, relieving their Spanish climbers Beltran, Rubiera, and Roberto Heras, who'd be refreshed to lead out Armstrong on the Alpe. Or, at least, that's how it appeared—that another "Coup de Lance" was in the making.

Things had started to unravel, though, even before the final climb was reached. "I was having trouble even staying there [behind my tempo-riding teammates]," Armstrong later revealed. "I discovered on the descent that somebody at the start or before the start [in Sallanches] had moved my back brake, and for the first [part] of the race the back brake had been rubbing the wheel. And obviously, you ride 4 or 5 hours, which include the Télégraphe [and] the Galibier, it takes a lot out of you with the brake on."

Then, on a straight, flat section of the valley road, Heras and Armstrong nudged bikes. The Texan had to ride onto the grass shoulder, while his Spanish lieutenant put his foot down to avoid falling. It certainly wasn't serious, but Heras did have to chase back through the pack to retake his place near the front.

A few minutes later, Postal's Blue Train was racing into the first savage grades of L'Alpe d'Huez. Beltran was at the front followed by Rubiera, Armstrong, and Heras. It was assumed that the Postal team workers were going to set a fast pace to burn off as many opponents as possible before Armstrong made his expected move. But "Triki" Beltran's acceleration came more suddenly and at a higher velocity

After his attack on L'Alpe d'Huez is neutralized, Beloki is held in check by Armstrong (left) and Zubeldia (right).

than anyone expected. It was as if he were in the last 100 meters of a sprint at an American criterium.

Was it too fast? "There's no doubt about that," said Armstrong. "Triki's new to the team and I guess the system is not clear enough yet because that was . . . Okay, a fast tempo is a good thing, but that was supersonic. And that's not a good thing. I mean, you immediately put Chechu [Rubiera] in trouble . . . so obviously we're gonna talk about that tonight."

Beltran's burst, though, did explode the group. Race leader Richard Virenque was immediately put in trouble; British hope David Millar went backward; then Ullrich and Garzelli disappeared; and Vinokourov, too, couldn't keep up. It was later divulged that Ullrich was fighting a stomach virus and reportedly had a 100-degree fever that was kept secret by his Bianchi team.

By the top of the first steep ramps, 10 kilometers from the finish, only four men were left with Armstrong and his pacemaker Heras: Hamilton, Beloki, Mayo, and

Hamilton makes one of several accelerations toward the top of L'Alpe d'Huez.

Haimar Zubeldia. Right there, where the grade softens somewhat, Beloki attacked. This was a more determined Beloki—the rider who said he wasn't going to be satisfied with 2nd place again. He gained 10 seconds, but he then started looking around to estimate the size of his gap rather than focusing on creating a bigger one. Heras, with his last strong effort before falling back, was able to bring Beloki to heel.

Now the impetus of the climb was on Armstrong, and there was still 8 kilometers to go. It was unusual to see the Texan riding out of the saddle rather than sitting down and pedaling at his hallmark high cadence. Mayo clearly noticed Armstrong's laboring, and the dashing Spaniard shot away with 7.3 kilometers still remaining.

There was no reply to the Euskaltel rider's attack. Armstrong reasoned, "I decided just to let Mayo go and limit my losses and cover Beloki, because he's close on the G.C."

This was the first time Armstrong had been so calculating so early in the Tour, but a glimpse at the overnight classification showed that Beloki was in 6th place over-

Mayo flies to the stage win.

all (38 seconds behind the American) and Mayo was in 40th (3:34 back). It seemed to be a smart decision.

The message to those riding with Armstrong, however, was that he was vulnerable. As a result, Beloki tried another attack, and even the handicapped Hamilton made a couple of accelerations. "I had a hard time standing up," Hamilton said. "And my attacks, I'll admit, were pretty feeble. But under my circumstances that's about all I can do."

The uneven pace allowed four more riders to catch back to the group, Mancebo, Heras, Roberto Laiseka of Euskaltel, and finally, Vinokourov. As soon as the blond Telekom rider made contact, with 6 kilometers to go, he counterattacked. There was initially no reaction, which allowed Basso to make it up to the group. Hamilton did try to go after Vinokourov, as did Beloki, and each time Armstrong had to stand on his pedals to bring them back. Heras had again fallen off the pace.

Asked later about the many attacks, Armstrong said, "I don't understand the tactics of some of the riders in the group, because [if they] rode a little more consistent, steady pace, it would have been faster overall, given up less time to Mayo, and put more time on Ullrich." Armstrong wasn't just critical of his opponents. After the stage finish, he said, "You know, if you'd asked me a month ago, 'Hey, are you're gonna suffer like that on Alpe d'Huez?' [I'd have said], 'No way.'"

In front, Mayo continued at his elevated climbing pace, inspired by the biggest crowd ever assembled on L'Alpe d'Huez. The excellent Euskaltel rider won the stage and with bonuses took 2:24 back from Armstrong, while Vinokourov regained 31 seconds. As for Ullrich, he came in with Heras and two others, having conceded another 1:32 to the new race leader.

Up to 8th overall, the enigmatic German elicited this remark from Armstrong: "I still think he's one of the most dangerous riders in the race. Jan typically gets better as the Tour goes on, and this Tour has a long way to go. Anyway, he's a threat, he's *still* a threat."

Armstrong also knew that he was under pressure from a host of other challengers, all of whom seemed ready to attack, again and again and again. And judging by the Armstrong we saw on the Alpe, he and his Postal men were going to have a tough time. In 6 hours, Armstrong had gone from confident to confused. The Tour had only just begun.

STAGE 8: SALLANCHES TO L'ALPE D'HUEZ
1. Iban Mayo (Sp), Euskaltel-Euskadi, 219 km in 5:57:50 (36.775 kph); 2. Alex Vinokourov (Kaz), Telekom, at 1:45; **3. Lance Armstrong (USA), U.S. Postal–Berry Floor, at 2:12**; 4. Francisco Mancebo (Sp), ibanesto.com; 5. Haimar Zubeldia (Sp), Euskaltel-Euskadi; 6. Joseba Beloki (Sp), ONCE-Eroski; **7. Tyler Hamilton (USA), CSC**; 8. Ivan Basso (I), Fassa Bortolo; 9. Roberto Laiseka (Sp), Euskaltel-Euskadi, all s.t.; 10. Pietro Caucchioli (I), Alessio, at 3:36.
Overall: 1. Armstrong, 35:12:50; 2. Beloki, at 0:40; 3. Mayo, at 1:10; 4. Vinokourov, at 1:17; 5. Mancebo, at 1:27.

STAGE 9

Le Bourg-d'Oisans to Gap

Having scouted this final alpine stage in May and expecting more aggression from the men who had attacked Armstrong on L'Alpe d'Huez, Hamilton knew what he was talking about when he said before the stage-9 start in Le Bourg-d'Oisans, "Today's a difficult stage, so [I've] gotta be very concentrated." Just *how* difficult it was going to be, not even "Tyler the Warrior" could know.

The moonlike rockscape of the Casse Déserte frames the peloton as it descends the legendary Col d'Izoard.

Besides the day's almost 12,000 feet of climbing and the 90-degree temperatures, he couldn't have predicted the ferocious start. Climbing in bursts between flatter sections that cut through tunnels on the flanks of a deep glacial valley, the peloton split into two equal parts as twelve leaders came together halfway up the 34-kilometer-long Col du Lautaret.

Only one of the twelve was of immediate danger to Armstrong's yellow jersey, ONCE's Jörg Jaksche. This twenty-six-year-old German, in his seventh year as a pro, was 18th in his first Tour back in 1998 when he rode for Polti; and as a super-domestique for Beloki the last two years he has finished 29th and 31st in the Tour. Starting this stage 9, Jaksche was in 10th place, only 3:19 behind Armstrong, so his presence seemed to condemn the break's chances of success. Aussie Brad McGee was so sure they'd be caught that, despite looking strong on the Lautaret, he decided to drop back on the 19-kilometer-long, progressively steep climb of the *hors-categorie* Col d'Izoard.

Postal didn't want to sacrifice riders on the day's second climb, however, and the gap increased from 2:20 in Briançon to 5:50 at the 7,742-foot summit, where Bianchi's thirty-five-year-old Aitor Garmendia split from the break. The seasoned

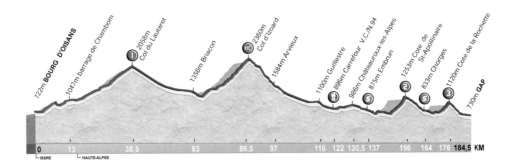

WEEK TWO

Spaniard opened up a 1:20 lead on the steep, technical descent but six of the break-aways caught him at the Guillestre feed zone, where the lead over the Postal-led pelo-ton had increased to 6:15.

This put Jaksche in the virtual race lead by 3 minutes, forcing the Postal troops to regroup and ride a team time trial along the Durance valley. In just 27 kilometers, the Blue Train gained 3:45 on the weary leaders to reach the much-anticipated Côte de St. Apollinaire with a 2:30 gap.

Though this 6.7-kilometer-long hill averaged only 7.4 percent, it erratically lifted a narrow, often bumpy back road to a ridge 1,470 feet above the blue waters of the vast Serre-Ponçon reservoir, with some pitches steeper than 15 percent. No wonder Hamilton said he feared this finale.

While Jaksche and Kelme's Ivan Parra left behind the rest of the breakaway group, Cofidis leader Millar closed to within 1:25 of them after a confident attack—although even the Scot was overgeared on the super-steep pitches toward the top. The pack exploded here. Heras and Beltran set the pace on the first 4 kilometers, but they were left behind when Beloki made a sharp attack that only Armstrong and Mayo could answer. Zubeldia and Ullrich trailed at a discreet distance, while Hamilton, only able to keep an even pace, was just behind with Vinokourov and Basso.

This was just a prelude to a similar battle on the last climb, La Rochette, still 15 kilometers away. In that distance, riding into a headwind, Millar was caught by the yellow jersey group, now thirty-nine strong, while the break's lead was cut to a minute. La Rochette, a 4-kilometer version of St. Apollinaire, climbs to the same ridge on a narrow road, but with a more consistent, near-8 percent grade.

Parra, the strong Colombian climber, attacked from the front in search of a solo stage win, and if Jaksche hadn't been in the daylong breakaway, Parra probably would have been successful. But the main group had closed to within 40 seconds when, 3 kilometers from the summit, Vinokourov launched a violent attack similar to those he made on the Ramaz and Alpe d'Huez in the previous two days.

HOW THE BELOKI CRASH UNFOLDED

And how Armstrong had the luckiest escape of his career.

IN THE MILLISECONDS that Lance Armstrong had to think as Joseba Beloki slammed sickeningly onto the baking-hot pavement of the D314 back road on July 14, the centennial Tour de France hung in the balance. Armstrong was racing two lengths behind Beloki down the twisting downhill from the Côte de la Rochette, the two of them taking turns to head a frantic chase after solo leader Alex Vinokourov. They were pedaling flat out on the straightaways and barely slowing for the frequent turns, moving even faster than Vinokourov, whose lead had been cut from 15 to 12 seconds in 3 kilometers of descending.

They had just two turns to go before joining the N94 highway where they'd complete the short run-in to the stage finish in Gap. The first of the two bends was a sweeping right curve that tightened and fell away steeply at its apex; the second was a long left switchback.

Seeing the potential danger of the combination, a Belgian fan was positioned above the first bend. "He was waving down the riders to warn them about the corner," said U.S. Postal team mechanic Geoff Brown, a friend of the Belgian fan. "He saw Beloki jam on his brakes as he was going into the corner too fast."

Armstrong later said, "The tire exploded. I was very afraid. It was my scariest moment on a bike."

Beloki's rear wheel fishtailed to the left, and as he tried to correct his path the rear tire came unglued. The locked-up wheel fishtailed to the right and the Basque plummeted sideways at perhaps 80 kilometers per hour. The impact smashed his right femur near the hip, shattered his right elbow, and snapped his right wrist. His bike clattered to the left, forcing Armstrong to make his millisecond decision: continue making his turn and try to dodge Beloki's sliding body, or swerve left past the bike, not knowing what lay beyond the curve. He chose to go left, which took him across a gravel shoulder and into a sloping hayfield.

Retracing his trajectory the next morning, I followed the indentations Armstrong's tires had made through the dust, small rocks, and scrubby straw and weeds.

The first shock was to see that where he left the road, Armstrong was within 6 inches of falling into a 2-foot-deep ditch that leads from a drainage culvert under the road. If a wheel had gone into that hole, Armstrong would have somersaulted down the hillside and likely suffered injuries as serious as Beloki's.

Having dodged Beloki's bike and the culvert, the race leader then traced a wide arc across the fall line of the hill's 25-percent grade. His narrow tires just missed several rocks and the spiky stems of chicory plants. Had he flatted, Armstrong would have been stranded in the middle of a field. As it was, he rumbled on, deciding to steer left to where the road curved around below the second turn rather than trying to get back to the upper level.

Armstrong's adventure had still not ended. As he said right after the stage: "I saw the cliff. I went, 'Oh, oh,' and got off my bike and jumped."

Beyond the edge of the field was a steep bank (Lance's "cliff") and a ditch before reaching the road. On standing in the ditch, the field was about level with a person's chest. Jumping from a standing start (without a bike)

across the 6-foot-wide gap down to the grass shoulder was a daunting exercise. Armstrong's momentum helped him do it safely with his bike in his hands.

In the perhaps 15 seconds it took Armstrong to cross the field, poor Beloki remained lying in the dirt screaming in pain.

The first to reach him were his teammates Jörg Jaksche and José Azevedo, who did their best to comfort him. But they knew that they'd lost their leader for this Tour. The twenty-nine-year-old Spaniard's continued presence would have made life even more difficult for Armstrong, who said, "Joseba Beloki could have been the spoiler here. He could have been better than Jan and he could have been better than me. And I know that."

Yet Armstrong was still in the yellow jersey, still in the race, but as he later reflected, "That was one of the luckiest days I think I've ever had." No kidding. ∎

Starting the stage in 4th place overall, only 1:17 behind Armstrong, Vinokourov ("Vino") was proving to be as solid a podium prospect as he said he'd be. Riding out of the saddle, his strong legs punching the pedals, Vino soon tore past the hapless Parra. At first, Heras led the chase, but the gap was 20 seconds and growing when Armstrong himself took over. The race leader's surge was so strong that only Beloki and Mayo could initially hold his wheel, followed by Zubeldia, Hamilton, and a few others. Vino's lead was 15 seconds at the top of La Rochette, 8 kilometers from the finish, but that gap was cut to 12 seconds as Beloki and Armstrong swapped pulls in pursuit of their dangerous opponent.

Who knows what would've happened had Beloki not crashed near the foot of the hill with only 4 kilometers to go (see "How the Beloki Crash Unfolded"). As it was, with Beloki missing and Armstrong stunned, Vinokourov stretched his lead to 36 seconds on a chase group of ten.

Vinokourov, whose effort was very similar to his winning move at April's Amstel Gold Race, crossed the line doing a "rocking the cradle" victory salute. "I wanted to win for my little twins," said the Kazakh. "I was good today, even better than yesterday. I'm very proud." He was also now in 2nd place overall, only 21 seconds behind Armstrong.

Second place was taken by a fast-finishing Paolo Bettini of Quick Step from Mayo, Armstrong, and Ullrich—who all sprinted in search of a top-three time bonus.

At the time, none of them knew that Beloki was seriously injured and still lying in agony where he crashed. A cruel stage had suffered a savage ending.

STAGE 9: LE BOURG-D'OISANS TO GAP
1. Vinokourov, 184.5 km in 5:02:00 (36.656 kph); 2. Paolo Bettini (I), Quick Step–Davitamon, at 0:36; 3. Mayo; **4. Armstrong**; 5. Ullrich; 6. Basso; 7. Totschnig; 8. Mancebo; 9. Zubeldia; **10. Hamilton**, all s.t.
Overall: 1. Armstrong, 40:15:26; 2. Vinokourov, at 0:21; 3. Mayo, at 1:02; 4. Mancebo, at 1:37; **5. Hamilton, at 1:52.**

STAGE 10

Gap to Marseille

On paper, there were many similarities between this 219.5-kilometer stage 10 from Gap to Marseille and the 1971 Tour's stage 12, which followed an almost identical route, except that the peloton thirty-two years earlier started at the ski resort of Orcières-Merlette and had already completed 30-odd kilometers before they passed through Gap.

For most of this year's stage, there were nine riders in a daylong break that reached the Marseille city limits 24 minutes ahead of the pack. Their only goal was a stage win. In 1971, too, nine men were in the front, but their mission was very different.

Leading the break were three Molteni team riders—Eddy Merckx, Julien Stevens, and Rini Wagtmans—who attacked from the very start, through the tight switchbacks of a 5-kilometer descent from Merlette. It seemed like a crazy move, but Merckx was desperate to make up the almost 9 minutes he'd lost to Spaniard Luis Ocaña on the previous stage.

Remarkably, even though Ocaña's Bic team chased all day, Merckx powered the break for 251 kilometers at an astonishing average speed of 45.351 kilometers per hour to finish in Marseille 2 minutes ahead of the pack. There were few spectators to see Merckx lose the sprint for 1st place to Italian Luciano Armani because the race arrived almost 2 hours ahead of the expected schedule!

When Marseille Mayor Gaston Deferre showed up to present the prizes, the riders had gone and the barriers were being packed up. Deferre, a powerful figure in French politics, was so angry that he stopped the Tour coming to his city. It didn't return to Marseille until 1989, three years after Deferre's death.

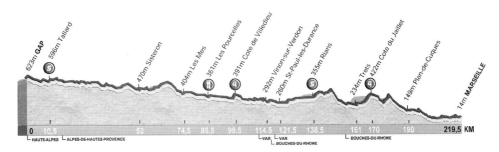

WEEK TWO

The nine men who made up this year's breakaway group arrived right on time. They rode hard all day to average 42.546 kilometers per hour—almost 3 kilometers per hour slower than that Merckx-led break more than three decades ago. Observers say that today's riders are much stronger and fitter than those of the past, and that Merckx would have a hard time winning a modern Tour. That 1971 stage to Marseille indicates otherwise.

As for this Tour's stage-10 finale, the key move came from the Italian veteran Fabio Sacchi of Saeco, when he counterattacked 18 kilometers from the finish. Along the seafront, before passing the 1971 finish at the Vieux Port, Sacchi was chased down by CSC's Jakob Piil, and the pair came into the long, straight downhill finish more than a minute ahead of the rest of the break.

Piil has been in similar situations before. He lost the 2001 Tour's Montluçon stage in a two-man sprint with Serge Baguet of Belgium; and in the 2002 stage to Bourg-en-Bresse, the Dane lost a three-man sprint to Thor Hushovd of Norway when his foot unclipped as he began his finishing effort. Piil made no mistakes this time, perhaps feeding off the confidence he gained in beating breakaway partner Jackie Durand to win the October 2002 Paris-Tours classic.

Denmark's Piil outkicks Italy's Sacchi in Marseille.

In any case, when the worried voice of one of his team directors came through his radio earpiece, Piil said, "Stay calm, there's no problem." So after making an initial acceleration, Piil let Sacchi wind up the sprint, followed the Italian across the wide avenue to the right-hand barriers, then back to the left, before diving past Sacchi on his right to take a perfect win.

It was a sprint of which even Merckx would have been proud.

STAGE 10: GAP TO MARSEILLE
1. Jakob Piil (Dk), CSC, 219.5 km in 5:09:33 (42.546 kph); 2. Fabio Sacchi (I), Saeco, s.t.; 3. Bram De Groot (Nl), Rabobank, at 0:49; 4. Damien Nazon (F), La Boulangère, at 2:07; 5. René Haselbacher (A), Gerolsteiner, s.t.
Overall: No change.

STAGE 11

Narbonne to Toulouse

Even when there's nothing much in play at the Tour, there's always a spectacle. If you'd been having a coffee in the bar of the Montagne Noire hotel at Saissac just before 3 p.m. on July 17, you'd have been watching the Tour's live telecast with a group of club cyclists from England. On the terrace, in the shade of colorful umbrellas, some locals were watching the Tour publicity caravan roll by on its cacophonous way to Toulouse. And in an ibanesto.com team support vehicle parked outside the hotel, the Spanish squad's manager, José Miguel Echavarri, was talking into his cell phone.

No doubt, Echavarri was relaying information to his directeur sportif, Eusebio Unzue, who was driving the No. 1 team car directly behind the peloton 25 kilometers away in Carcassonne.

A low-angle image on the bar TV was showing the pack racing past that city's walled, medieval fortress with its round towers and cone-shaped roofs. The cameras then panned ahead to a break that was just taking shape. Three Spaniards started the move. Iñigo Cuesta of Cofidis jumped first, followed by ONCE-Eroski's Isidro Nozal, and Echavarri's man, Juan Antonio Flecha. Five others quickly bridged: Aussies

Stuart O'Grady of Crédit Agricole and Michael Rogers of Quick Step; Frenchmen Carlos Da Cruz of fdjeux.com and Nicolas Portal of ag2r; and the Dutchman Bram De Groot of Rabobank, who finished 3rd on the previous stage into Marseille.

On reaching the Montagne Noire, the eight leaders would be 3 minutes ahead of the peloton. That gap was the same 1 hour later as they reached the outskirts of Toulouse. This is familiar territory for both O'Grady and Flecha. The Australian owns a house just south of the city, where he was planning a barbecue that night, while Flecha often visits his girlfriend, Lourdes, an aeronautical student in Toulouse who was waiting for him at the finish.

O'Grady was the most seasoned sprinter in the group, but he knew that he'd have a hard time controlling seven others on the flat run-in to the finish at the Montaudran aerodrome, which was the original home of French aviation nine decades ago. The only ones flying this day, though, were Spanish. With 15 kilometers to go, Nozal jumped away from the break, and as soon as he was brought back, Flecha counter-attacked to take an immediate 15-second lead.

"I often train on these roads," Flecha said later, "so I knew exactly where I wanted to make my move." At twenty-five years old, Flecha is one of Spain's most promising classics riders, and earlier in the year he even finished 25th at Paris-Roubaix. No doubt the toughness he learned in the spring helped him hold on to a 20-second gap all the way into the aerodrome finish.

By now, the hundreds of vehicles in the publicity caravan were parked in Toulouse. Back in Saissac, the English cyclists were probably watching the TV images of Flecha heading to his stage win. And Echavarri, waiting near the ibanesto.com team bus, was probably thankful that one of his guys was going to win the stage. It may not be as epochal as his longtime prodigy Miguel Induráin winning five Tours, but a win is a win, especially at the Tour.

Once Flecha saw that he was home safe—De Groot was coming in 2nd this time—he knew what he was going to do. "Whenever I win a big race," said Flecha (whose name means "arrow" in Spanish), "I do it." "It" was an elegant victory gesture, as if he were firing an arrow from an imaginary bow. Another ending to another show.

STAGE 11: NARBONNE TO TOULOUSE
1. Juan Antonio Flecha (Sp), ibanesto.com, 153.5 km in 3:29:33 (43.951 kph); 2. De Groot, at 0:04; 3. Isidro Nozal (Sp), ONCE-Eroski, s.t.; 4. Iñigo Cuesta (Sp), Cofidis, at 0:15; 5. Carlos Da Cruz (F), fdjeux.com, at 0:23.
Overall: No change.

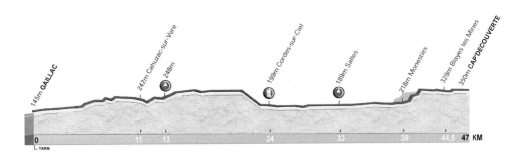

STAGE 12

Gaillac to Cap'Découverte Time Trial

To best understand the dynamics of this vital 47-kilometer time trial in the hill country of the Tarn, let's go back 24 hours to the start of stage 11 in the ocher-brick town of Narbonne. There was excitement in the humid air. With the first rest day and more than half this suspenseful Tour behind them, the 171 survivors seemed refreshed, ready to continue.

That wasn't the case with all of them, though. When Hamilton was asked whether he'd tried out his time-trial bike on the rest day in preparation for stage 12, he was uncharacteristically curt. "No. I'm just thinking about today's stage," he almost snapped. The reason for his darker mood was the concern that the pain would return from a trapped nerve in his back, a problem he hoped had been solved by the magic hands of his team physiotherapist.

As Hamilton rode back to the CSC team bus, followed at a trot by a *soigneur* protecting the American's broken shoulder from back-slapping fans, a ceremony was taking place on the start podium. Race leader Armstrong had just signed in and was about to return down the steps when he was called back. From backstage came a barrel-chested middle-age man with rust-dyed hair. It was Arnold Schwarzenegger, who'd come to the Tour for a day to promote his *Terminator 3* movie.

The two icons smiled and politely shook hands for the cameras. Armstrong, wearing the yellow jersey for the forty-ninth day in his career, is used to the adulation and daily duties that cut into his recovery time. He had just come off a rest day, but even then a TV crew and press photographers followed him on a 2-hour training run, and reporters camped out in the lobby of the Novotel at Montpellier, hoping for a glimpse of Armstrong with his wife and three children, who'd made the short trip from their Gerona, Spain, home.

As the Texan and the Terminator briefly chatted, Ullrich was riding away from the podium. He turned his head when some fans shouted his name from behind the barriers, but instead of continuing to his team bus's air-conditioned refuge, he decided to ride over to the fans and stood for 5 minutes under the leaden sun, signing anything that was proffered: Tour T-shirts, yellow Crédit Lyonnais cycling caps and musette bags, big green PMU cardboard hands, and even newspapers.

The man they dubbed the Tourminator when he won the Tour in 1997 was relaxed, smiling, happy to be a center of attention again. He said he was recovered from the stomach virus and fever that affected his performance in the Alps, and he was ready to do battle in his favorite event, the time trial.

Later that day, Armstrong said, "It's the most important time trial in the past five years because the G.C. is so close. It's a good course, not easy, not very hard, but with the wind and the heat . . . " He left that last word hanging, as if he knew that when he launched himself down the starting ramp in Gaillac at 4:18 p.m. the next afternoon, he'd be riding into a cauldron.

And it *was* a cauldron.

"It was 35 degrees [95 degrees F] when we were driving over, so I knew it was a hot day," Armstrong said. It was actually the hottest day of the race so far, with a maximum shade temperature of 100 degrees F, while the road temperature topped out at 141 degrees F.

The shoe-baking heat was the day's biggest factor, particularly before the start. Armstrong warmed up as usual on a turbo trainer in the shade of a canopy stretched between the Postal team bus and equipment truck, but he later agreed that he hadn't drunk enough water during his warm-up. It was exceptionally hot and humid in medieval Gaillac, where thousands of fans and tourists jammed the streets around the town's tree-lined Place de la Libération. To avoid the crush and the heat, the Bianchi team set up Ullrich's bike in an air-conditioned bike shop, where he warmed up for a couple of hours beneath a cooling ceiling fan.

Out on the road, the hotter afternoon temperature was a clear factor in slowing the times. In the relatively cool midmorning, Gerolsteiner's Uwe Peschel set a mark of 1:01:58 that 143 riders in the ensuing 5 hours failed to beat. The former East German, who won a gold medal in the team time trial at the 1992 Olympics, was riding his first Tour at age thirty-four. Among those who didn't get close to his time were some ace time trialists, including Quick Step's Laszlo Bodrogi and Michael Rogers, Postal's Olympic champion Viatcheslav Ekimov, Telekom's world champion Santiago Botero, and Cofidis's David Millar.

In fact, Millar, 19th from the end of the field, riding in the late afternoon, was the first to come within half a minute of Peschel's time. The first to beat it was Euskaltel's

Zubeldia, the prologue surprise who again stunned the experts. His 1:01:12 was eventually 4th fastest.

An analysis of the time splits showed that Zubeldia was faster than Peschel by 22 seconds on the opening 13 kilometers, which was mainly uphill; 15 seconds slower over the next 20.5 kilometers, which included a fast downhill to the feed-zone town of Cordes; and 39 seconds faster than Peschel on the final 13.5 kilometers, which contained a winding hill that climbed 384 feet in 2 kilometers out of the shady riverside town of Monesties.

Zubeldia had been on the course for just 8 minutes when Ullrich left the start house and was quickly into his stride. The Bianchi leader was already on his aero bars before the first turn, and then smoothly negotiated a series of curves through Gaillac, including a sharp left into the Rue Maurice Garin, a short street appropriately named for the 1903 Tour winner.

Ullrich was benefiting from the Union Cycliste Internationale's mandatory helmet rule, because in the past he'd have worn a back-turned cotton cap, rather than the aerodynamic, dimpled Rudy Project helmet that seemed to help his penetration through the sticky air. He passed the first checkpoint, at the top of a short, out-of-the-saddle hill, in 16:26, which was 19 seconds faster than the previous best split set by Millar.

Two minutes after Ullrich, Hamilton made a more hesitant start, going onto his aero bars too soon and returning to the hooks before the first turn. Next starter Mayo looked calm, but his expressionless look probably reflected the pressure of attempting to defend his 3rd place on G.C. Next-to-last starter Vinokourov was both focused and energetic in his starting effort.

Then came Armstrong.

Normally, the American makes a steady start (he was *too* steady in the Paris prologue, remember), but his first few pedal strokes seemed to reflect the gravity he'd placed on this day. Instead of quickly finding the high cadence that has been his hallmark in Tour time trials, he was launching a big gear all the way to the first corner before he sat down and moved his hands to the aero bars.

His fast, almost too frantic, start took Armstrong through that 13-kilometer split in the same second as Ullrich; but was it the wisest of opening efforts on this sizzling afternoon? Hamilton said later, "You had to be very careful from the start because if you went over your limit—it's a headwind pretty much all day—and with the extreme heat, it was difficult. I felt I just went hard tempo the whole time because if you go above that you're gonna explode."

A smooth Ullrich stays in the saddle on the last short rise before the finish of the time trial ... while a dehydrated Armstrong, his lips covered with salt, stands on the pedals.

Several of the race leaders did explode, but not Hamilton. He felt that, ideally (i.e., no broken shoulder or pinched nerve), he would have used a one-cog-heavier gear ridden at the same cadence. And though he steadily lost time to Ullrich (roughly 3.5 seconds per kilometer), the New Englander was faster than all but Ullrich and Armstrong over the first 33.5 kilometers; and he probably would have remained in 3rd place had he been able to stand on his pedals and pull on the bars up the Monesties hill.

On finishing, Hamilton stopped just after the line, dropped his bike, and doubled over to ease his back pain, while his face was sprayed with water by his *soigneur*. That was in contrast to the man who finished ahead of him, Ullrich, who came barreling through and flashed by the cameras and microphones to reach his team bus as fast as possible.

What no one knew at the time was that Ullrich, too, was suffering big-time. The German told *Super Illu* magazine after the Tour that he even felt like abandoning the Tour. "I'd already told my team director, Rudy Pevenage, that I couldn't do more," said Ullrich. "I was dizzy, I couldn't continue." Perhaps the fact that he had to wear that helmet instead of a racing cap caused his touch of heatstroke. In the end, after getting some acetaminophen (the main ingredient of Tylenol) from the race doctor, he pushed on. Ullrich added, "The human body is amazing. You think that it's finished but it carries on even so."

> **SPLITS**
> **FIRST 13 km:** 1. Ullrich, 16:26 (47.462 kph); 2. Armstrong, s.t.; 3. Millar, 16:45; 4. Vinokourov, 16:45; 5. Zubeldia, 16:52; 6. Hamilton, 17:01.
> **NEXT 20.5 km:** 1.Ullrich, 24:02 (51.178 kph) 2. Armstrong, 24:42; 3. Peschel, 25:13; 4. Hamilton, 25:15; 5. Zubeldia, 25:28; 6. Vinokourov, 25:25.
> **LAST 13.5 km:** 1. Ullrich, 18:04 (44.833 kph); 2. Vinokourov, 18:18; 3. Zubeldia, 18:52; 4. Hamilton, 18:59; 5. Armstrong, 19:00; 6. Chaurreau, 19:15.

The German was the only one to break the 1-hour barrier, with a time of 58:32. He made most of his gains on the middle 20-kilometer stretch, where he averaged more than 51 kilometers per hour despite the rollers before the Cordes downhill that was followed by a long, false flat up the winding valley of the Cérou.

Armstrong was still in 2nd place at the 33.5-kilometer split, halfway up the valley road, but he had a huge shock when he heard his time: He was 40 seconds slower than Ullrich. He didn't know it then, but the Texan's day was about to get a lot worse.

"From the second time point till the hill, I had an incredible crisis," Armstrong later revealed. "I felt like I was . . . going backward. I mean, I ran out of water. I was certainly the thirstiest I've ever been in a time trial, but I was thirsty from the very beginning."

Dehydrated and overheating, Armstrong slowed dramatically on the 8 kilometers before Monesties. Perhaps his crisis was accentuated by this stretch being exposed to the hot sun, whereas overhanging trees shaded the first half of the valley road. The climb away from the ancient stone bridge over the Cérou River was also shady, and perhaps helped the yellow jersey recover. "On the hill, I tried to start easy and just go regular, and actually felt a little bit better after that," he said.

Even so, Armstrong was only 5th fastest over the final 13.5 kilometers, where he conceded a second to Hamilton; 41 seconds to a fast-finishing Vinokourov, who really punched it on the hill; and a whopping 56 seconds to Ullrich (more than 4 seconds per kilometer!).

Nothing was going as expected in this Tour de France. Armstrong still had the jersey, but his 34-second lead over Ullrich was tiny going into four giant stages in the Pyrénées. Was the Tourminator back?

STAGE 12: GAILLAC TO CAP'DÉCOUVERTE TT
1. Ullrich, 47 km in 58:32 (48.178 kph); **2. Armstrong, 1:00:08**; 3. Vinokourov, 1:00:38; 4. Zubeldia, 1:01:12; **5. Hamilton, 1:01:15**; 6. Uwe Peschel (G), Gerolsteiner, 1:01:58; 7. Millar, 1:02:27; 8. Iñigo Chaurreau (Sp), ag2r, 1:02:33; 9. David Plaza (Sp), Bianchi, 1:03:09; 10. Botero, 1:03:32.
Overall: 1. Armstrong, 50:16:45; 2. Ullrich, at 0:34; 3. Vinokourov, at 0:51; **4. Hamilton, at 2:59**; 5. Zubeldia, at 4:29.

STAGE 13

Toulouse to Ax-3 Domaines

There were more questions than answers after a flurry of attacks by Zubeldia, Ullrich, and Vinokourov on the climb to the stage-13 finish at Ax-3 Domaines forced race leader Armstrong to fight for his life. That he managed to keep his yellow jersey by a 15-second margin over Ullrich was testimony to the Texan's resilience, and also a mark of his champion's mentality.

It was clear that Armstrong hadn't fully recovered from his dehydration crisis in the time trial, but he and his team still contained the challenges from his main rivals. "It was difficult today, but I expected that," said Armstrong after the finish. "I had a hard time yesterday in the time trial, and it's impossible to recover from an effort like that within 24 hours."

Champions of the past have shown similar qualities of being able to hide their true strength (or weakness). Bernard Hinault, the five-time Tour winner of twenty years ago, was perhaps the best at bluffing his opponents. To make his rivals think he was strong when having a bad day, he would ride at the front, or even make a brief acceleration at a critical point on a climb.

Armstrong showed some of that ability on the long, very steep Port de Pailhères, the Cat. I climb that immediately preceded the finishing hill out of Ax-les-Thermes. A photo taken by *L'Équipe* photographer Bernard Papon about 6 kilometers from the Pailhères summit captured the difficulty of the climb and the intensity of the situation.

Armstrong is sitting down spinning his lowest gear, his hands pulling on the tops of his bars; he's riding to the right of Spanish teammate Beltran, their wheels over-lapping. Ullrich follows on Armstrong's right, his hands on the drops as he rises out of the saddle to tackle the 10 percent grade. The eyes of Armstrong and Ullrich reveal how hard they are riding. They're totally focused on the narrow road climbing in front of them; sweat glistens on their faces, their jersey zips are opened to the chest, and their helmet straps are loosened. Immediately behind the Tour's two protagonists are Hamilton, Vinokourov, and Zubeldia, their concentration just as intense, while Mayo can be seen in the far left of the photo, out of the saddle and slightly gapped. All of the Tour's athleticism and passion are encapsulated in that one shot.

By that point on the 15-kilometer-long Pailhères climb, the last of Ullrich's Bianchi teammates had disappeared from the front group, a fact that probably dissuaded the German from testing Armstrong's mettle until later.

The Port de Pailhères was being climbed in the Tour for the first time. It crosses a remote grassy ridge at 6,565-feet elevation via what was once a goat track linking the deep, wooded valleys of the Aude and Ariège. The last 5 kilometers of the climb are on a road barely 10 feet wide that zigzags up a clifflike escarpment in a dozen tight switchbacks. It was here that Mayo made two surges, each of them followed by Armstrong, which forced Ullrich to go on the defensive, rather than being able to test the Texan.

Over the summit, where vast crowds of fans had been waiting all day in the 90-degree heat, the small Armstrong-Ullrich group was 1:37 behind three attackers. Two

WEEK TWO

Vinokourov makes a bold attack 2.5 kilometers from the summit finish at Ax-3 Domaines.

of them, ibanesto.com's Juan Miguel Mercado and CSC's Carlos Sastre, had attacked near the foot of the climb to join Postal's Rubiera, who was the only survivor of a ten-man group that escaped just 25 kilometers into the 197.5-kilometer stage.

The gap increased to 2:10 on the 20-kilometer-long descent, which proved a big enough gap for Sastre to launch a solo attack for the stage win. The Spaniard had asked his CSC teammate Hamilton if he could attack before making his move. Hamilton gave Sastre the nod, but he probably wished he still had the Spaniard at his side when he ran out of water.

The CSC team car couldn't get up to Hamilton on the narrow, crowd-lined switchbacks of the Pailhères, and when the American tried to grab a water bottle from the metal rack of a stationary feed motorcycle with his right hand, his arm was yanked back and undid much of the work done on his injured clavicle.

Without that incident, Hamilton would no doubt have not lost the 1:20 he conceded to Armstrong and Ullrich at Ax. Mayo, too, dropped back on the last climb, partly because the other high-ranking Euskaltel rider, Zubeldia, twice made attacks to break up the Armstrong group.

But the catalyst of the American's defeat was a surge by 3rd-placed Vinokourov about 2.5 kilometers from the top. Ullrich chased, then he raced past the Kazakh toward 2nd place, while Armstrong couldn't follow. He was looking vulnerable.

The defending champion, however, showed his fighting qualities to overtake a fading Vinokourov and then surge over the easy final kilometer (which included a short downhill) to finish within 7 seconds of Ullrich, whose time bonus of 12 seconds brought him very close to the overall lead. The race leader later admitted that this was one of his lowest points in the Tour. He hadn't recovered from the dehydration, and his big rival was attacking him on the climbs.

Armstrong's bad mien hit a high about 20 minutes after the finish, when his *soigneur* was trying to guide him to an awaiting helicopter through a bottleneck caused by official vehicles trying to evacuate the area, along with the usual mobs of fans, journalists, and TV crews. Suddenly, a frustrated driver laid on his horn. He hadn't seen that the yellow jersey was right in front of the van, so he had quite a shock when Armstrong turned and glared at him. Moments later, as he walked past the vehicle's open passenger window, Armstrong squirted water from his bottle right in the guy's face. And it wasn't meant as a joke. There was a reason for that sticker on one of the Postal wagons: "Don't mess with Texas."

Perhaps that rush of adrenaline was a sign that Armstrong was on the way back. But what if Ullrich and Vinokourov had attacked farther down the difficult 9-kilometer Ax climb? Would they have been able to put the Texan in real trouble, or was he stronger than it seemed? They had blown a possible opportunity, and Armstrong would surely be stronger by the next day's six-climb stage to Loudenvielle. Or would he?

STAGE 13: TOULOUSE TO AX-3 DOMAINES
1. Carlos Sastre (Sp), CSC, 197.5 km in 5:16:08 (37.484 kph); 2. Ullrich, at 1:01; 3. Zubeldia, at 1:03; **4. Armstrong, at 1:08**; 5. Vinokourov, at 1:18; 6. Basso, at 1:20; 7. Juan Miguel Mercado (Sp), ibanesto.com, at 1:24; 8. Mayo, at 1:59; 9. Moreau, at 2:32; **10. Hamilton, at 2:34.**
Overall: 1. Armstrong, 55:34:01; 2. Ullrich, at 0:15; 3. Vinokourov, at 1:01; 4. Zubeldia, at 4:16; **5. Hamilton, at 4:25.**

STAGE 14

St. Girons to Loudenvielle

In the four months since his friend and countryman Andreï Kivilev was killed in a racing accident, Vinokourov had been saying that the Tour podium was his goal. His subsequent victories in Paris-Nice, the Amstel Gold Race, and the Tour of Switzerland made that goal a true possibility. His motivation came not only from his desire to memorialize his friend, but also from something he and Kivilev had discussed earlier in the year. "Kivi trained hard last winter, because he wanted to improve on his 4th place at the 2001 Tour," said Vinokourov, Telekom's sturdy Kazakh. "His words gave me the inspiration to try for what *he* wanted at the Tour."

But could a rider whose only Tour finishes were 15th in 2000 and 16th in 2001 become a contender, especially when it looked like Vinokourov would come to the Tour as only the 4th-ranking team member behind Telekom's high-priced newcomers: the 2002 Giro winner Paolo Savoldelli of Italy, the 2002 Tour's 4th-place finisher Botero of Colombia, and the promising Cadel Evans of Australia?

Well, Evans twice fractured his collarbone before the Tour and couldn't start; Savoldelli was returning from an early-season accident when he went down with a stomach virus that ruled him out; and Botero showed up in Paris looking overweight and underprepared. So Vino got his chance.

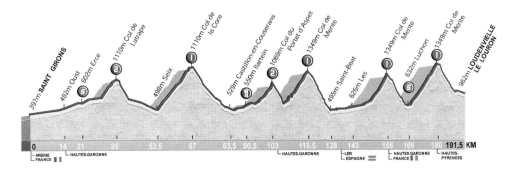

The peloton crosses the Garbet creek before tackling stage 14's opening climb, the Col de Latrape.

His attacks on every mountain stage in the Alps, his stage win into Gap, and his solid 3rd-place time trial put him in contention, but when he made a late move on stage 13 it fizzled before the line. Everyone wondered whether he was cooked, or if he had the courage to try again.

Well, he did have the courage, and he did try again, in his most impressive performance to date.

The six-mountain stage from St. Girons over the Latrape, Core, Portet d'Aspet, Menté, Portillon, and Peyresourde climbs seemed to be headed to a tame conclusion on this day of cooler, more humid conditions. Admittedly, there was a seventeen-man daylong break that saw 2003 Giro winner Simoni of Saeco, along with Quick Step's Virenque and Alessio's Laurent Dufaux, break clear on the Portillon, but none of them was a G.C. threat. Virenque, the best placed overall at 14:25, was in front to wrap up his King of the Mountains jersey, while the other two were hoping for a face-saving stage win.

Then, about 9 kilometers from the summit of Peyresourde—where the mass of spectators was so thick it covered the roadway as well as the roadsides—Vinokourov found the opening he was looking for. After Euskaltel's Mayo counterattacked a solid move by Crédit Agricole's Christophe Moreau, and just after Laiseka, a second Euskaltel man, attempted to join his teammate, Vino sprang from the back of the dwindling yellow-jersey group. This attack was even stronger than those he made on the other mountain stages—the Col de la Ramaz, L'Alpe d'Huez, the Côte de la Rochette, and Ax-3 Domaines.

There was even greater conviction in his acceleration. Mayo and Moreau grabbed Vinokourov's wheel; but Moreau couldn't hang for long, while Mayo was happy just to follow. Behind, there was a wait-and-see attitude—until the gap became 1 minute and Ullrich decided 5 kilometers from the top of the Peyresourde that he should take over the pacemaking of the still nine-strong group of G.C. leaders.

Armstrong took some criticism for not taking the initiative himself, but there were reasons. First, as he said later, "I regard Jan and me as co-leaders of this race. He never asked me to take a pull. I wouldn't have taken a pull, anyway, because my only concern was him . . . not Vinokourov." Second, Armstrong was still not himself, and if he could continue to recover from his stage-12 crisis by following Ullrich, that was just fine.

In the end, his decision proved smart. Instead of exerting himself on the climb, Armstrong decided to make his effort on the descent, and he helped close what was a 55-second lead for Vinokourov at the summit to a 43-second gain at the line. That put Vino in 3rd place overall, just 3 seconds back of Ullrich, but Armstrong was still the leader.

As for the stage win, that went to a joyful Simoni, who outsprinted the former discredited Festina pair, Virenque and Dufaux. But all three were almost beaten by another man from the daylong break. CSC's Andrea Peron closed a 1-minute gap in the last 10 kilometers and came hurtling past the three leaders with a kilometer left. "I almost surprised them," said Peron, "but Virenque turned and saw me just before I caught them."

CSC's hardworking Italian would have been a worthy winner, but this stage will be remembered for another near miss—the one for the yellow jersey by the irrepressible Vino.

STAGE 14: ST. GIRONS TO LOUDENVIELLE

1. Gilberto Simoni (I), Saeco, 191.5 km in 5:31:52 (34.622 kph); 2. Dufaux; 3. Virenque, both s.t.; 4. Andrea Peron (I), CSC, at 0:03; 5. Walter Beneteau (F), La Boulangère, at 0:10; 6. Vinokourov, at 0:41; 7. Mayo; 8. Steve Zampieri (Swi), Vini Caldirola, both s.t.; 9. Zubeldia, at 1:24; 10. Basso, s.t.

Overall: 1. Armstrong, 55:34:01; 2. Ullrich, at 0:15; 3. Vinokourov, at 0:18; 4. Zubeldia, at 4:16; 5. Mayo, at 4:37.

SUNDAY, JULY 13

L'ALPE D'HUEZ—*What a difference a week makes. Last Sunday night was a pretty low point for me and everyone on the CSC team. But here we are seven days later, reflecting on a day we couldn't have imagined was possible.*

It really is impossible to explain the range of emotions this team has been through since the start of the Tour. But everyone has rallied around me and my effort to continue. I don't know where I'd be without their support. My being able to stay in this race has been the result of a full and collective effort by all the riders and staff. Everyone has tried to stay as positive as possible.

Figuring out a game plan hasn't been easy. Friday morning I had an informal meeting with my wife and our team's doctor. By that point I had made it through four days of relatively flat racing and I was still in a lot of pain. We had to be realistic about my chances of being able to climb in stages 7 and 8. We made a pact. If I lost 15 minutes or more on either stage, I would have to stop the race.

I finished yesterday's stage with a lot of pain in my back and ribs. The consensus was that my other bruises were becoming more apparent since the pain in my collarbone was starting to become a little bit more manageable.

It hasn't subsided very much, it's more like I'm just starting to get used to it. But on the bright side of things, I was happy to be able to stand up a little bit on the bike today. I'm still not able to accelerate with 100-percent effort, but I do feel like I'm gaining a little bit of my strength back, which is good for my morale.

The climb up to L'Alpe d'Huez was loaded with people today. The fans were crazy. They were throwing water on us and crowding the roads in ways you expect on the big climbs. But a few fans went a little overboard with the cheering and back patting. I wound up getting smacked in my right shoulder twice. But, luckily, no harm was done.

I had a surprise visitor last night. My University of Colorado cycling coach, Eric Schmidt, was at the Tour de France on vacation and stopped by my hotel. He said he nearly didn't recognize me since I'm about 25 pounds lighter than I was back in college. I guess I drank a little more beer back then. It was great to see him, especially since he was one of the guys who helped launch my career in cycling. Neither of us would have ever thought I would ride in seven Tours de France. I guess that goes to show that you never know where certain opportunities will lead.

Behind the Scenes

I've been concentrating on using a higher cadence in this year's Tour de France. I've been riding a 56–36 chainring combination, instead of a typical 53–39 setup.

WEDNESDAY, JULY 16

MONTPELLIER—*Yesterday was a great day for our team. Jakob Piil spent most of the stage in a breakaway, and then he duked it out in a two-man sprint for his first Tour de France stage victory. I'm really happy for him. He had a few tough moments during the first week of the race, but fought back hard and came up with an incredible result. The team celebrated with a little champagne at dinner last night.*

Thankfully today is a rest day. Ten stages into this year's Tour de France, and I'm feeling about ten years older. There are days when cycling can make you feel like an old man. And for me, yesterday was one of them.

The pain in my collarbone is now being matched by pain in my spine. I started feeling a jabbing pain in my back and rib cage a couple of days ago. We just figured it was a bruise making it's way to the surface and that it would get better each day. But the problem is that it has been getting worse.

On Tuesday morning, the pain woke me up about an hour ahead of our scheduled wake-up call. No one gets up earlier than they have to at the Tour. So this was serious. I couldn't take a deep breath. It was like I got an instant cramp every time I tried to suck in a lot of air. And the pain would dart around my side into my chest. The feeling made me a little more than nervous.

As I ate breakfast, Ole spent a little time working on the area trying to get a feel for what was wrong. He figured the culprit was probably a nerve being pinched somewhere in my now twisted spine. Since I'm stronger on one side at the moment, I'm pulling things a little out of whack. I practically squirmed out of my seat every time Ole got close to the spot where the pain was the most intense. To make matters a little more challenging, we had about an hour's worth of a transfer from our hotel yesterday. We had stayed at the base of a ski station in the middle of nowhere.

The roads were about as twisty and up and down as they come. By the time we made it to the start town of Gap I was ready to get out of the car. But we got stuck in a traffic jam. We inched along for about as long as we could stand, and then finally started hauling down the wrong side of the road to get to the start.

We made it with about 20 minutes to spare, which isn't a whole lot of time when you need to get taped up, sign in, and get your act together to get into the race. I didn't sign in. Something had to give, and that seemed to be the least important demand at the time. It was a pretty stressful morning.

To make matters a little worse, Bjarne had tried to take a shortcut to the start and wound up getting the lead team car stuck in a ditch. Our mechanic Frederick had to beg a guy with a Jeep to help tow the car out. They got the job done just in the nick of time.

I started the race feeling pretty awful and spent the entire day counting the kilometers to the finish. I'm glad Jakob had such a great day. His success was a good distraction from my misery. We had another long transfer after the stage. We finished in Marseille and had to drive to Montpellier.

It didn't look like a long way on the map, but there was an accident halfway on the main highway to Montpellier that basically shut down traffic for 20 km in both directions, which meant we had to take the national route to our hotel. I lost count of how many traffic lights and rotaries we passed. It was a long day.

Monday's stage to Gap was really tough. I had previewed the climbs in June, so I knew that we were going to have our work cut out for us. It was a dangerous ride as well since the tar was soft and pretty slippery in some spots. It was really a shame to see Beloki go down like he did.

My read on the crash was that he had hit a slick spot where the tar had melted, had his wheel slip out, and then got caught on dry pavement. The speeds combined with the elements made it impossible for him to control his bike.

But how about Armstrong? I've never seen anything like what he did. The guy just keeps making bike-racing history. We could see him crossing the field as we made our way around the switchback. When he darted back into the road I couldn't believe what I was watching him do.

I instinctively threw out my arm to try and give him a push to help get him up to speed, but then I realized I had reached out with my right arm, which is the side with my collarbone fractures. At the last second, I pulled my hand away. I don't think I would have been much help to him anyway. He seemed to have the situation under control—although his heart rate must have been over 200 at the time!

FRIDAY, JULY 18

TOULOUSE—*Today's individual time trial was pretty brutal. The route was difficult with a lot of uphills, false flats, and a headwind. I guess you could say today was a* warm-up for the four tough days that lie ahead. The heat was also a huge factor this afternoon. It was nearly 100 degrees F out there. I finished exhausted and dehydrated. I think I was half delirious on the bus ride back to Toulouse.

I was happy with today's result in light of the fact that I thought I was out of the race for good on the rest day. I went to bed with a pinched nerve the night before, and awoke with some of the most excruciating pain I've ever felt the next morning.

Anyone who has dealt with a nerve problem must know what I'm talking about. For me, this was a first. The pain radiating from my spine dwarfed the pain I was feeling in my collarbone. It was incredible. I could barely get out of bed, and taking more than a half-breath was out of the question. I was really lucky we didn't have to race on Wednesday, because I don't know if I could have started in that condition.

But once again, Ole came to the rescue. He hadn't been able to crack or adjust my back since the crash in stage 1. In addition to my fractures, I had hit my head pretty hard, which left my neck in rough shape. Add ten days of riding while favoring my left side, and it added up to trouble for my back. My spine had apparently twisted just enough that the bones about halfway down started pressing together on a nerve.

Ole had to work step-by-step, but was finally able to crack my back. He was afraid of hurting me, but I kept telling him if it was going to fix things to keep going. By the time he got me straightened out, it felt like someone had finally reversed the truck parked on my back. I can't explain in words the kind of relief I felt at that point. I nearly lost it.

Yesterday, I was still a little sore from the whole ordeal since my muscles had spent about a day and a half completely clenched. But by this morning, I was feeling a little better. So, hopefully, the nerve thing is behind me. Okay, quick—everyone knock on wood. It's not unusual to have one injury lead to another. I was lucky we could get the situation with my back under control. It's not always that easy.

Some people may have already said that the Tour really started today. It was a difficult time trial that certainly shook things up and spread things out a bit. There's still a lot of racing left to do, though. The Pyrénées are looming, and I have a feeling they are not going to be very forgiving. Especially with the heat wave we're having here in Europe. There's going to be some serious water-bottle-run traffic in and out of the caravan in the days ahead.

Tyler Hamilton

MONDAY, JULY 14

GAP—*The Alps . . . what an experience they were. And the people. I have never ridden through so many crowds. Whatever happens, it is a Tour I will never forget.*

With the Alps behind us now, I'll have a bit of time to reflect on the experience; well, that is, until the Pyrénées come under our wheels and the road goes painfully up again.

Today's stage was hard, hot, and hurt as the result sheet shows (I was 78th, at 15:38, along with 13 others). This time I couldn't finish with the leaders, as I did on stage 7 where I was 4th, or even as I did in stage 8 where I hit the last climb up to L'Alpe d'Huez with Lance Armstrong's group before finishing 34th at 9:29—a result that was naturally influenced by the circumstances of our defense of the yellow jersey.

It's true that I've done a fair bit of work recently, probably more than I had anticipated as Richard Virenque's yellow jersey added to the demands. That can only help me in the long run, experience-wise. It was great to see the crowds support Richard like they did. You can hear about the French loving Richard, but you have to really witness it firsthand to believe it.

It was a great day, to L'Alpe d'Huez. I was pretty happy with how I went, especially getting back onto Armstrong's group after the Col du Galibier. I lost touch when the U.S. Postal Service team did a big surge. I just couldn't stay with them. But I also knew that if I could just not lose too much time, I could regain it on the descent. I did, and by the time we hit the base of L'Alpe d'Huez, I was tucked nicely into Armstrong's group ready to ride for Richard.

I had no idea Richard wasn't feeling that well when I came back to him on the descent of the Galibier, so I thought we could have a good crack at defending his jersey. But I knew he was in trouble when I took his helmet from him to hand back to the team car at the bottom of the climb and he didn't come through to go in front of me.

In that situation there wasn't much I could do. The only thing left for me was to help Richard as much as possible. That meant I had to ride in front of him and set as high a tempo as I could, but one that he could maintain in my slipstream. On television, it may have looked like I was riding within myself. But trust me, it was a hard climb.

Cycling's most famous mountain, L'Alpe d'Huez is not that hard in itself. But when you get there after racing over three or four passes—and with 200 km under your belt—it is pretty hard.

Also, riding tempo like I had to for Richard—to suit someone else's pace rather than one you would feel more comfortable in setting—can also make it harder mentally as much as physically. Not only do you have to ease up at times, breaking your rhythm, you also have to constantly look over your shoulder to make sure he is all right. That creates added strain.

Throughout the climb I tried to encourage him, saying not to lose too much time on Armstrong. But he didn't say a lot back as we rode up to the finish. In the heat and with the noise of the crowds surrounding us, I realized the best thing to do was to stay focused and concentrate on the job at hand. Despite our best efforts, we lost the yellow jersey. And while Richard is fixed on winning the King of the Mountains jersey, we know he was really disappointed for us. He knew we loved having the yellow jersey in the team.

THURSDAY, JULY 17

TOULOUSE—When it comes to negative racing, the performances of two French riders alongside me today in the winning eight-man break really takes the cake. All Carlos Da Cruz (fdjeux.com) and Nicolas Portal (ag2r) were worried about was marking me. I couldn't scratch my arse without them getting on my wheel.

When you have two guys like them, who ride as if their lives depend on chasing you down, it's not easy to get away. How they raced today was a disgrace. And what did they gain from it? Fifth and 7th places!

I tried to make something of it, right up until the end when Spaniard Juan Antonio Flecha (ibanesto) broke away. Who was there on my wheel? Da Cruz.

Yes, placing 8th in those circumstances was a disappointing end to what could have been a great—and very rare—winning opportunity for a rider like me in his first-ever Tour.

I've never raced for so many days, and with the stage-12 time trial next up on the menu of pain, I had intended to save myself by hiding in the bunch. But what's done is done, and now all I can do is recover and pray the legs will return for the 47-km race of truth in which I had hoped, with a good ride, to finish in the top five.

One of the great things about this team is that you are allowed to make choices, but at the same time Quick Step works hard to ensure that you are on a solid and progressive career plan. That's one of the reasons why I re-signed with Quick Step for another two years. The news was announced a couple of days ago, but I actually put pen to paper two weeks ago.

Sure, I have job security for a couple of years now, but for me Quick Step–Davitamon is the perfect team right now. I'm trying to develop into a rider who can perform in stage races. The Tours of Belgium and Germany are perfect races for me now. But we have talked about setting out a time line of development with certain goals for me to achieve along the way. That includes working on a really good program with the team trainer.

The goals are to train and progressively get my weight down with the guidance of a dietician. It takes time for a body to develop into that of a Tour rider. You can't change it overnight. Ideally, for me to perform at my maximum in the Tour, I want to be about 71 kg. I am 73 kg now, the same as what I weighed when the Tour started. That may surprise you. But I have kept eating and drinking heaps, up to 20 bidons a day in the heat that has hit 40 degrees Celsius (104 degrees F) on occasion.

Luckily, I haven't been really sick like some riders have. The only upset I had was after the stage to L'Alpe d'Huez. It was literally an upset tummy. On a day like that you eat so many sugars to get the calories down. I think it overloaded my system. Eating thousands of calories like we do . . . the body is not made to do that.

Then again, as I am reminded every day on the Tour, the body can be stretched to limits I never imagined.

SATURDAY, JULY 19

AX-3 DOMAINES—It was a big day in the Tour de France today. With one of four days in the Pyrénées down, all I am really thinking about now is making it to the finish in Paris—and making the best of next Saturday's time trial along the way.

If you were in the bus—the laughing group—like I was today, there was one thing very funny about today's stage 13: hearing the Italians crying as we tackled the major climbs.

You could hear them. **Crying.** Why? They just thought we were going too hard up the 15-km-long Port de Pailhères and then the final climb to the finish at Ax-3 Domaines.

We had 48 riders in the bus at the finish, 33 minutes and 14 seconds behind stage winner Carlos Sastre (CSC)—including 6 Italians. I won't give away the names of those who cried.

It was quite an experience riding in the bus for the first time in the Tour, though. I took it easy because tomorrow, stage 14, is going to be a real hard day, as will stage 15.

Everyone just took their turn at the front and rode tempo to keep within the time limit. We knew it was about 50 minutes, so we knew all along that we were safe.

In many ways, it was almost a day off. Well, kind of. It surely won't be tomorrow. Since I am here at the Tour to learn, I will try and go with the main group and see how far I can go.

After Friday's time trial—in which the heat got to me a bit—I actually felt pretty good the whole day. Sure, there was a lot of talk about the two climbs ahead—especially the first of them, the Port de Pailhères, which rises to 2,001 meters (6,565 feet) elevation.

It was a big climb all right, especially nearer the summit. It was so steep there, and the roads were narrow and twisting. With huge crowds near the summit, I can tell you there was not a lot of room for a bunch the size of what I was riding in.

Michael Rogers

Week 3: Gladiators

ARMSTRONG–ULLRICH COMBAT
GOES DOWN TO THE WIRE.

———————————◉———————————

Heading into its final week, the Tour de France is usually all wrapped up. Take the first four years of Lance Armstrong's reign: With seven days remaining, his overall margin on his closest rival was 7:44 in 1999, 7:26 in 2000, 5:05 in 2001, and 4:21 in 2002. As the 2003 Tour began its final week, Armstrong led Jan Ullrich by only 15 seconds, while Alex Vinokourov was only 3 seconds behind the German, and two others were within 5 minutes. Just about the only thing sewn up before stage 15 to Luz-Ardiden was the climber's polka-dot jersey competition, in which Richard Virenque had an unassailable lead—he would thus equal the six titles of Spaniard Federico Bahamontes and Belgian Lucien Van Impe.

Five, not six, was the number of overall wins that Armstrong was aiming for when he pedaled out of the crowded little town of Bagnères-de-Bigorre on the final Monday morning of the race. Ahead of him was a stage that included the Aspin, Tourmalet, and Luz-Ardiden climbs, on which potential Tour winners have faltered in the past.

Back in 1983, Australian Phil Anderson was the designated leader of the powerful Peugeot team. He was lying in 3rd place when he started the Pau-Luchon stage that included the Tourmalet and Aspin. When Anderson fell and lost a shoe on the day's first climb, the Aubisque, none of his team waited, and the Aussie was exhausted by his subsequent chase. On reaching the Tourmalet, Anderson could do nothing when his French teammate Pascal Simon broke away, finished 3rd on the stage, and took the yellow jersey. Two years later, the race leader was Bernard Hinault, who faltered on the Tourmalet and was dropped on Luz-Ardiden, but just managed to keep the yellow jersey.

Then, in 1990, overall leader Claudio Chiappucci actually attacked over the Aspin and Tourmalet before losing more than 2 minutes on Luz-Ardiden to his closest challenger, Greg LeMond, who went on to win the Tour. The positions were reversed the following year, when the American was dropped on the Tourmalet and Chiappucci went on to win the stage ahead of breakaway companion Miguel Induráin, who took the first yellow jersey of his career.

The Tourmalet and Luz-Ardiden would again be arbitrators in 2003, this time between Armstrong, Ullrich, and Vinokourov. That's why the American said, "When we started the climb [to Luz-Ardiden], I knew that was where I needed to win the Tour. And at the finish I was confident that that was enough."

Armstrong was lucky that there were no serious consequences from the heavy fall he suffered just when he began the attack that he hoped would win him the Tour. By the time he had won the stage a minute (including bonus seconds) ahead of Iban Mayo, Ullrich, and Haimar Zubeldia, Armstrong was conscious that he was only five stages from the Champs-Élysées, with just the penultimate day's time trial standing between him and Tour win No. 5.

The brave Vinokourov was knocked out of the picture at Luz-Ardiden, so the ninetieth Tour became a two-man battle: Armstrong versus Ullrich. As both are great time trialists, the suspense would continue to the final weekend—just like the

Between Basque flags and fans, Vinokourov heads to an eighth-place finish at Luz-Ardiden.

Jacques Anquetil–Raymond Poulidor duel in 1964, and the Greg LeMond–Laurent Fignon showdown in 1989. Those earlier epics also featured deep fluctuations in fortune, along with the eventual champion having to use tactical nuance to overcome physical vulnerability.

With just over a minute separating Armstrong from Ullrich going into the final weekend, the time trial from Pornic to Nantes could still send the Tour the German's way. But even before Ullrich had a spectacular spill 12 kilometers from the stage finish, he was leading the defending champion by only 2 seconds. The crash simply confirmed that Ullrich was going to finish as the Tour runner-up for the fifth time in his career. For Armstrong, it meant he was going to finish in 1st place for the fifth time. "When I heard that Jan crashed," he said, "for me, the race was finished."

A drained, but exultant, Armstrong said later that day, "This was absolutely the most difficult year. Physically not superb, technically, some mistakes made, some bad mistakes; but this close one feels different, feels better than all of the others. It's very satisfying."

This was a different Armstrong. His setbacks and crises, and those of his opponents, seemed to humble him. "I was able to survive in the bad moments," he said. "Sometimes you have to survive in order to win. I was able to do that."

Armstrong's average winning margin in his first four Tour victories was 6:55. But in 2003, instead of obliterating the opposition early with a dominant time trial or a solo climbing recital, he had to limit his losses and eke out his gains—and then hope that he had enough resources to make a big push in the final week.

STAGE 15

Bagnères-de-Bigorre to Luz-Ardiden

Shots of a radiant Lance Armstrong in the yellow jersey at Luz-Ardiden flashed around the world on July 21. The photos showed the day's winner leaning forward and pointing. If you're wondering, he was pointing at teammate George Hincapie, the only Postal rider who has been with Armstrong on all of his winning Tours. Hincapie had just reached the mountaintop finish in 52nd place, 19:49 behind his boss. At first, he didn't see Armstrong on the podium, but he then turned to his right and the two made eye contact. That's when the leader of the Tour, beaming, leaned forward and thrust his right index finger at Hincapie. He even seemed to consider throwing him the little stuffed lion that he'd just received with the yellow jersey from the Crédit Lyonnais hostesses.

His yellow jersey, bouquet, and Crédit Lyonnais lion in hand, Armstrong catches the eye of teammate Hincapie.

Hincapie wasn't surprised to see his friend on the podium. When asked that morning, before the stage-15 start in Bagnères-de-Bigorre, whether he thought Armstrong had it in him to attack on the last climb, Hincapie replied, "I think so. Just seeing his face . . . After the time trial it didn't look like Lance. The next day, he looked a little better. Yesterday he started looking more like Lance. Then this morning and last night, he looked like Lance, just happy, confident, joking around, and not tired . . . didn't look tired at all. So I have a good feeling about today."

Having a good feeling about a friend is one thing, but it's vastly more complicated for that friend to translate his good mood into defending the Tour de France lead in one of the tightest situations in race history on one of its most challenging stages.

History tends to repeat itself, particularly Tour history. Twenty-eight years before this Tour, on a stage finishing with the same two climbs, the Tourmalet and Luz-Ardiden, the man trying to win his fifth Tour was Bernard Hinault. The Frenchman fell back on the Tourmalet, and it looked like he might lose the Tour. Hinault only survived because his young teammate, Greg LeMond, was ordered to drop back and help him.

Armstrong, too, appeared to be struggling on the Tourmalet when archrival Ullrich made a strong surge just as the riders headed into a bank of swirling cloud on the steep approaches to La Mongie—where a year before Armstrong attacked to

win the 2002 Tour's first mountain stage. This time, with 41 kilometers still to race, he was digging deep just to stay in contention.

The German surged again, and this time the Texan couldn't (or didn't want to) follow. "He was going strong there," Armstrong admitted, "[and] I said, 'Okay, if you're gonna ride like that all day, you can win the Tour de France,' because I can't continue [at that pace]. This was a very strong attack, but I felt at the time that it was not the time to do that. For me it's better to establish my own rhythm, let him have 5 seconds or 10 seconds and keep him there—we can both ride our own little time trials—and then try to come back."

Cool under pressure, the hard-riding Armstrong dropped Vinokourov, Mayo, and the rest, but remained some 25 meters behind Ullrich. Had the Bianchi leader been able to sustain his attack, the "little time trial" could have continued for the remaining 6 kilometers to the 6,935-foot Tourmalet summit, down its spectacularly fast 20-kilometer descent to the streets of Luz-St. Sauveur at 2,388 feet, and back up to the 5,626-foot elevation of Luz-Ardiden.

However, by the time they emerged from the clouds, Armstrong had clawed his way up to his prey, while first Mayo and then Zubeldia caught back on. But Ullrich's surge wasn't totally wasted as 3rd-placed Vinokourov (only 3 seconds behind Ullrich on G.C.) wouldn't return. Indeed, he'd concede more than 2 minutes by the stage's end.

Ahead of the Telekom rider, seventeen riders came together after the descent and the up-and-down approach to the 13.7-kilometer Luz-Ardiden ascent. In the next half hour or so, the 2003 Tour would likely be decided. Helmets came off. Postal's Beltran and Rubiera came up to help Armstrong, and Bianchi's David Plaza and Felix Garcia Casas moved to the front to pace Ullrich. Before the 10-kilometers-to-go archway, though, the domestiques' duties appeared to be over.

First, Mayo set the thousands of orange-shirted Basques cheering with a sudden attack, and Armstrong responded. The race leader pounced by the Alpe d'Huez winner, and Ullrich accelerated after them. This was the battle everyone had been waiting

WEEK THREE

for. But suddenly the cheers turned to gasps. Armstrong was leading, moving at perhaps 30 kilometers per hour on his uphill attack, close to the fans packed along the inside of a right-hand curve, when he dramatically tumbled to the tarmac. Mayo crashed over him, his bike sliding out, and Ullrich swerved around it. Armstrong later admitted that he was riding too close to the fans, and said that his bars got caught in the strap of a yellow Tour musette food bag hanging from a fan's shoulder. Luckily, neither Armstrong nor Mayo was hurt beyond road rash. But to crash like that when you're making the effort that you think will win you the Tour was traumatic.

Hamilton rode up to the front to make sure that Ullrich and the others slowed until the two men who had crashed were back at the front. Meanwhile, from behind, Rubiera was able to catch back to the fallen Armstrong and begin pacing his leader again. But Armstrong's problems weren't over. As the Texan got out of the saddle to follow Rubiera, his chain skipped a cog as he shifted gears and he was thrown forward onto his crossbar, but just avoided falling again.

After this double dose of adrenaline, Armstrong seemed immune to any pain from his crash, and on catching back he didn't hesitate to follow when Mayo made another attack. This time it was a springboard to one of those ferocious solo accelerations that Armstrong first displayed at Sestriere in 1999.

When asked the day before why he was standing up more than usual on the climbs, Armstrong said, "When you're lacking, missing form, you've just got to rough it." But there was no roughing it on Luz-Ardiden. By progressively accelerating, Armstrong left Mayo behind then slowly opened up a gap on the desperately chasing Ullrich: 15 seconds . . . 22 seconds . . . 25 seconds . . . 43 seconds . . . and 45 seconds with 4 kilometers to go. By then, Armstrong had passed start-of-the-day attacker Sylvain Chavanel of La Boulangère, whom the leader gave a friendly tap on the back as if he were saying, "Good job, boy." That was quite a gesture when you're racing at the red line, calling upon every last sinew and focusing your whole mind on applying the killer punch to a gritty opponent.

Maybe Armstrong *was* roughing it, though, because he didn't have the smooth, almost mechanical, 90- to 100-rpm cadence that took him to his mountaintop stage victories at La Mongie and Plateau de Beille in 2002, L'Alpe d'Huez and Pla d'Adet in 2001, or Sestriere in 1999. Instead, there was pain on his face as he rode with his head dipped and his eyes looking manically upward, while sweat oozed down his sunken cheeks and dripped from his proud, protruding jaw.

His lead was pegged to 50 seconds by Ullrich, who never turned to ask for help from those who followed him: Zubeldia, Mayo, and Fassa Bortolo's Ivan Basso. The

WEEK THREE

Armstrong's face
says it all.

Ullrich rides himself to a standstill at Luz-Ardiden.

finish couldn't come soon enough for Armstrong. He battled around the last series of tight turns, heading into a swirling mist that engulfed the ski lifts and cow pastures of Luz-Ardiden, and kept up the pressure all the way to the line. He'd literally ridden himself to a standstill. There was no strength left to lift his arms in a victory salute. His yellow jersey soggy with sweat, Armstrong was grabbed around the shoulder by his *soigneur*, who wheeled him through a gap in the crowd barriers to the camper van where winners have a space to clean off.

It was a gutsy, knockout performance, but Armstrong didn't know how close he'd been to disaster (once again!) when he crashed. Mayo's bike had smashed into his Trek, and the right chainstay had cracked. That partly explained why his chain jumped a cog as he chased back. But good fortune enabled him to complete his winning attack on the broken frame. "When we took the back wheel out of the bike," Armstrong later revealed, "the frame fell apart."

In the last kilometer, Armstrong conceded 10 seconds of his 50-second lead as Mayo sprinted with Zubeldia and Ullrich for the 2nd- and 3rd-place time bonuses. The German later complained that Mayo shouldn't have gone past him to take the 12-second bonus, but in his defense the Spaniard did kick off the attacks, he had crashed, and his final accelerations did help Ullrich get closer to Armstrong. But would that 4-second difference between the 2nd- and 3rd-place bonuses be a factor in Paris?

For now, though, it was the American who was celebrating. With a lead on Ullrich expanded from 15 to 67 seconds, no wonder he had a big smile on his face after he'd recovered and then shared that podium moment with Hincapie.

STAGE 15: BAGNÈRES-DE-BIGORRE TO LUZ-ARDIDEN
1. Armstrong, 159.5 km in 4:29:26 (35.519 kph); 2. Mayo, at 0:40; 3. Ullrich; 4. Zubeldia, both s.t.; 5. Moreau, at 0:43; 6. Basso, at 0:47; 7. Hamilton, at 1:10; 8. Vinokourov, at 2:07; **9. José Luis Rubiera (Sp), U.S. Postal–Berry Floor, at 2:45**; 10. Sylvain Chavanel (F), La Boulangère, at 2:47.
Overall: 1. Armstrong, 65:36:23; 2. Ullrich, at 1:07; 3. Vinokourov, at 2:45; 4. Zubeldia, at 5:16; 5. Mayo, at 1:27.

WEEK THREE

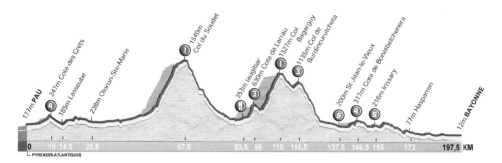

STAGE 16
Pau to Bayonne

For more than two weeks, Hamilton had been astounding the whole world with his resilience. Some even doubted that he had really broken his collarbone in that stage-1 crash. Most called him a hero, although that's not a designation he would choose himself. But if you had been standing a kilometer from the summit of the savage Col Bagargui on this final mountain stage and seen Hamilton as he headed off on one of the most remarkable solo break's in the Tour's 100-year history (and that's no exaggeration), you would never doubt his bravery.

Let's first go back to the start of this 197.5-kilometer stage in Pau. It was overcast and humid, with temperatures in the seventies as the 151 survivors headed back into the Pyrénées after a too-brief rest day. In the CSC team bus that morning, director Riis had told his men that it was a dangerous stage, and that they had to stay focused and not start thinking about Paris quite yet.

It was advice that Hamilton almost ignored. The stage began at a crazy speed (48 kilometers in the first hour) and the CSC team leader was in the wrong place when the strung-out peloton hit the day's first climb, the not-insignificant Cat. IV Côte des Crêts, just 10 kilometers out of Pau.

"I made a mistake, a big mistake," Hamilton said after the stage. "We went over that Cat. IV climb and it was a windy, twisty descent. There were a lot of attacks from the front, and the peloton was single file. I was just too far back in the peloton, and all of a sudden the peloton split, and I was in the second group. I had to call for help [on my team radio], and luckily I had four or five teammates drop back and help me. Without their help, I don't know whether we'd have caught [up]."

In fact, two riders who did fall behind in that opening stretch never returned. Both Rabobank's Remmert Wielinga and Lotto-Domo's Nick Gates were sick and simply couldn't follow the fast pace. Both of them abandoned after riding alone in the hope that the peloton would slow down. But that didn't happen.

By the time Hamilton returned to the front end of the peloton, a seventeen-man break had developed on the narrow back roads approaching the formidable Col de Soudet, a Cat. I climb rising to 5,064 feet. Having just about caught his breath, Hamilton had a conversation with Riis. "Bjarne told me if I felt good to try an attack, so I did," Hamilton said. The CSC team leader then made an attack that everyone saw, but no one could follow, on the first 12-percent pitch of the 14-kilometer Soudet, as it headed up a vivid green valley of pregnant beauty.

Hamilton quickly closed a 90-second gap to the front group, from which his Danish teammate Nicki Sörensen dropped back to help him close the last few meters. Once at the front, Hamilton took charge, upping the pace to such an extent that only seven men were left with him as the leaders crested the Soudet, already 3:35 ahead of the peloton. That gap came down to 2 minutes in the next 30 kilometers on mainly descending roads, running intimately alongside cascading mountain creeks, before climbing up again to the short, but very steep, Côte de Lareau. From the top of this hill, exactly halfway through the stage, the eight leaders raced single file down a narrow road that spiraled into the bowels of a deep valley beneath a canopy of ancient oaks.

This was the approach to the Col Bagargui, which opens with 2.5 kilometers of easy grades, climbing away from a small creek, before hitting a wall—or that's what it feels like to a cyclist. "I've never ridden as hard in my life," said Aussie Michael Rogers. The next kilometer *averages* 13 percent, and it continues like that on a paved goat track barely 10 feet wide whose tight hairpins lift the riders up a mountainside of emerald green grass and ebon black rocks that, on this momentous day, disappeared into a thick fog.

This was where Hamilton, after a strong lead-out by Sörensen, began his solo break. Most riders were on gears of 39x25 or 39x26, and even then it wasn't easy. Hamilton, to enable him to sit for much of the impossibly steep mountain, chose a 36x26 combination. He flew up the climb, pushing his lead over the dwindling Armstrong group from 2 to 4 minutes in the 6 kilometers.

As he entered the Bagargui's last kilometer, his face was a vivid crimson, covered in sweat, his eyes screwed up in pain, his mouth gulping in the humid air. His unzipped jersey revealed the white bandage strapped over his fractured clavicle. A river of cheering followed him as he swept through the last steep curves, where the shouts and applause of the fans reverberated through the clinging clouds. The Basque fans massed at the 4,353-foot summit urged him on as if he were one of their own.

WEEK THREE

Hamilton had already been on the attack for 54 kilometers over some of the toughest terrain that any mountain range can offer. To win the stage, and perhaps move up in the overall standings from his 7th place, he still had the prospect of racing alone for almost another 2 hours. In fact, he would complete the remaining 87.5 kilometers in just 1:54:00—despite having to overcome a sweeping technical descent; another two short, but steep, climbs; and a long run-in toward the Atlantic coast hammered by crosswinds. His average speed for his solo flight from Bagargui to Bayonne was 46 kilometers per hour, which was exactly the same speed he'd done in the 48-kilometer Gaillac time trial! But this effort was twice as far, over far more difficult terrain, and on a regular bike. No wonder Armstrong said that this was the most outstanding athletic feat of the Tour. And he should know.

Despite being alone, Hamilton kept on gaining over the yellow-jersey group that grew from twenty to seventy riders as his lead grew to a maximum of 5:21 with 43 kilometers still to go. "I knew if I could keep the gap at 5 minutes and hold it as long as I could," said Hamilton, "it would break their morale."

His plan worked, even though the Euskaltel, Telekom, Quick Step, and Fassa Bortolo teams all took turns to ride their hardest in an effort to pull him back. Despite the chase, Hamilton was still 2 minutes clear as he wearily pedaled up the

For the final 54 kilometers of his magnificent breakaway through the Pyrénées, Hamilton averages 46 kilometers per hour (almost 30 mph)!

Avenue des Allées Paulny in Bayonne, waved up the CSC team car to shake hands with Riis, then celebrated by first tapping his bars with a fisted right hand, then giving a half-dozen short claps, briefly covering his face in his hands, and finally raising his arms in glorious relief.

Asked how he felt about his stupendous stage victory, Hamilton simply replied, "I'm exhausted." And what did he think of all those "hero" stories that had been printed during the Tour? "I don't think I'm a hero," he said, "I'm just doing my job."

STAGE 16: PAU TO BAYONNE
1. Hamilton, 197.5 km in 4:59:41 (39.542 kph); 2. Zabel, at 1:55; 3. Yuriy Krivtsov (Ukr), Jean Delatour; 4. Gerrit Glomser (A), Saeco, all s.t.
Overall: No change.

STAGE 17

Dax to Bordeaux

After four stages in the Pyrénées and just four stages remaining in the fastest Tour in history, only the occasional rider could say his legs were still feeling good. But in

Before stage 17, Hamilton receives the red numberplate for taking the previous day's most aggressive rider award, along with a little lion as a member of the Tour's leading team, CSC.

this modern Tour, with so much pressure to win to get massive worldwide exposure for your sponsors, there's no such thing as an easy stage. No more *tranquillo*. No more *piano*. It's just go, go, go.

Of the twenty-two teams that started this ninetieth Tour, only ten of them so far had a stage winner, while all the main overall competitions were being led by one of the stage-winning teams. In fact, the only team that had a chance of usurping the establishment was Lotto-Domo, whose sprinter Robbie McEwen was just a handful of points behind green jersey Baden Cooke of fdjeux.com.

Traditionally, it's the sprinters that contest the flat stages into Bordeaux. Even the inaugural stage into Bordeaux in 1903 ended in a six-man sprint, taken by a

WEEK THREE

Belgian, Julien "Samson" Lootens—although the stage was officially awarded to Swiss rider Charles Laeser, who was in a later group of riders that had abandoned the race on a previous stage but were allowed back in the Tour to contest for the stage prizes. The ceremonial finish was at Bordeaux's big outdoor velodrome, where stages would culminate through the mid-1970s, and where the stands would be packed every year.

Track finishes have since become obsolete at the Tour because of the dangers of sending a pack of 200 riders onto a banked velodrome or the necessity to move the finish should there be rain. The finish in 2003 was downtown, on one of Bordeaux's Paris-like boulevards, the Cours de Verdun; but there would be no sprinters in sight when stage 17 ended.

From the very start in Dax, ten of the 149 starters broke away, and because ten different teams were represented its chances of survival were very good. Cooke was happy to see the break go as it virtually ensured that he would keep the green jersey. First, he had French teammate Christophe Mengin up there who might win the stage. Second, the young Aussie knew that the ten leaders would take all the points at the intermediate sprints. And third, the point differential at the finish for 11th on down was only one per place, while between 1st and 3rd place, for instance, there was a six-point difference.

Teams not represented in the break gave chase initially, particularly Crédit Agricole and Alessio, which held the ten leaders to a 20-second gap as they headed out into the flat terrain of the Landes; but once the gap reached a minute after 25 kilometers the chasers gave up. By the 50-kilometer mark—reached in less than an hour—the break was more than 10 minutes ahead.

It wasn't, however, a totally effortless day for the peloton. Its pace picked up when the gap reached 16:11 midway through the 181-kilometer stage, just as the course headed along a straight, narrow back road between tall turpentine pines toward the feed zone. Crédit Agricole again took up the chase because the 8th place of its leader, Moreau, was being threatened by the break's best-placed rider, Peter Luttenberger of CSC (18th at 26:52).

Coming into the suburbs of Bordeaux, the gap was down to a safe 8 minutes, and the attention returned to the leaders. The sprinters had been blown away, but another Bordeaux tradition was still alive: that Dutch riders always win at Bordeaux. (It's not exactly true as there have been only seven Dutch stage wins here in the past thirty years; the last was in 1992 when Rob Harmeling was the fastest finisher in a big breakaway group.)

This time, three Dutch riders had a chance of success: Rabobank's De Groot (who placed 3rd in Marseille, 2nd in Toulouse), Lotto's Leon Van Bon (a Tour stage winner in 1998 and 2000), and Quick Step's Servais Knaven (the 2001 Paris-Roubaix winner). Knaven was the first to attack as the break headed past the airport with 18 kilometers to go, and as with his solo into the Roubaix velodrome two years before, the tall Dutch domestique was home dry. He didn't even need to sprint.

STAGE 17: DAX TO BORDEAUX

1. Servais Knaven (Nl), Quick Step–Davitamon, 181 km in 3:54:23 (46.344 kph); 2. Paolo Bossoni (I), Vini Caldirola, at 0:17; 3. Christophe Mengin (F), fdjeux.com; 4. Leon Van Bon (Nl), Lotto-Domo; 5. Salvatore Commesso (I), Saeco, all s.t.
Overall: No change.

STAGE 18

Bordeaux to St. Maixent-L'École

For a long time in this race through the vineyards it looked as though the record speed for a Tour road stage was sure to be beaten. It started out like stage 17 with attacks from the gun, but this time the pace of the peloton was *so* fast (almost 56 kilometers per hour for the first hour!) that none of the breaks could stick. And when an attacking group of thirty-four riders *did* get some air, it contained top-ten contenders Mayo, Zubeldia, and Moreau, and was soon closed down by the Postal team.

And so the peloton was basically together when it approached the first of the day's two intermediate sprints, at Montendre, 50 kilometers out of Bordeaux. With only six points separating Cooke from McEwen in the green-jersey competition, a new episode in their battle looked to be in the cards. But a near-collision prevented

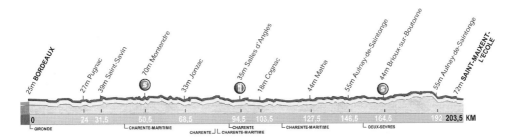

WEEK THREE

Cooke from making his sprint, and his Aussie rival dashed away to get the six points. At the same time, on the other side of the road, Ullrich hurtled to the front around the last turn and decided to bid for the 2nd-place, 4-second time bonus—and he took it ahead of Armstrong. The two rivals laughed about their sprint and Ullrich tapped Armstrong on the shoulder, perhaps thinking ahead to their more serious battle in the next day's time trial.

Within a few kilometers of the Montendre sprint, a break finally went clear, as none of its sixteen riders was remotely dangerous on G.C. Thanks to a nice tailwind, the leaders averaged 48 kilometers per hour over the last 3 hours, but they fell just 2 minutes short of breaking the road-stage record of 50.355 kilometers per hour set by Mario Cipollini on a 194.5-kilometer stage from Laval to Blois in 1999.

The sixteen men did have the pleasure of contesting the stage win, though. Having seen Knaven's success the previous day with a solo attack 18 kilometers from the finish, Thomas Voeckler from the local team, La Boulangère, tried his luck with 20 kilometers to go. But on this stage, the lone move didn't work.

Another Frenchman, Andy Flickinger of ag2r, made a move at the 10-kilometer mark, then Spaniard David Cañada went with 5 kilometers to go. It looked as though he would score Quick Step's second win in 24 hours, but Cañada died 300 meters from the line, and those chasing him suddenly found themselves sprinting for the victory.

After a stage win at the 2001 Giro d'Italia and two stage wins at the 2002 Vuelta a España, ibanesto.com's Pablo Lastras came through to become one of the few men to take stages at all three grand tours.

STAGE 18: BORDEAUX TO ST. MAIXENT-L'ÉCOLE
1. Pablo Lastras (Sp), ibanesto.com, 202.5 km in 4:03:18 (49.938 kph); 2. Carlos Da Cruz (F), fdjeux.com; 3. Daniele Nardello (I), Telekom, all s.t.; 4. David Cañada (Sp), Quick Step–Davitamon, at 0:04; 5. Massimiliano Lelli (I), Cofidis, at 0:18.
Overall: 1. Armstrong, 79:07:49; 2. Ullrich, at 1:05; 3. Vinokourov, at 2:47.

STAGE 19

Pornic to Nantes Time Trial

Armstrong knew that with only a 65-second cushion on Ullrich going into this final time trial that he would probably have to win the 49-kilometer test between Pornic and Nantes to clinch his fifth consecutive Tour. "I was extremely nervous this morning," he said later, "although I was confident and I felt good."

Ullrich, too, was obviously nervous, and yet, despite riding in the only heavy rain of the three weeks, he started like a whirlwind. The Bianchi rider was 6 seconds faster than Armstrong in the first mile. At that rate, he would have beaten his rival

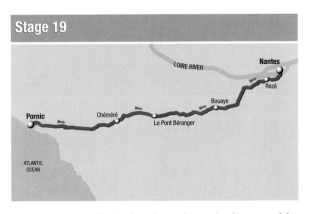

by 3 minutes. He didn't, of course. Instead, the two gladiators were soon moving at the same speed, Ullrich windmilling a huge fifty-six-tooth chainring, Armstrong spinning some 20–30 rpm faster in a much smaller gear.

It was an emotional contest. They were both hurtling through the rain, blown by a gale, their wet, contorted faces revealing the intensity of their efforts. They both averaged 57.324 kilometers per hour over the first 15 kilometers, a speed that made the dangers of riding on wet roads even higher, particularly in the latter part of the stage where a proliferation of roundabouts, sharp turns, and painted crosswalks awaited them.

"There were times when both wheels [were] sliding out," said Armstrong. "It just reminded us that, 'Hey, the difference between staying upright and going down sometimes is a very fine line.'"

Indeed, this spectacular Armstrong-Ullrich duel, in what looked like the fastest long time trial in Tour history, was turned sour by a series of crashes on the course's dangerous run-in to Nantes.

Overnight, an Atlantic storm hit land and on this humid Saturday afternoon its ferocious winds blew the riders toward the finish as torrential rains turned the roads into rinks. This was particularly dangerous in the final 18 kilometers, from where the course turned off the straight, wide D751 highway until it reached the ancient heart of Nantes. Along this stretch, riders had to negotiate some narrow village streets, tricky downhills, and a seemingly endless number of roundabouts and traffic islands.

One of the first to find that the rain and run-in were a deadly mix was twentieth starter Uwe Peschel. The thirty-four-year-old German sped away from Pornic's umbrella-lined streets as if he were determined to make his mark on a time trial that suited his big-gear-wielding style much better than stage 12's hilly course in the south. Peschel averaged almost 57 kilometers per hour on the first 15 kilometers with a 15:54 split that would remain the fastest until Ullrich and Armstrong beat it more than 4 hours later. Peschel carried that speed into the finale, where he crashed, and then crashed again. He managed to struggle home with a 57:35, but his chest injuries, including a broken rib, were serious enough to prevent him starting the final stage.

WEEK THREE

Millar's average speed of 54.361 kilometers per hour is only 12 seconds short of breaking Greg LeMond's Tour time trial record set in 1989.

Peschel's two falls were followed by many others, including, 2 hours later, that of Italian Marzio Bruseghin of Fassa Bortolo—who had just completed the second split (17.5 kilometers in 19:42) faster than Peschel.

A half hour later, the unlucky prologue runner-up, David Millar—who had been sick for much of the Tour and almost quit in the Pyrénées—was riding faster than both Peschel and Bruseghin. Over the opening 42 kilometers, Cofidis's tall Brit averaged 55.629 kilometers per hour (much faster than Greg LeMond's Tour record of 54.545 kilometers per hour over the 24.5-kilometer Versailles-Paris course in 1989). Using a gear of 55x14, with occasional use of the 13 and 15 sprockets ("I like to keep a high cadence," he said), Millar at times was spinning at 130 rpm on the windblown sections. Then, heading downhill into a tight right turn before one of the roundabouts, he suddenly had to swerve to miss a stationary sponsor's van that stopped when Millar's 2-minute man Mikel Pradera misread the curve and crashed into some hay bales on the outside of the turn.

Millar squeezed through the narrow opening and raced on, but just 4 kilometers from the line, on a right-angle left turn, the Cofidis rider's tires skidded and he slammed into the hay bales. "I had not been taking any risks," he said later. "I was like, 'Ooh, crash.' Nothing I could do about it. I didn't stress. Got back up, waited for my mechanic to come. [He] tried to get the bike going but the chain was off, and it was me who just calmly said, 'Nico, put the chain back on.'"

The crash delayed Millar just over 20 seconds, and he probably lost another 10 seconds in refinding his rhythm, and he was far more cautious on the remaining five turns and two roundabouts. He still crossed the line in 54:05, only 12 seconds outside the time he needed to beat LeMond's all-time record. The crash cost Millar a place in history. Would it cost him the stage, too?

> **SPLITS**
> **FIRST 15 km:** 1. Ullrich, 15:42 (57.324 kph); 2. Armstrong, s.t.; 3. Peschel, 15:54; 4. Millar, 15:58; 5. Hamilton, 16:06.
> **NEXT 17.5 km:** 1. Millar, 19:36 (53.571 kph); 2. Hamilton, s.t.; 3. Ullrich, 19:37; 4. Armstrong, 19:39; 5. Bruseghin, 19:42.
> **NEXT 9.5 km:** 1. Millar, 9:44 (58.561 kph); 2. Peña, 9:55; 3. Hamilton, 9:57; 4. Hincapie, 9:58; 5. Ekimov, 10:07.
> **LAST 7 km:** 1. Bodrogi, 8:13 (51.177 kph); 2. Hamilton, 8:35; 3. Bruseghin, 8:46; 4. Millar, 8:47; 5. Armstrong, s.t.

The next rider to come close to beating Millar was Hamilton. The CSC hero had started cautiously, but then he picked up his pace and equaled Millar's split between 15 and 32.5 kilometers—even riding faster than Ullrich and Armstrong on this section. But although he didn't crash, Hamilton was just 9 seconds short of demoting Millar on the leader board.

By now, all eyes were on the ferocious duel between Armstrong and Ullrich. But as Millar said: "When I saw Ullrich go in the first kilometer, I said he's going down.

WEEK THREE

Ullrich puts everything into his bid to win the final time trial …

. . . but, surging through the rainstorm, Armstrong keeps him in check.

He was taking risks today and he was going so fast that it was gonna happen."

The inevitable crash did happen. Not to Armstrong, for whom it could have spelled the end of his No. 5 Tour dream, but to Ullrich. Whereas the American had ridden the course in the rain that morning, and then received firsthand accounts from his teammates who raced before him, Ullrich relied on a description given to him by his team director. "I don't see the need to look over courses beforehand," the German commented.

So while Armstrong tried to balance his focus on speed with the necessity for caution, Ullrich was simply riding as fast as he could, knowing that this was perhaps his only chance to win the Tour. Most people have seen the replays of his negotiating the left-right-left slalom through a roundabout, when Ullrich's rear wheel slides out as he makes the right-turn part of the maneuver and then skates sideways and crashes into the plastic-covered hay bales. Ullrich's speed and the slick road (he thought he hit a patch of oil) were factors in his fall, but it's possible that a wind gust (they were measured at up to 70 kilometers per hour) caught his rear disc wheel at the wrong moment.

By the time Ullrich crashed, 12 kilometers from the line, he was just 2 seconds ahead of the remorseless Armstrong. This was a different Armstrong from the dehydrated one who conceded 1:36 to Ullrich at Cap'Découverte. The Texan, spinning as fast as Millar, was able to contain the German, who tried to blast his opponent out of the water. The tactic didn't work, but it was a great try. And in the end Armstrong was able to cruise through those scary final turns and then pump his fist in celebration. Tour No. 5 was in the bag.

Because he scaled back the power in those last kilometers, Armstrong didn't win the stage. He stopped the clock 3 seconds slower than Hamilton and 12 seconds back of Millar—who thus took the win that was so cruelly plucked from him three Saturdays before in Paris.

Stage 19: Pornic to Nantes TT
1. David Millar (GB), Cofiidis, 49 km in 54:05 (54.361 kph); **2. Hamilton, 54:14**; **3. Armstrong, 54:17**; 4. Ullrich, 54:29; 5. Bodrogi, 54:31; 6. Viatcheslav Ekimov (Rus), U.S. Postal–Berry Floor, 55:01; 7. Peña, 55:05; 8. Hincapie, 55:13; 9. Chavanel, 55:17; 10. Marzio Bruseghin (I), Fassa Bortolo, 55:31.
Overall: 1. Armstrong, 80:02:08; 2. Ullrich, at 1:16; 3. Vinokourov, at 4:29; **4. Hamilton, at 6:32**; 5. Zubeldia, at 7:06.

STAGE 20
Ville d'Avray to Paris (Champs-Élysées)

Back in Sedan, three weeks before this finale on the Champs-Élysées, a wild field sprint saw Cooke take a great lead-out from Aussie teammate Brad McGee, then wearing the yellow jersey, to win the first Tour stage of his young career. To achieve

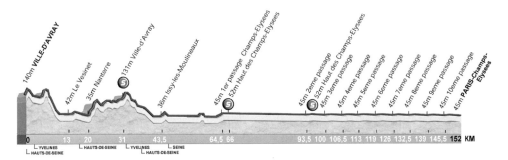

WEEK THREE

that result, after McEwen got boxed in, Cooke dashed through a gap in the final meters to squeeze out French sprinter Jean-Patrick Nazon.

Since that stage, Cooke, Nazon, and McEwen had survived the mountains, the heat wave, and the record pace, and were ready to do battle again.

With only two points separating leader McEwen from Cooke in the green-jersey competition, they'd have to contest both of the day's intermediate sprints—which were located at the top end of the Champs-Élysées, and not where the stage would finish near the foot of the world's most famous avenue. In the first sprint, McGee gave a perfect leadout to fdjeux.com teammate Cooke, who dashed clear using his twelve-tooth sprocket to win the uphill sprint, while McEwen challenged too late. That put the pair dead level on overall points.

The tide turned in defending champion McEwen's favor in the second sprint. This time, the more experienced Lotto-Domo rider jumped on the left of the McGee lead-out as Cooke made his move on the right. "I got greedy," said Cooke later, "and went into the 11. It was too big and I was chugging on it."

That gave McEwen the lead by two points again, and so the sprint for the stage victory would also decide the fate of the green jersey. "I lost confidence after that [second sprint] and honestly felt like shit," said Cooke. "I was hurting and couldn't position myself. But all of a sudden I came to life when I heard the bell."

Into the final 6.5-kilometer lap, the remnants of an eight-man break still had an 8-second gap, but the pack was chasing hard in one long line as it headed into the last 3-kilometer loop around the Tuileries Gardens. The attackers were overtaken one by one and then it was the turn of the sprinters' teams to start the lead out.

Telekom's Zabel, the six-time points winner who had been outsped in every sprint so far, was still hoping for a win, while Cooke and McEwen were still fatigued from their earlier efforts when the final sprint started a long way out. Also, this final dash is always extrahard because it's contested on the small-cobblestone pavement of the Champs-Élysées.

Cooke holds off McEwen to grab the green jersey from his fellow Aussie on the Champs-Élysées.

Cooke was the first to hit the front, but in his fatigued state, he moved wide toward the left on the 36-foot-wide boulevard. That forced the challenging McEwen to go to his left, while Nazon, who'd been on McEwen's wheel, was given an opening to Cooke's right and sped through for the stage win. In the last pedal strokes, and with his final grams of energy, McEwen attempted to take Cooke on his left. But the younger Aussie kept his wheel in front as they crossed the line leaning their shoulders into one other.

The intensity of the sprint split the peloton in two, and the back half that included Armstrong crossed the line 15 seconds adrift, to cut the Texan's final overall margin on Ullrich to 1:01.

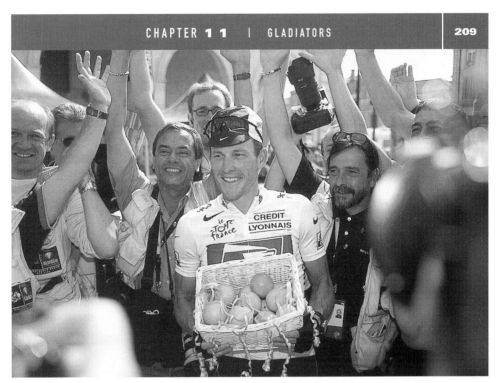

The Tour photographers award Armstrong their *Prix Orange* award as the most cooperative rider.

WEEK THREE

Almost lost in the focus on the yellow and green jerseys was the fact that also being decided in this sprint was the big-money *Prix de Centenaire*—a challenge that totaled every rider's placings at the six stage towns of the original 1903 Tour. With almost $60,000 for 1st overall and $24,000 for 2nd, this was almost double the 1st- and 2nd-place prizes for the green and polka-dot jersey competitions. By finishing consistently high in the sprints at Lyon, Marseille, Toulouse, and Bordeaux, and also placing respectively 11th and 27th at the Nantes time trial, Stuart O'Grady and Thor Hushovd came in 1st and 2nd overall, to give their Crédit Agricole team its only true success of the Tour. Hushovd took 5th, O'Grady 6th in this last sprint to complete their smart domination of an interesting, but almost unpublicized, competition.

There were plenty of other reminders of the Tour's 100-year history in the huge parade that followed the presentations of the four distinctive jerseys: white (for best rider twenty-five years or under) to Denis Menchov of ibanesto.com; polka-dot (for best climber) to Virenque of Quick Step–Davitamon; green (for best sprinter) to Cooke of fdjeux.com; and yellow for Armstrong. The winning team (based on its top three finishers each stage) was Hamilton's CSC squad; the *super-combativité* award (most effective attacks) went to Vinokourov of Telekom; and the photographers' *Prix Orange* (for the most cooperative rider) went to Armstrong—which is a turnaround from a few years earlier when he was given the *Prix Citron* for the least-cooperative rider.

Armstrong's change from being the photographers' least favorite to most favorite subject reflects the public's view of the American. In 2003, those folks holding the stars-and-stripes flags and pro-Lance placards were just as likely to be French as American. And there were no cries of "*dopé, dopé*" as Armstrong climbed the mountains, as there were in 2002. His vulnerability made him more accessible, more popular than any of the other five-time winners. Frenchmen Jacques Anquetil and Bernard Hinault were certainly not universally liked in their own country, while Eddy Merckx and Miguel Induráin were respected rather than admired.

But when you've suffered crises and had narrow escapes, and then picked yourself off the floor to deliver a knockout blow in the mountains to win one of the most dramatic Tours in history, what is there not to like?

STAGE 20: VILLE D'AVRAY TO PARIS (CHAMPS-ÉLYSÉES)
1. Jean-Patrick Nazon (F), Jean Delatour, 152 km in 3:38:49 (41.679 kph); 2. Cooke; 3. McEwen; 4. Luca Paolini (I), Quick Step–Davitamon; 5. Thor Hushovd (N), Crédit Agricole, all s.t.
Final Overall: 1. Armstrong, 3426.5 km in 83:41:12 (40.940 kph, RECORD); 2. Ullrich, at 1:01; 3. Vinokourov, at 4:14; **4. Hamilton, at 6:17**; 5. Zubeldia, at 6:51.

MONDAY, JULY 21

PAU—*My apologies for the lag in getting an update out. I've been a little tapped the last few nights. This feels like the fifth week of the Tour de France for me, not the third. Most G.C. riders spend the first week of the race laying low, conserving energy. But I feel like I've been on the rivet since the get-go. Adrenaline and disbelief probably got me through the first ten stages of the race. But all the effort to keep going has taken its toll. And as a result, the Pyrénées have been a bigger challenge than I would have liked.*

Today's stage started out with a 2-km climb from the gun. There was one attack after another and the peloton was single file for the first 50 km. It was not the ideal way for a long, hard day to get rolling. After suffering over the two previous days I tried to concentrate on riding as steady as I could. Without being able to respond to accelerations with 100 percent of myself, I've found that being as consistent as possible is the best strategy. Attacks can't go forever, and the pace will eventually fall back a bit. I've just had to hope that when it did, I would still be within striking distance. Today, my tactics played out pretty well and I was able to stay in contact with the first group.

Seeing Lance bounce back after taking a couple of hard knocks on the final climb today shows he still has the fight left in him. I think people were starting to count him out for this year's Tour. Big mistake. His crash happened when his handlebar caught a bag being held by a spectator. While these kinds of incidents are part of the sport, they shouldn't decide the outcome of the race. I motioned to everyone in the group they should hold up and not attack while the yellow jersey was in the process of rejoining the group. It was only a couple of years ago that Lance made the same gesture toward Ullrich when he crashed on a descent during the Tour. Waiting was the right thing to do.

Yesterday was a brutal day for me. The climbs were punishing and it was the first day I could feel that the power that had been in my legs throughout the first two weeks was starting to fade. It was a humbling stage in the sweltering heat. And those are about the nicest things I have to say about it.

Saturday's stage proved to be a big success for our team, but was tough for me personally. First, the day started out with my taking a hit from an elevator door on the way out of the team hotel. Apparently the sensors weren't working, because I got clocked pretty good on my collarbone . . . not a good omen heading out to the race.

It was our first day in the Pyrénées, and it was more than 100 degrees F. The Port de Pailhères was the big challenge of the day. It's a massive Cat. I climb stretching over 18 km. I knew when I previewed it in May that it was going to be a killer. And it didn't disappoint. I felt like I was riding pretty well, though, under the circumstances. Although I, like almost everyone else, was feeling the effects of dehydrating so badly during the time trial the day before.

During the team meeting that morning, we discussed that Carlos Sastre and I were both still G.C. leaders since it seemed at that point that we both stood a shot at contending for the top ten. Halfway up the Pailhères, Carlos was feeling pretty good and asked me if I minded if he attacked. There was no way I could ask him to give up an opportunity for himself after all he's done for me so far this season. Things went well for him and he was able to rack up a second stage win for the CSC team. But things didn't work out so well for me personally. After Carlos took off, I spent the next 25 km calling on the radio and raising my arm for food and water. Due to congestion on the road and some communication problems, Bjarne couldn't move the team car up to where I was. So I was in a pretty dangerous situation.

Bjarne finally reached me just before the base of the last climb. But by then I was digging pretty deep. I downed a couple of gels out of necessity, but this isn't the smartest idea at the base of a big climb. It can cause you to cramp, or get sick, especially when it's as hot as it has been. When the attacks went I really started to suffer, and there hadn't been enough time for the gels to take effect. I had to let them go and just ride at my own pace. If I had tried to follow the surges, I would have exploded. And then who knows what would have happened?

In my desperation for water I tried at one point to grab a bottle from one of the Aquarel motorbikes parked on the side of the road. What I didn't realize was how deep the bottles were situated in the carrier at the back of the bike. When I reached to grab one as I rode past, it felt as though I had grabbed a lamppost. The bottle didn't budge. And not only did I miss my opportunity to get a drink, I made the mistake of reaching out with my right arm, which is the side with my collarbone fractures. Any healing that had been done in the previous days felt like it had been undone in that moment. I guess you could say I was having one of those days.

WEDNESDAY, JULY 23

BAYONNE—*Well, what a day this turned out to be! With Paris on the horizon and a day off from racing yesterday, I started letting myself feel a little disappointed about this year's Tour. I had really centered my entire season around my objectives for July. With five stages to go, I knew my initial hopes of finishing on the podium by the end of the race were not going to be realized. I was trying to convince myself that 7th overall with my injuries was still respectable. But part of me was having a little trouble justifying all the suffering I had put myself through since the first stage.*

Last night, Bjarne pulled everyone together just to remind us that the Tour wasn't over. He told us to maintain our focus on the race and to avoid thinking about Paris.

He said there was a stage similar to today's in the 1996 Tour. It was one of the last of the most difficult days of that year's race. He noted that some of the guys had started to relax a bit, and on that day missed an opportunity when an important break went up the road. He shared this story with us to remind us that the race was still in full swing, and there were still opportunities to be made or missed . . . and that none of us should be asleep at the wheel.

The ironic thing was that I almost fell into the very trap Bjarne was warning us about. I started today's stage riding at the back. Suddenly a gap opened up in front of me and I was in the second group. Four of my teammates dropped back to where I was and hauled me back up to the front of the first group. There was already a break up the road that included my teammate Nicki Sörensen.

When we hit the day's first climb, I radioed Bjarne and asked him what I should do. He told me if I felt good, I should try to go across. So I attacked and bridged up to the group that was away. Nicki and I then worked together for the next 30 km until we hit the base of the steepest climb in this year's Tour de France, the Col Bagargui. That's when I decided it was time to make a go of things. And then, with more than half the stage still to cover, I was off the front and on my own.

The profile made it look as though there were just two hard climbs and then flat roads leading into the finish. Unless you previewed the stage, you really had no way of knowing how steep the two climbs were . . . or just how technical the descent was coming off the first climb.

Being there, I can also assure you that the flat stretch on the course profile wasn't so flat. It was up and down all the way home. The last 20 km seemed to go on forever. I think my tongue was hanging out the entire time. I don't know if I've ever worked so hard for anything in my entire life. This stage win was not only special for me personally, but also for everyone who has helped me stay in this race and supported my decision to keep going.

If you told me two weeks ago that this day was possible, I would have offered to sell you some swampland. But that's bike racing. Extreme lows can easily be matched by extreme highs. And there's no telling where or when you will find either experience.

Today was a day I will never forget. I have to send special thanks out to my teammates who towed me back up to the front today. And to Nicki who broke out his Liège legs to shred the breakaway group on my behalf. The team rode really well together today and that made all the difference.

Behind the Scenes

In case you ever wondered what cyclists eat for breakfast, I'll give you a little insight. Here's what's in our team's "breakfast box," which is a clear plastic crate that not only makes its way to breakfast, but to every meal.

Inside you will find no fewer than four kinds of cereal, a large jar of Nutella, soy milk, sugar-free jam, ketchup and mustard (for our eggs, rice, and pasta), instant decaf coffee, honey, parmesan cheese, olive oil, balsamic vinegar, nuts, low-sugar cookies, rice cakes, water, and fruit.

SATURDAY, JULY 26

NANTES—We had a pretty long transfer last night from St. Maixent-L'École to Nantes. It took us a couple of hours to get to our team hotel. It was a crowded highway with everyone in the race, including the publicity caravan and all the organizers headed along with the teams in the same direction. It started to rain as well, which probably made things a little slower.

Dark clouds have been hanging over the race since we entered the Pyrénées, but we haven't seen any significant rainfall until now. We woke up to pouring rain and pretty fierce winds this morning. I guess you could say we were overdue, but no one is happy to see weather like this on the day of a time trial, especially at the Tour de France.

Everyone who follows cycling has been waiting all week for the showdown between Armstrong and Ullrich in the final time trial. The weather only added to the last-minute speculation and suspense.

We previewed the time-trial course by car this morning since it was raining pretty hard. One of our riders has been suffering from influenza since descending from Luz-Ardiden in the cooler temperatures after the race. I've managed to pick up his cold over the last day or two, so I wasn't in the best mood before the time trial.

Still, all things considered, the stage went pretty well. There was a fairly significant tail wind out there, so I figured the times were going to be fast and close together. I'm glad we previewed the course because it was pretty technical with a lot of roundabouts and turns. It was really hard to make a couple of them with all the water on the road. At one point there was so much water on my wheels my brakes weren't working at all, so I had to unclip a foot from one of the pedals just to brace myself if I lost control.

Finishing 2nd by 9 seconds is close enough to make you wonder just **where** you could have been a little faster. But on this day, in that weather, I think I went as quickly as I could have. Taking any of those wet turns with more speed was out of the question. Everyone had to ride at a controlled tempo through the corners. Between that and the wind, I still felt like I had a little gas at the end. I'm sure that I'm not the only one who felt that way. The race might have been a lot more interesting if there had been a long straightaway to the finish.

I changed in the Cofidis team bus after the race. David Millar was inside watching Lance and Jan duke it out on television. It was hard to be that close to the guy and not root for him. Being that the fight on screen was for the overall lead, I figured that was okay. I was happy to see David get a well-deserved stage victory.

Tomorrow we transfer by train back to the outskirts of Paris. I know we started this journey there, but it feels like that was a lifetime ago.

Thanks for reading.

Tyler Hamilton

WEEK THREE

MONDAY, JULY 21

LUZ-ARDIDEN—*Well, despite what happens between here and the Tour de France finish in Paris on Sunday, I know for sure that I won't go home empty-handed. It has been a successful Tour for the Quick Step–Davitamon team. As of today, we have managed to win the most prize money of any team: 48,597 euros (about $50,000). That has come from virtually securing the King of the Mountains title for Richard Virenque, who has also won a stage in the Alps, and hauling Paolo Bettini into 3rd place in the same competition.*

To top it off, I've got a new nickname, thanks to Richard. He calls me "Scooter" because, he reckons, I'm like one and that he's ridden it to help him up the mountains. I'm not sure if the nickname will stick, but he seems pretty happy with it. And if he's happy, I'm happy.

It's been a great experience riding with and for Richard here. He's a good guy and I look forward to more races with him. I had never ridden with him before the Tour, and it has been great having a role in his success, which he deserves. It was also nice to hear of his recognition in the media for the work that I, Paolo, and the rest of the team have done for him. After all the support I got from the team in the Tours of Belgium and Germany and Route du Sud, it has also been great to be able to give something back to him and the team.

With one mountain stage to go—and after a rest day—I can say that I feel pretty good right now. It's great to know that I can get through such a long race and still be able to push myself hard in the third week. I wouldn't say today's stage 15 was my best, but it was still okay. Compared to stage 14, though, I'd have to say the latter was my best for the Tour.

Riding in the mountains has been great. As each day has passed I've even heard my name a lot more from fans on the side of the road. Trust me, it makes a difference. It did today, especially when the U.S. Postals started to drive it a bit near the top of the Col du Tourmalet. I had to dig in and grit my teeth. But then I felt good, got to the bottom, and rode with Richard to help him get into position at the foot of Luz-Ardiden. That done, I eased up and was happy to ride in the next group that came in at 16:26.

The only thing I missed was the drama up front! Boy, I wish I could have seen that. You wouldn't have imagined the drama, but I did predict that Lance Armstrong would pull something off today. So how does Lance keep so calm under pressure? He certainly has shown that he can—and quite well for that matter. You only have to look at what has happened to him in the Tour this year—how he averted a crash when he rode off course near the finish to Gap where Joseba Beloki fell, how he recovered from his first crash today, and then later when he pulled his foot from the pedal.

The closest I have come to what Lance did today was in last year's Tour Down Under in Australia. On one of the last stages, and the last climb, I crashed while in the leader's yellow jersey. It was just as the attacks were going and there I was, on the deck with a broken bike. But from nowhere came a spectator with a black bike, offering it to me. Not only was it the same size, and of the same components, but it was also the same brand I was riding. I didn't hesitate, though, and before I knew it I was on it and racing for the next 80 km as my life depended on it to chase the lead group. Guess what? I kept the leader's jersey.

WEDNESDAY, JULY 23

BAYONNE—If the Col Bagargui looked steep on television, it was . . . plus some. I can honestly say I have never climbed a road as steep as that one—let alone race up it like we did in today's stage 16. It felt like we were pedaling up one giant wall forever.

We all knew it was a steep climb, but we never expected it to be that steep. I think a lot of riders were really caught off guard by it today. Me included. I have never ridden so hard on the bike. I heard Tyler Hamilton had trained over it and you can see the time taken doing that paid off today.

One thing I have to say about my fellow VeloNews diarist is that fella is all class and guts. What a ride from him today.

As for everyone else? Well, they were pretty much at their limit even though we were supposed to have had a rest day. It was like a war zone in the pack—riders were looking okay and next to you one moment then suddenly—boom—dropping off the next.

For the Col Bagargui I used a 39x25 gearing for almost the whole way up. There were only a couple of times I dropped down to the 23, but doing that quickly told me "no way," and I was back up to the 25 again. It was the first time this year I have used that 25.

The mist at the top was amazing too. You couldn't see what was ahead. Maybe that was for the best. The only way you knew where riders were ahead of you was by following the sounds of the cheering crowds, especially the Basques who came out by the thousands.

WEEK THREE

The climb was made harder by a little stuff-up earlier in the stage, at the feed station in Laugibar after 93.5 km, just before a Cat. III hill that preceded the Col Bagargui.

Unfortunately, our cars were in last place at the feed zone, which ended near the foot of the Larrau climb. By the time I got my musette, the race was picking up again. Also, when the pace went right up, I was still putting stuff in my pockets. Before I knew it, I was out the back and chasing. The effort I put in there was one I never really recovered from. And to think at that point I didn't realize what was waiting for us on the next climb!

Still, it's great to have the mountains behind us. As you may have seen, we didn't waste any time getting involved in the mix once we hit the flats. A few people were asking why we chased Hamilton when Richard Virenque was our best rider overall in 14th place, at 22 minutes.

Actually, we still felt like we could get the stage win. We wanted to get Paolo Bettini up for the win. He has ridden very strongly throughout the Tour and he said he had good legs today. So it was normal that we thought if the bunch could bring Hamilton back, we would have a good chance of seeing Paolo win the stage.

Okay, it didn't happen that way. Hamilton stayed away to claim a very popular win. We'll keep trying though.

FRIDAY, JULY 25

ST. MAIXENT–L'ÉCOLE—We're 18 stages down and still racing at breakneck speed after nearly three weeks, and there's no letup. I couldn't believe it today when I looked at my computer after the first hour of racing in the third-to-last stage to see we had flown over nearly 53 km.

You'd reckon that riders who were not there at the Tour start in Paris were joining the race fresh, sneaking into the bunch rather than dropping like flies, as the result sheets show. You can imagine my shock when a little more than 4 hours later we sped into the finish. The stage average was 49.938 kph—the second-fastest stage in Tour history.

Then, as if that were not enough, what a crowd it was to ride into at the finish today. It may not have been captured on television, but the mass of humanity that was in the road after the finish line was incredible. There they were: jammed chest first, back to back, and 10 deep into the sides of our team buses. There we were: one moment flying into the finish and then, meters after the line, *weaving our way through a thin tunnel of humanity, heading toward our buses. It never ceases to amaze me how much people love cycling here.*

With the Quick Step–Davitamon bus, I've learned another lesson. Having Richard Virenque on the team is bad for one thing: His being there absolutely ensures that outside the bus door there always will be a wall of people you have to walk through.

Still, to be fair, while they are crying out "Richard, Richard" all the time, they do respect your space when you come out. Hey, a team would rather have fans than not!

One who deserved to receive their cheers today was our Spanish teammate David Cañada. Previously with ONCE and then Mapei, he is a gutsy rider, and a good time trialist. That was a big effort to get away like he did. Not that I was surprised he had it in him. But then, to get caught so close to the finish. Watching the replay on television, you hurt for him.

Michael Rogers

WEEK THREE

Centennial Tour Records

Besides Lance Armstrong equaling the record of five overall Tour victories, the 2003 Tour de France saw several other records beaten or threatened. Here is an update on the major statistics:

Record prizes

To mark the historic centennial Tour, the organizers added three-quarters-of-a-million dollars to the prize list, making it more than $3 million, with 400,000 euros (about $445,000) to the winner.

Most days in yellow jersey

By wearing the yellow jersey for 13 days in the 2003 Tour, Armstrong moved above Jacques Anquetil and came to within one day of third-placed Miguel Induráin in the all-time rankings.

1.	Eddy Merckx	96
2.	Bernard Hinault	77
3.	Miguel Induráin	60
4.	**Lance Armstrong**	**59**
5.	Jacques Anquetil	51

Most stage wins

Armstrong scored only one stage win in 2003, and he is now within four victories of moving into the top five of all-time stage winners.

1.	Eddy Merckx	34
2.	Bernard Hinault	28
3.	André Leducq	25
4.	André Darrigade	22
5.	Nicolas Frantz	20
6.	Francois Faber	19

7. Jean Alavoine	17
8. Lance Armstrong	**16**
Jacques Anquetil	16
Charles Pélissier	16
René le Greves	16

Fastest Tours

In a Tour that saw incessant attacks both in the plains and the mountains, the overall average speed record was shattered by overall winner Armstrong.

1. Lance Armstrong 2003	40.940 kph
2. Lance Armstrong 1999	40.273 kph
3. Marco Pantani 1998	39.938 kph
4. Lance Armstrong 2000	39.572 kph
5. Miguel Induráin 1992	39.504 kph

Fastest road stages

Stage 18 winner Pablo Lastras came within two minutes of breaking the all-time stage speed record, set in 1999 by Mario Cipollini.

1. Mario Cipollini (1999)	Laval-Blois (194.5km)	50.355 kph
2. Pablo Lastras (2003)	**Bordeaux-St. Maixent-L'École (203.5km)**	**49.938 kph**
3. Johan Bruyneel (1993)	Evreux-Amiens (158km)	49.417 kph
4. Adri Van de Poel (1988)	Tarbes-Pau (38km)	48.927 kph
5. Tom Steels (1998)	Tarascon-Le Cap d'Agde (205.5km)	48.764 kph

Fastest individual time trials

Stage 19 winner David Millar came within 12 seconds of breaking the all-time time-trial stage speed record set by Greg LeMond in 1989.

1. Greg LeMond (1989)	Versailles-Paris (24.5km)	54.545 kph
2. David Millar (2003)	**Pornic-Nantes (49km)**	**54.361 kph**
3. Lance Armstrong (2000)	Freiburg-Mulhouse (58.5km)	53.986 kph
4. Miguel Induráin (1992)	Tours-Blois (64km)	52.349 kph
5. Miguel Induráin (1994)	Périgueux-Bérgerac (64km)	50.539 kph

Fastest team time trials

Despite racing on a course that had sections directly into a head win, the U.S. Postal team still recorded the fourth fastest team time trial in Tour history.

1. Gewiss-Ballan (1995)	Mayenne-Alençon (67km)	54.943 kph
2. Carrera (1987)	Berlin-Berlin (40.5km)	54.201 kph
3. Ariostea (1991)	Chassieu circuit (36.5km)	52.919 kph
4. U.S. Postal-Berry Floor (2003)	**Joinville-St.Dizier (69km)**	**52.772 kph**
5. Panasonic (1992)	Libourne circuit (63.5km)	52.049 kph

Fastest prologues

Tour prologue time trials are always held on a circuit, so they are a record of pure speed, with the effects of wind neutralized. Brad McGee did well to break into the top-five club of fastest prologues, but he remains a long way back of 1990s ace Chris Boardman.

1. Chris Boardman (1994)	Lille circuit (7.2km)	55.152 kph
2. Chris Boardman (1998)	Dublin circuit (5.6km)	54.193 kph
3. Brad McGee (2003)	**Paris circuit (6.5km)**	**52.466 kph**
4. Chris Boardman (1997)	Rouen circuit (7.3km)	52.465 kph
5. Thierry Marie (1991)	Lyon circuit (5.4km)	52.365 kph

References

Chany, Pierre. *La Fabuleuse Histoire du Tour de France*. Paris: Editions O.D.I.L, 1983.

García Sánchez, Javier. *Induráin: A Tempered Passion*. United Kingdom: Mousehold Press, 2003.

Godaert, Joël, Robert Janssens, and Guido Cammaert. *Tour Encyclopedie*. Volumes 1-7. Ghent, Belgium: Uitgeverij Worldstrips, 1987-2003.

Goddet, Jacques. *L'Équipée Belle*. Paris: Éditions Robert Laffont, 1991.

L'Équipe editors. *Tour de France: 100 Ans*. Paris: L'Équipe, 2003.

Photo Credits

Part I, History of the Tour

Photos by Presse Sports, ABACA

Part II, Americans at the Tour

AFP: pages 72, 73 (Julich), 81, 98

Graham Watson: pages 73 (Hincapie), 75, 76, 88 (LeMond, 1986 Tour)

John Pierce/PhotoSport International: page 74

Presse Sports, ABACA: pages 64, 78, 88 (LeMond, 1989 Tour), 90, 94

Tom Moran: page 68 (Roll)

VeloNews file: pages 65, 67, 68 (Pierce, Kiefel), 70

Part III, The 2003 Tour de France

Photos by Graham Watson, with the following exceptions.

AFP: pages 158, 159

About the Author

John Wilcockson, editorial director of *VeloNews*, has written ten books, including *John Wilcockson's World of Cycling* (VeloPress 1998). A graduate of the University of London, he raced as a Category-I amateur in the 1960s when he spent two seasons competing in France.

Wilcockson has been the editor of five cycling magazines—*International Cycle Sport, Cyclist Monthly, Winning: Bicycle Racing Illustrated, Inside Cycling*, and *VeloNews*—and was the cycling correspondent for *The Sunday Times* and *The Times of London* before moving to the United States in 1987.

He has received two awards from the organizers of the Tour de France: the Medaille de la Reconnaissance and the Plaque de la Reconnaissance. Wilcockson reported the Tour for the 35th time in 2003. He lives in Boulder, Colorado, with his wife Rivvy Neshama.